DERIVATIVES

ALSO BY DAVID M. WEISS

Financial Instruments

After the Trade Is Made

DERIVATIVES

A GUIDE TO
ALTERNATIVE INVESTMENTS

DAVID M. WEISS

PORTFOLIO / PENGUIN

PORTFOLIO / PENGUIN

Published by the Penguin Group
Penguin Group (USA) LLC
375 Hudson Street
New York, New York 10014

USA | Canada | UK | Ireland | Australia | New Zealand | India | South Africa | China
penguin.com
A Penguin Random House Company

First published by Portfolio / Penguin, a member of
Penguin Group (USA) LLC, 2014

ISBN 978-1-59184-572-0

1 3 5 7 9 10 8 6 4 2

Set in Fairfield LT Std 45 Light
Designed by Neuwirth & Associates, Inc.

This publication is designed to provide accurate and authoritative information
in regard to the subject matter covered. It is sold with the understanding that
the publisher is not engaged in rendering legal, accounting, or other professional
services. If you require legal advice or other expert assistance, you should seek
the services of a competent professional

To my wife and best friend, Marcia;
to my family: Randi, Craig, Ruth, Nicole, Jenna, and Carly,
who collectively brighten my day.

| CONTENTS |

Introduction   1

CHAPTER 1
Derivatives Defined   3

CHAPTER 2
Overview of the Debt Market   8

CHAPTER 3
Types of Risk in Debt Markets   22

CHAPTER 4
Debt Markets and Lending Rates   28

CHAPTER 5
Forms of Mutual Funds   36

CHAPTER 6
Real Estate Investment Trusts   43

CHAPTER 7
Exchange-Traded Funds   48

CHAPTER 8
Other Exchange-Traded Products   63

CHAPTER 9

Options Products   69

CHAPTER 10

Option Strategies   83

CHAPTER 11

Greek Terms for Option Strategies   95

CHAPTER 12

Nonstandard Options   104

CHAPTER 13

Futures and Commodity Products   121

CHAPTER 14

The Futures Market   137

CHAPTER 15

Future Margin Page Ratings   152

CHAPTER 16

Forward Contracts and Forward Rate Agreements   165

CHAPTER 17

Swaps and Their Participants   171

CHAPTER 18

Range of Swaps   177

CHAPTER 19

Credit Default Swaps   194

CHAPTER 20

Swaptions   202

CHAPTER 21

Collateralized Debt Obligations   206

CHAPTER 22

Structured "Packaged" Products   218

CHAPTER 23

Regulators and Industry Associations   230

CHAPTER 24

Derivative Transaction Processing and the Dodd-Frank Act   238

CHAPTER 25

Using Indexes   256

Acknowledgments   265

Glossary   267

Index   299

DERIVATIVES

INTRODUCTION

This book has been written to meet the needs of users in a changing marketplace. The financial industry has always been in a constant state of change—certain aspects of the industry change faster than others, creating an imbalance, and then those areas left behind catch up, prompting the process to start over again. This consistent change keeps industry professionals on their toes, trying to stay abreast of the latest developments.

The financial market has completely changed from when I penned my first book in 1986. Within that time span there has been a consolidation of assets from individuals' accounts into the professional management of financial institutions. With that consolidation came the accumulation of huge sums of assets that needed to be invested, drastically increasing the scale of investments.

Also, during that time automation and electronic markets did away with many manual processing steps, which greatly reduced the processing time of the more traditional products. As time was freed up, the way was paved for new types of products, and more complex variations of existing products could now be offered in the marketplace. Most of the newer products are a result of technological advances that permit complex computations to be made at split-second speeds and make way for spontaneous analysis and projections of outcomes. Products designed to take advantage of new technologies can magnify profits and minimize losses. They can also be combined or packaged with other products, thereby allowing for a new set of results.

These same technical advances broke down country borders and boundaries, making our once domestic market into an international and then a global one. This, in turn, demanded the development of computer software programs that permitted twenty-four-hour trading, which led to a major increase in the use of foreign currency exchange and trading on foreign markets, shrinking the globe even more. The algorithms that were developed allowed for the solving of complex and time-consuming formula calculations, permitting new classes of products to enter the fold and new methods for assessing risk to be employed. Some of these new products are classified as "derivatives," others are referred to as "structured products," and still others simply broadened the base of those "steak and potatoes" products, such as equities and bonds.

As the participants became more familiar with these new products, their applications led to the need for other new products. For example, over-the-counter options existed for centuries but the establishment of "exchange listed" options in 1973 gave forth a new type of option product, which in turn gave way to a rash of other types of option products. Today, the buyer, seller, or trader who is involved with this last range of products is actually three layers away from the underlying product. For example, using products that are explained throughout the book: the trading of an option contract (layer #1) that is based on a future product contract (layer #2) that is based on a predetermined quantity of a commodity (layer #3) or the trading of an exchange-traded fund (ETF) (layer #1) that is based on an equity index (layer #2), which is based on a select group of underlying common stocks (layer #3). If the professional takes the time to deeply understand the products as well as the relationship of products to one another, a profit may be anticipated and a loss may be controlled. Those who don't bother to learn hurt not only themselves but also others in the market.

The reader must keep in mind two very important facts throughout this book. First, all examples in the book are fictional situations isolated to serve as examples, whereas real-world examples are dynamic and change rapidly. Second, in some of the examples assumptions are made to facilitate the explanations, sometimes oversimplifying the situation to make the point. Armed with those facts and with a mind eager to understand new and exciting products, you will be in good shape to approach the book. I trust you will find the material here both informative and interesting.

CHAPTER 1

DERIVATIVES DEFINED

As the derivatives market evolved, traders developed specialized terms for discussing its various products. A basic understanding of these terms is essential to a study of derivatives, so this chapter will focus on providing a few essential definitions.

· WHAT IS A DERIVATIVE PRODUCT? ·

A derivative product is one that *derives* its value from another product or other products. For example: the value of a future contract (a type of derivative) on wheat is based on the current price of wheat—it derives its value from the price of wheat. Many other factors contribute to the wheat future's value, but it is still based on the price of today's wheat.

Types of Derivatives

There are many ways to sort or categorize derivative products. One way is to divide derivatives into two categories. The first category contains the derivatives that benefit the issuer of the derivative's underlying product, the second is the derivatives that give the issuer no direct financial benefit. The derivatives in both of these categories derive their values from the value of the underlying product.

An example of the first type occurs when a corporation issues a bond with warrants attached. What they are issuing is a debt product (the bond) with which they are borrowing money for a period of time (the duration of the bond) and will have to pay interest over the bond's life: they are also issuing an opportunity for the warrant holder to invest in the common stock of that company at a later time, should that investment appear appealing at that point. In other words, the warrant has a life of its own with an expiration date and the price the warrant holder will have to pay if he or she wants to take advantage of the opportunity. Both products, the bond and the warrant, are offered initially as a "unit." With this unit the issuer has the possibility of raising funding from two sources: the borrow, which is made against the bond, and the potential investment, which is made later by the warrant holder in the issuer's common shares, thereby benefiting from the issuance of those shares.

Options, forwards, futures, forward rate agreements, exchange-traded funds, mutual funds, unit investment trusts and other mortgage-backed securities, asset-backed securities, and covered bonds are all types of derivatives that do not benefit the issuer of the original or underlying product.

For an example of these other types of derivatives, we will use a listed option product that trades on an exchange. The buyer and seller of the option contract are anticipating changes in the underlying issue's market value that will benefit them. The issuer of the underlying product does not receive compensation of any kind from the buying and selling of the option.

In the arena of derivative products, those benefiting the issuer include warrants, rights, units, and privately placed options. Included, although stretching the concept a bit, is the initiation of collateralized debt obligations (CDOs), which we will discuss in depth in chapter 21 to the extent that they represent packages of loans made by a financial institution and through their sale, the institution can recoup its expenditures in order to continue to make loans.

• WHAT IS A STRUCTURED PRODUCT? •

A structured product is a combination of two or more products designed in the anticipation of achieving a particular goal. The important word is "anticipation," as the result is not guaranteed. The component parts are offered as a package. Sometimes the "package" is issued under a trust. One of the simplest examples of a structured product can be found within the option world. It is called the buy/write. The principal buys shares (100 shares is a trading lot) of a stock because the corporation that issued it pays a good-size quarterly dividend and the stock purchaser is not anticipating capital appreciation. In this particular strategy the principal wants the value of the stock to remain stagnant. Against the purchase, the principal sells an "out of the money" call on the same stock, thereby earning the option premium. As long as the stock doesn't rise in value to the point where the owner of the option will call the stock away, the principal can earn the dividend and enhance that income with the premium received from the option.

Here's an example:

Mr. Chuck Spear purchases a package consisting of the acquisition of 1,000 shares Marnee common stock @ $38 per share (the stock pays a dividend of $1.00 per share annually, which is paid quarterly) and the sales of ten call options (option represents 100 shares) expiring in six months with a strike price of $40 for $1 per underlying share. Putting commission and fees costs aside, the package cost $37 ($38 − $1) per share. Assuming the stock does not rise above $40 per share, the option will expire and be worthless. Mr. Spear has earned $0.50 in dividends during the six-month period and $1 from the sale of the now worthless option for a total of $1.50, versus just the dividend of $0.50 had the options not been sold. This strategy and others, including risks, are discussed later in this book.

• THE BASICS •

The financial industry, like most industries, runs on credit. Some participants arrange financing for their clients, who use it to finance their own company's operation—often by arranging private loans, underwriting their company's securities, and advising on mergers, acquisitions, or consolidations. This financing originates with lenders, known as clients. Banks lend money received from depositors, and broker-dealers offer securities for their clients to buy (more funding). These same clients acquire and sell the securities using financing as the conduit. The use of all this financing involves interest charges. The amount of interest charged depends on the creditworthiness of the borrower.

What Is a Broker-Dealer?

"Broker-dealer" is a catchall term for any firm that must be registered with the Securities and Exchange Commission (SEC) to do brokerage business with the public. This general term encompasses broker-dealers whose customers are institutions, those that focus on retail customers, and those that are national, international, or multinational firms.

What Does an Investment Bank Do?

An investment bank may or may not be a broker-dealer; the usual operation either is or has an affiliation with one. Typically an investment bank is the intermediary between a corporation or other institution and the public markets. An investment bank can assist a young company in raising short-term funding by introducing the company to lending operations such as venture capitalists or broker-dealers that specialize in the placement of this type of financing.

As the company grows, its need for financing grows and the investment bank assists it in preparing to issue securities to the public. This process is known as underwriting an initial public offering (IPO). As the company continues to grow the investment bank will continue to assist it if it is issuing securities.

Corporate Actions

Investment banks also assist their corporate clients through the steps necessary to execute a merger or acquisition. This assistance ranges from locating prospective candidates to helping to thwart an unwanted takeover.

Of importance to this book is the role investment banks play in the derivative and structured markets. It is the clients of the investment bank that need and use these products. It is these firms that have the financial strength to support these strategies, to take the opposite side when necessary, and to facilitate the transaction through their contacts. They are basically set up to focus on a few large transactions per day.

Investment banks bring new issues to market. They underwrite the issue, meaning they buy the issue from the issuer and sell the product into the market. Once issued, the product begins secondary trading as the new buyers sell their new issue to market makers, who in turn sell them to new buyers, and the trading begins. Many of these products will be serviced by the initial issuer.

CHAPTER 2

OVERVIEW OF THE DEBT MARKET

The debt market forms the base for many of the products we will be discussing throughout this book. The market actually serves two purposes. The first is that many derivatives products use as a base the underlying issues that trade in this market, such as Treasury debt instruments. The second is that many of the derivatives products discussed in this book trade in the debt markets themselves. Collateralized mortgage obligations are an example. This chapter will focus on the debt instruments operating in that market.

• THE GLOBAL ECONOMY •

Everyone is connected to the debt market in some way. Individuals and governments both come to the market to borrow funds.

On the other side of the equation are the lenders, many of whom are also borrowers. A lender's business model is to borrow other people's money at one interest rate so that it can lend the same money to others at a higher interest rate. Paying an interest rate for the funds that is less than the rate received means a profit. The duration of these borrows ranges from overnight to decades.

The additional payment made by the borrower for the use of these funds is referred to as interest. The amount of interest charged by the lenders depends on several factors. The three primary factors are: the availability of funds, the risk that the borrowed sum may not be returned, and the length of time the borrowed funds will be outstanding. Therefore, interest cost can be looked at as another commodity or another product.

Since interest rates change and the timing of interest payments to the lender can differ, there is a market to trade interest rates and/or interest payments. If supply of funds exceeds demand for funds, interest rates will fall; whereas, if demand for funds exceeds the supply of funds, interest rates will rise. This symmetry excludes government intervention. The supply of funds is affected by monetary policy and the willingness of lenders, in general, to offer funds. In the global economy, economic events in one part of the planet may cause economic reactions in other parts, which in turn affect not only major corporations' activities but even individuals' daily lives.

Take this simple exercise:

Assume a local manufacturer makes a $5.00 product. The manufacturer buys $2.00 worth of material per product from a company two towns away, and spends $2.00 on labor, etc., therefore earning $1.00 profit for a total revenue source of $5.00—all of it domestic. Somewhere in some country on another continent is a company that makes the same material, and the domestic manufacturer can acquire the material from this foreign vendor for $1.25 per product. How long would it be before the manufacturer would switch vendors? The manufacturer would have the ability to see its profit increase from $1.00 to $1.75 per unit. If this manufacturer doesn't do it, its competitors will.

Let's make it even more realistic by looking at the variables. The manufacturer has to have a factory, which raises a lot of issues. Is the factory owned outright or is there a mortgage? What rate of interest is being paid on the mortgage versus the current rate? Does the manufacturer carry inventory? How is it paid for? Is it pledged against a loan; at what rate is it financed? Does the manufacturer have long-term debt, and if so, what interest rate is being paid? What is the current going rate for this class of debt? Are the bonds callable? Would it be beneficial for the manufacturer to call the debt in and pay for it with new debt at a lower interest cost? Is the company using its funds and resources to its best advantage? These questions, and many more that the company faces every day, assist it to better manage its businesses. As interest is an expense, it chews away at profits. And a company's use of cash, owned or borrowed, is a very dear commodity—perhaps now more than ever.

• THE FINANCIAL CRISIS •

The financial markets, like any other markets, are vulnerable to abuse. The most recent example is the financial crisis that began late in the last decade. There are many fingers pointing in different directions as to who is to blame. Many people made a lot of money; many more lost. Among the abuses were high-risk loans. It will suffice to say that loans were made to individuals who couldn't afford them, to purchase homes they couldn't afford, at inflated prices the homes couldn't sustain. As the housing market began to cool and housing prices started to fall, homeowners found themselves with outstanding mortgage amounts that exceeded the value of their homes.

Many of the homeowners walked away from their obligations. Those houses were eventually sold by the mortgage companies, depressing the housing market even more. On top of this, many "flippers" began buying homes with the intention of dumping them in a few months when homes price rose, capturing the profit. Instead, as the prices were falling, those speculators wound up dumping these investments on an already weak market, causing the prices to fall even faster. Many of these mortgages were securitized into derivative products. By the end of the downward spiral, it was a global disaster.

The financial crisis has brought a slew of regulations in the United States under the Dodd-Frank Act, also known as the Wall Street Reform and Consumer Protection Act, many provisions of which are still pending. In addition, the European Central Bank and its seventeen member states found themselves in a sovereign debt crisis with the possibility of countries' defaulting, which led to European Market Infrastructure Regulation (EMIR). These regulations are designed to head off another financial crisis.

As a law of physics states, each action has a reaction. Many banks and other financial institutions must raise the amount of reserves they are required to keep against their loans. Therefore the banks have less money to lend, borrowing becomes more difficult, and interest rates rise. The Volcker Rule, which is included in the Dodd-Frank Act, restricts certain financial entities from engaging in different types of proprietary trading, with the result that markets become less liquid. As that happens, traders face bigger risks in their proprietary (market making [trading against the public markets]) activity, and certain markets may become unattractive for trading due to the lack of liquidity and trading activity. In the face of a weak economy, different countries must take care to ensure continuity in the implementation of these actions.

• FIXED- VERSUS FLOATING-RATE DEBT INSTRUMENTS •

Lenders are always trying to find innovative ways to offer their funds at the highest possible return and yet acquire these funds at a rate that is attractive to the investor or other lending institutions. This search has led to many interesting and complex products. Yet there are still many investors who want straight uncluttered simple debt, such as bonds, notes, and short-term paper (known as commercial paper). These simple instruments pay interest payments periodically, and their principal sum at maturity. However, during the life of the debt instrument, the owners of the issuer's loans are at risk due to no fault of the borrowing entities.

If interest rates in general rise, the prices of those fixed-interest instruments already outstanding decrease, in order to remain competitive with the yield of newer products coming to market. Therefore, should the bond owner have to sell these bonds before maturity, and while interest rates are higher than when the bonds were issued, the bond owner would suffer a loss.

Here's an example:

As the interest rate is fixed on a bond with a 5 percent "coupon" rate, the bond is expected to pay 5 percent of its principal amount annually. If interest rates in the debt market rise in general so that new bonds coming to market carry a 6 percent coupon, the value of the 5 percent bond has to fall so that its return on investment is comparable to the 6 percent newly issued bonds. The bond is still paying the 5 percent annual interest owed, but it is now priced so that it is yielding the equivalent of the newly issued 6 percent bond.

The reverse is true also; if a 5 percent bond is trading in the markets when interest rates fall and newly issued equivalent bonds are carrying a lower interest rate, the price of the 5 percent bond will rise so that its return is competitive. In both cases the bond is paying 5 percent of its face amount, with a $1,000 bond paying $50 a year. However, if newly issued bonds, equal in quality and longevity, are trading at their face value but paying out at a different rate due to interest rate changes, the outstanding fixed-income instrument's price must change to remain competitive in the marketplace.

There are investors who value the principal of their investment more than the income it produces. In an attempt to attract these debt investors, wanting not to expose their capital investment to interest rate swings, borrowers will issue floating or adjustable rate instrument bonds. The interest rate paid by these instruments taps into the rates at which short-term debt instruments are borrowing. As short-term rates change, the rate of interest paid on these longer-term bonds is reset periodically to reflect current debt market conditions. As the interest rate paid on newly issued debt rises or falls, the interest rate on these outstanding instruments is adjusted accordingly. It is also important to remember that the real or perceived financial strength of the issuer of the debt also affects the price of its debt instrument.

• CALLABLE BONDS •

Bonds may contain a call feature: this allows the issuer to retire a bond earlier than the debt's maturity date. Usually a bond with a call feature will contain a premium price at which the bond will be called.

Here's an example:

A thirty-year bond has a call feature that allows the bond to be retired (called in) after twenty years, but it may be called at a premium price. The premium will diminish over the ten years that are between the call date and the maturity date of the bond. Furthermore, call features in debt instruments work for the benefit of the issuer, not the investor. An issuer will call bonds in either when it can refinance those loans for less cost, or when it simply does not need the borrowed funds any longer. The former is brought about as general interest rates have fallen and money is easier to borrow. If the issuer can finance the loans for less cost, it means the current bondholder will have the bond called in and then, if desired, reenter the debt market buying other bonds, of equal ratings, that are paying less than the bonds that are being retired.

The call feature may permit a full call, the retiring of the entire issue, or a partial call. In the process of the full call, the bonds must be surrendered by the bond owners by a predetermined date. The issuer's agent will pay the bondholders the required amount when the bonds are retired. On the due date of the call, the bond will stop paying interest, and if any bonds are not retired on time, the issuer can continue to use the borrowed funds free of any interest cost until these bonds are submitted for retirement. Bond positions that are maintained by industry institutions for proprietary use or for their clients will deliver the bonds to the issuer's agent by the due date so they can pay the debt owners their due.

In the case of a partial call, the main repository, the Depository Trust Company (DTC), will allocate the amount being called among all of their members who have those bonds in position. Those member companies, in turn, will allocate their required portion of the call among their clients' and proprietary accounts that have those bonds in their positions. Therefore there is a chance that a bondholder may have his or her bonds retired early, or have them not retired.

Naturally, most bond owners do not want their bonds retired early, as they would miss out on the higher interest income they could receive. Broker-dealers and other financial institutions are under strict rules to carry out their fiduciary responsibility in this allocation process fairly and in accordance with established procedures. On a partial call, the quantity being called may be prorated against those customer accounts holding the bonds. As an investor, it is important that you trust the firm you are doing business with to make sure they are following proper rules and regulations as to the allocation of calls.

The Rule-of-Thumb Method

In dealing with callable bonds, the bond dealer must offer the bonds to the investor at the lower of yield to maturity or yield to call price—whichever is less advantageous to the client. Let's take a look at an example using the rule-of-thumb method—a quick, but inaccurate way of getting near the correct answer. (We'll look at the actual computation for yield to maturity later in the book.) Using the rule of thumb method, a $1,000 5 percent thirty-year bond is issued that is callable in twenty years at a price of 105 ($1,050.00). The bond is currently trading at "97" ($970.00).

Rule-of-Thumb Calculation (ROT)

1. Calculate the difference between the market price and the value at maturity, divided by the bond's years remaining. The answer is the annual amortization amount (for a bond priced at a discount) or annual depletion amount (for a bond priced at a premium).
2. Add (in the case of a bond trading at a discount) or subtract (in the case of a bond trading at a premium) the amortization/depletion amount to the annual bond's interest payment to get an adjusted payment amount.
3. Add the current value and the value at maturity together and divide by two to obtain an average price over the bond's remaining life.
4. Divide the adjusted payment amount by the average bond price to get the ROT.

Yield to Maturity

$1,000.00—Value at maturity

Less: $970.00—Current market value

$ 30.00

$30 amortized over 30 years = $1 per year

Average theoretical value over the life of the bond: = $1,000 + $970
= $1,970/2 (for average) = $985

$5% interest on $1,000 bond = $50 + $1 (annualized amortization)
   = $51.00
51/985 = 5.17%

Yield to Call

$1,050.00—Value if called
Less: **$970.00—Current market value**
           $ 80.00

$80 amortized over 20 years = $4

Average theoretical value up to call = $1,050 + $970 = $2,020/2 (for
   average) = $1,010
Annual interest of 5% on $1,000 bond = $50 + $4 (annualized
   amortization) = $54
54/1010 = 5.34%

Using the above example, the client would be quoted a basis price of
5.17 percent. If the bonds should be called at the twenty-year mark, the
client would do better. By using the worst outcome as the quote, the floor
is set by which the client can do no worse, but get that return or better.
Bear in mind that these yields are obtained through corporate actions
and not by market activity. Once the bonds are acquired, selling them in
the market will involve profit or loss on the total transaction. This computation has nothing to do with the rate of return on the investment.

Sinking Fund Provision

There are some investors who may, as part of a strategy, want their
bonds to be called early, since the normal yield curve slopes upward
the longer a debt is outstanding. Let's look at an imaginary investor, Mr.
Ian Long, who wants to invest a sum of money for twenty years. Using
the chart below, and assuming a straight-line yield curve, Mr. Long
could acquire a twenty-year instrument and receive slightly more than
a 5 percent rate, or he could buy the thirty-year bond and receive 6
percent interest, hoping to be called at twenty years.

Some bonds are issued with a sinking fund provision to accommodate investors like Mr. Long. This fund allows the issuer to retire the bonds earlier by buying them in the open market and paying for the purchases from the company's earnings. Under the provision of the sinking fund, the issuers are not permitted to pay more than face amount for the bonds. When the sinker is active, participants surrender the bonds to the issuer's agent, which will retire enough of the particular bond issue to satisfy the sinker's provision.

| SINKING FUND PROVISIONS |

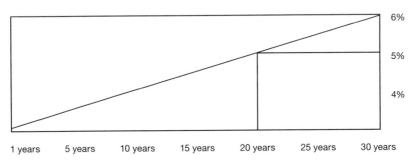

Refunding

Refunding must be looked at from the point of view of the issuer as well as from the point of view of the investor.

Investor's Point of View

The bond issuer exercising a call feature may offer to pay cash for retiring the bonds, or go through a refunding whereby the bondholder is offered a new bond in place of the called one. This refunding applies to the relationship between the investor and issuer. Refunding by the issuer, who is using a new debt to replace the old one, may have incentives for the bondholder to accept the refunding. One such enticement is to issue the new bond with an interest rate below the existing bond's rate, but slightly higher than competitive bonds that are trading in the market. As the bonds are about to be retired, the current bondholders will be receiving cash represented by the call price. The bondholder may reinvest this cash in any product he or she wants to acquire. The most attractive investment may be the issuer's new offering.

Issuer's Point of View

To the issuer who is offering substitute bonds to the current bond holders, they are attempting to refinance the older debt on more favorable terms yet sweetening the offer so as to retain the previous owners' investment.

If the issuer is retiring one bond by offering a new bond in the marketplace and not directly to the previous owners, that would be referred to as refunding also. Simply put, the retiring of one debt by issuing another is refunding. The U.S. Treasury Department refunds the Treasury bills every week. They retire Treasury bills that are maturing by paying for them with Treasury bills that are brand new. If they issue more than they retire, they will expand the national debt; if they issue fewer bills than they are retiring, they reduce the national debt. This type of refunding does not include the owners of the older bond. They simply surrender their maturing bonds and receive the payoff proceeds. The new bonds are offered in the market to anyone who wants to acquire them.

• Put Bonds •

The term "put bond" is deceiving. It should mean that the bondholders have a right to "put" the bond back to the issuer, given certain terms and conditions. Few bonds are issued with this provision; however, a putable bond carries a mandate that the bond be returned to the issuer. If the issuer has the right to mandate that the bondholder must put the bonds back to them, that is the same as the call feature of a bond.

Let's look at the call feature more closely. If a corporation comes to market and wants to issue $10 million worth of thirty-year bonds based on the current interest rate, the company must pay 7 percent. At 7 percent of $10 million, the bond is paying $700,000 a year in interest, and over thirty years that will be $21 million in interest. If interest rates should fall over time, so that this company could now issue a 5 percent bond and the investors would be able to get par, it can now be in a position to issue a $10 million 5 percent bond. Assuming that one is also going out for thirty years, that will cost the company $500,000 a year or $15 million in thirty years. It would save $6 million by retiring the bond. There is some expense involved in the retiring or reissuance of bonds, of course, but $6 million saved covers a lot of expenses.

Another reason for calling in bonds is the difference in interest rates as the thirty-year bond goes through its life. The thirty-year bond will be paying 7 percent for as long as it's outstanding. After fifteen years, the corporation that issued the thirty-year bond may be able to issue a fifteen-year bond paying less interest, let's assume the proverbial 5 percent. By calling in the thirty-year bond that has fifteen years to go, and issuing a fifteen-year bond that is carrying a 5 percent coupon, the company can save $3 million a year. Therefore, in the case of a callable bond holder, the threat of a bond's being called is not only caused by a drop of interest rates, it could be caused by a change in the bond's longevity as it goes along the yield curve from thirty years to fifteen years to zero.

• SINKING FUND •

Some bonds are sold with the understanding that a sinking fund has been activated. A sinking fund is the ability of an issuer to buy its bonds back out of earnings. Therefore in the above example, a corporation issuing a thirty-year 7 percent bond, with a sinker in force, can buy the bonds back whenever it wants, depending on the terms of the sinker, and retire the bonds at the current market price.

Not all bonds have sinkers. The advantage to buying a bond with a sinking fund is that if the issuer bought back early in the bond's life it will pay as long as it at par or less, and the owner of the bond will receive a high rate of interest for a short period of time—much better than if he or she had invested in a short-term bond. Some bonds are traded at dollar prices, which means they settle in currency. A price in the United States of a bond trading at 96 would be $0.96 on a dollar, so a $1,000 bond would cost $960. A bond trading at 101 would be $1,010.

Bonds that trade below their principal amount are said to be trading at a discount. Bonds that trade above their principal amount are said to trade at a premium. As the interest rates change due to many economic conditions, the price of bonds will change accordingly. In a fixed-income instrument, as interest rates rise bond prices fall; as interest rates fall bond prices rise. Since the bond can't change its interest rate to reflect the current interest rates, it must adjust for the difference somehow.

• How Debt Instruments Trade •

Fixed-income instruments will change their price to accommodate the changing in interest rates. Some debt instruments trade at basis prices. The term "basis price" is short for a yield-to-maturity basis, which means that if the buyer of that particular bond holds the bond to maturity, that is the rate of return they would receive. It includes the interest received, plus any amortization of the difference between the purchase price and par, assuming the bond was procured at a discount, or the depletion of the amount that the customer paid over the bond's face amount if the bond was bought at a premium.

Some debt instruments, like municipal securities and U.S. Treasury bills, trade on a yield-to-maturity basis. That means that the price they're paying has to be converted from the yield to maturity or the basis price into a dollar price. Generally speaking, if the basis price is higher than the coupon rate, the bond is trading at a discount. If the yield to maturity is less than the coupon rate, the bond is trading at a premium. For example, if a bond has a 6 percent coupon and is yielding a basis price of 5.9 percent, the customer must be paying more than the face amount to get the reduction in the yield. If that same bond has a basis price of 6.15, the customer would be getting the yield to maturity of 6.15, or 6.15 percent on their money. Since the bond only pays 6 percent interest they must be paying less than par to get the increase in the rate of return.

The relationship between the interest rate or coupon rate of the bond and the basis price is very important to understand, especially when discussing credit derivative products. The closer those two are to each other, and the closer the bond is to trading at par, the further the conversion to dollars will be from par. So an 8 percent bond trading at an 8.05 percent yield is trading very close to par. An 8 percent bond trading at 12.5 percent yield basis price is trading far from par and is trading at a deep discount to par.

• TAX ON INTEREST PAID •

Another feature peculiar to bonds is the tax or applicable tax on the interest paid. Concerning United States Treasury bonds, the interest paid is free from state and local taxes, but is taxed by the federal government. It may sound counterintuitive, but once again, the interest paid on debt issued directly by the federal government is taxed by the federal government but not taxed by state and local governments.

The interest paid by some municipal bonds is fully taxable, including by federal, state, and local governments; however, the interest paid by most municipal bonds is free from federal tax and, if you live within the state of issuance, free from state and local taxes. Therefore, for people who live in New York City, the city's own municipal bonds are usually free from federal, state, and city taxes. That freedom from federal income tax is applicable across state borders also; however, once you cross the border, the bonds become taxable for state and local purposes.

Corporate bonds are fully subject to federal, state, and local taxes. Therefore people who buy tax-free bonds may be getting a small advantage, but the adjustment in the yield between a taxable bond and a tax-free bond normally includes in the calculation the tax rates of those various states. Concerning bonds issued by federal agencies, like Ginnie Mae and Freddie Mac, the interest paid on those bonds is fully taxable on the state, federal, and local levels.

• DIFFERENCES BETWEEN MUNICIPAL BONDS AND CORPORATE BONDS •

An important point to bring out regarding bonds is the issuance. At the point of issuance, U.S. Treasury bonds and corporate bonds have one

CUSIP number. Municipal bonds, however, are issued in serial form. Because their various component bonds mature at different times, there are millions of municipal bonds outstanding. Therefore a customer buying your typical corporate bond on Monday, and telling a friend about it that night, might find that friend buying the same bond on Tuesday. However, should that investor have bought a municipal bond on Monday, and told his friend about it on Monday night, chances are that bond would no longer be available.

The corporate bond and the government bond form of issuances is called a "bullet," which means the entire bond offering has one coupon rate and one maturity date. Municipal bonds, on the other hand, are issued in serial form; therefore, while the issue itself may be as large as a corporate bond, the individual bonds making up the total are relatively or comparatively small and would have their own coupon and maturity date.

CHAPTER 3

TYPES OF RISK
IN DEBT MARKETS

O ne of the main reasons derivatives are used with debt products is to hedge or mitigate the potential risks inherent in debt ownership. These risks emanate from different sources, the product itself, its issuer, the market sector, the market in general, the domestic economy, the global economy, a disaster, or force majeure. Unlike other products, debt products incur liabilities almost at issuance. Any event or happening that may jeopardize the ability of the debt to meet its obligations, now or in the future, constitutes risk.

In understanding the credit markets, one must focus on the three core elements that make up risk. Each of these risks in turn affects pricing. There are three primary types of risk in the debt market: credit risk, market risk, and operational risk.

• CREDIT RISK •

Credit risk is a reflection of the financial strength of the issuer, or the financial strength and marketability that is behind the product itself. There are several tests one might use to determine the creditworthiness of the issuer and/or the issue. One test is how easily the borrower can pay off its debt. Another test is whether, if all of its assets were liquidated at reasonably anticipated prices, the borrower would still face a deficit. Another simple test is to look into how many times over the interest payments are covered by the company's earnings. The true market value of the collateral potentially supporting the instrument can be another test, considering whether the collateral is marketable and fungible. The relative security of the source of funds that will be used to the meet the debt obligations is still another.

There are many more tests and many different types of analysis that research analysts who work for financial institutions use. Besides these sources are the rating agencies that report on the financial worthiness of the party being studied. Their focus ranges from the workings of Standard & Poor's, Moody's, or Fitch, three companies among others that rate government, corporate, and municipal debt, to TransUnion, Experian, and Equifax, which rate individuals' financial status.

The ratings given by these agencies affect the borrower's ability to secure funding. Interest rate, or the rate charged for the use of others' money, increases with risk. At certain points certain lenders will not accept the borrower's risk and will not make loans. Therefore, we have terms such as "investment grade" securities, where certain institutions are not permitted to invest in companies whose debt has not achieved this standard rating.

A term that was constantly in the news over the last few years was "subprime mortgage loans." These loans were offered to individuals whose credit scores did not qualify them for a regular loan. These mortgages carried a higher interest rate than a conventional mortgage because the risk of default was much greater. As a debt instrument falls below investment grade, the investment company that is not permitted to own that instrument may have to liquidate and replace it with a better-suited instrument. The need for substitution and the process of doing so can be found in the offering documentation of the product.

Variance in Yield

The rating given to a bond affects its yield. In its simplest form, the yield is an issue's required annual payout divided by its market price. A $1,000 bond with a 5 percent "coupon" is supposed to pay $50 annually. If the bond has a current market value of $800, its current yield is $50 divided by $800 = 6.25 percent. If the bond's current market value is par (face amount, or in this example $1,000) the current yield would be 5 percent. If the bonds were valued at $1,250, the current yield would be 4 percent ($50 divided by $1,250 = 4 percent). We will discuss bond pricing in the section on market risk.

Yield is also affected by credit risk. Two bonds issued by two different companies, on the same day, with the same degree of financial strength backing them, with the same coupon rate and the same maturity date, will probably be trading at slightly different prices. The difference will be due to the market's perception of the issuers. This difference in pricing is reflected in the two bonds' yields and the difference in the prices of one bond to another bond, called the "basis spread."

"Basis points" is a term used to express interest rates, with 100 basis points equaling one percentage point. Therefore, 25 basis points equates to one quarter of a percent and 50 basis points equates to one half of a percent. In the above example of two bonds from different issuers, which have the same characteristics and the same level of securities, let's assume one bond is yielding 5.25 percent while the other is yielding 5.30 percent. It would be said that the bonds would be trading at a 5-basis-point spread. Some debt trades at a trusted rate or bellwether rate, such as LIBOR (London Interbank Offered Rate). If the LIBOR rate is at 3 percent, a debt instrument trading "200 over LIBOR" is priced to yield 5 percent.

Bonds at the same ratings may have different yields. This structure is similar to the tiered grading system in schools where grades of 90 to 100 is an A, 80 to 89 is a B, and so on. Taking three students, whose averages are 98, 91, and 88 respectively, and using this logic, a student with a 91-point average would receive the same grade as a student with a 98-point average even though the 91-point average student is closer in grade to a student with an 88-point average. That student would receive a B.

Bond yields are more sensitive to their rating. The yield on the 91 average bond would be priced closer to the 88 average bond than it would be to the 98 average bond.

Bond Ratings

Bonds are rated from triple-A downward. Bonds with triple-B rating or higher are considered investment grade. Certain institutions cannot acquire bonds below a triple-B rating. These are higher-risk bonds, but are above "junk" status. Bonds rated triple-C or lower are considered junk.

BOND RATINGS			
	Standard & Poor's	*Moody's*	*Fitch*
Best	AAA	Aaa	AAA
Investment Grade Minimum	BBB	BAA	BBB
Below Investment Grade (Riskier)	BB+	BA	BB+
Junk or Below	CCC	CAA	CCC
Default	D	C	D

Creditworthiness

The creditworthiness of an issuer is not static. Markets are dynamic and ever changing. Not only do interest rates change but the creditworthiness of a company fluctuates as well. These changes affect an issuer's financial status either positively or negatively. For instance, a manufacturer's receiving a huge contract would have a positive effect on that company, whereas should a competitor receive that contract instead, the effect on the manufacturing company could be negative. The forward projections or outlook for a company affects its bond pricing and by extension its yield.

• MARKET RISK •

Market risk is affected by current interest rates. As interest rates fluctuate, the rates of interest paid by newly issued bellwether instruments change accordingly. All other new issues coming to market key off these bellwether bond rates and their rates reflect the degree of additional interest the new issue must pay. Issues already trading in the secondary market will see their market price change. The rates change according to the difference in their perceived safety in relation to the bellwether instruments.

Here's an example:

> Let's assume a $1,000 bond with a 5 percent coupon rate trading at face amount (par) has a current yield of 5 percent. The bond pays $50 interest ($1,000 × 5% = $50) per year. If the bond was selling at par, its current yield would be 5 percent ($50/$1,000 = 5%). If a rise in overall interest rates causes this bond to now yield 6 percent, its market price must fall. Using only the current interest rate formula (interest payment divided by yield), the price would fall to $833.33 ($50/.06 = $833.33).
>
> Therefore, in the above example, someone who acquired the bonds at par would be losing $166.67 per $1,000 bond even though the financial strength of the issuer hasn't changed.

Market Liquidity

Market risk is also affected by the product's market liquidity. The thinner the market, the more likely the price will be affected by orders of size. The thin market may be caused by the size of the issue itself or the float: that is, the amount available for trading. On these types of markets it is difficult to obtain a true current market price due to the size of the spread. This figure is the difference between the bid and the offer. The less liquidity that is in the market, the wider the spread will be between the bid and offer because of the greater difficulty the contra side to the trade has unwinding or adjusting the position.

As we move into derivative and structured products, we run the gamut from highly traded products with rock solid prices to "one-offs" whose market price is based on the prices of similar products or on assumptions made as to their value. For example, in the trading of some future products, the near-term contract months are actively traded, whereas the farther out the contract month is the less likely to trade. Should trades occur in an inactive product's contract month, its price will be determined by extrapolating from a nearby active month. Through this process every future contract is priced, whether or not it actually traded that day.

• Operational Risk •

Operational risk is the possibility that a contract will not be completed because of logistical or other nonfinancial obstacles. It varies from product to product and from participant to participant. A firm trading a highly liquid instrument cleared through a central clearing party (CCP) has a minimum operational risk in regard to the contra party. This is partly because the contra party has satisfied the operational requirements of the clearing facility, besides also satisfying the financial and regulatory requirements. Second, the clearing corporation acts as a transaction matching facility, comparing the details of the transaction as reported by the buyer and the seller. This serves to bring an independent set of eyes to witness the transaction.

When the terms of the transaction are agreed to, the transaction is considered compared. To expedite transaction settlement, the clearing entity stands behind each compared trade and becomes the buyer for each seller and the seller for each buyer. The clearing entity then will net down the transaction per participant by reducing the number of receives and deliveries of the same issue each participant has to make.

Some clearing corporations act as central clearing party and guarantee the transactions. Should a party that is contra to a compared transaction default, the clearing corporation will stand in for the defaulting party. Operational risk grows as the central contra party is replaced by a clearing facility that is not a central contra party. The risk continues to grow as the product becomes less liquid and more customized. When it moves out of a third-party verification environment into a transaction for transaction, then both parties must rely only on each other.

Adding to the mix of potential problems are complications such as the use of different currencies, the distance some products must travel to satisfy delivery requirements, the quality requirements demanded by the contract, government intervention affecting international transactions, and so on. Many derivative products go on to form some of the other structured products covered in this book. At least one leg of the packaged product is affected or priced by the debt market.

Let's take a look at the debt market now to see what it provides.

CHAPTER 4

DEBT MARKETS AND LENDING RATES

L et's suppose that a new employee is hired and has negotiated a salary of X. The employee thinks X is very good and is proud of his negotiating skills. On the first day on the job, the employee discovers that another new employee doing the same job and having the same skill set is earning more. Suddenly the employee isn't happy. On the other hand, if he finds that another new employee doing the same job and having the same skill set is earning less, the employee is happier.

The same concept can be applied to interest rates on debt instruments. An issuer negotiates an interest rate for a bond offering that the issuer thinks is a good rate. The bonds are offered. Awhile later another corporation with the same finances et cetera issues a similar bond and pays a lower rate of interest. The issuer of the first bond isn't happy but if the opposite had occurred they would be very happy. The investor who acquired the bonds is on the opposite side of the emotional roller coster. In the middle is the market.

The market accommodates the disparity in the bonds' interest rates by the prices the bonds trade at. Other factors, such as the degree of risk, longevity of the debt, and so on all affect the interest rates the debt has to pay. With all the factors involved, there must be a base rate from which all other rates emanate. Some of these key rates are universal, others are domestic in origin. But they set the lending rates that are used.

• DEBT PRICING •

The pricing of bonds is quite an interesting process; it comprises the present value of all cash flows. Let's assume, for instance, that the reader tells a friend about a $10,000 bonus due in one year's time, which he or she would like right now. Since the bonus is guaranteed, the friend offers to buy it. If the friend was to pay $10,000 for the $10,000 bonus a year from now, that friend would be without the use of the money during that year. The reader would have a big advantage, having been paid one year earlier. Instead, the friend and the reader negotiate a price that is fair to both of them, settling on $9,500. Therefore, that $500 discount represents payment to the friend for doing without the money for a year as well as a penalty to the reader for obtaining the funds one year early. The present value of $10,000 receivable a year from now, in this particular case, is $9,500. Similarly, each payment in a bond's life has to be discounted to its present value and these present values added up to get to today's price.

The formula for Present Value = Pay Out times 1/[1 + Rate] times the number of times it happened, or $PV = PO \times [1/1 + R] \times t$. If a bond was to pay 7 percent on $1,000, it will be paying $70 a year or $35 every six months. The tricky part of the formula is the rate. It's not the interest rate of the bond; it's the current interest rate that the bond is trading at in the marketplace. In other words, for a 7 percent bond priced to yield 8 percent, the R would be 8 percent. If the 7 percent bond was priced to yield 6 percent, the R would be 6 percent. A 7 percent bond paying interest six months from now, priced to yield 8 percent, would be $PV = PO \$35/1/[1 + 4\%] \times 1$ (the number of times this event happened; the next payment, it would be 2).

Present Value at Work

The following are two examples of the present value calculations of a ten-year 7 percent bond that pays its interest twice a year. One bond is priced at a discount priced to yield approximately 8 percent, the other is priced at a premium to yield approximately 6 percent. In addition: both examples are followed by the quick "Rule of Thumb" method, which is used to estimate the yield.

(The calculation using this method, in the first example, is to take the bond's discounted price of $932.13 and subtract it from the bond's maturity value of $1,000.00, which leaves a gain of $67.87. Amortizing this gain over ten years comes to $6.79 per year. While the bond is paying $70.00 per interest per year, its value is theoretically increasing at a rate of $6.79 for a net of $76.79. To determine an average theoretical value of the bond over its life, add the current market value and the value at maturity together and divide by 2 to arrive at the average theoretical value of $966.06. Divide 76.79 by 966.06 = 0.0794878 or 7.95 percent. The calculation for the premium bond is different only in that the rate of depletion is subtracted from the interest payment.)

$1,000 7 PERCENT SEMIANNUAL INTEREST-PAYING 10-YEAR BOND, PRICED AT A DISCOUNT

Payment Number	Payout × Factor	Present Value Amount
1	35 × .961538	$33.76
2	35 × .924556	32.36
3	35 × .888996	31.11
4	35 × .854804	29.92
5	35 × .821927	28.77
6	35 × .790314	27.66
7	35 × .759918	26.60
8	35 × .730690	25.57
9	35 × .702506	24.59
10	35 × .676564	23.64
11	35 × .649508	22.73
12	35 × .624597	21.86
13	35 × .600574	21.02
14	35 × .577475	20.21
15	35 × .555264	19.43
16	35 × .533908	18.68
17	35 × .513373	17.97
18	35 × .493628	17.28

19	35 × .474642	16.61
20	1,035 × .456386	472.36
	Total:	$ 932.13

$1,000.00 − $932.13 = $67.87
$67.87/10 = $6.79
$6.79 + $70 = $76.79
($1,000.00 + $932.13)/2 = $966.06
$76.79/10 = 7.679 or 6.78 percent

$1,000 7 PERCENT SEMIANNUAL INTEREST-PAYING 10-YEAR BOND, PRICED AT A PREMIUM

Payment Number	Payout × Factor	Present Value Amount
1	35 × .970874	$33.98
2	35 × .942596	32.99
3	35 × .915141	32.03
4	35 × .888486	31.10
5	35 × .862608	30.19
6	35 × .837483	29.31
7	35 × .813091	28.46
8	35 × .789409	27.63
9	35 × .766416	26.82
10	35 × .744093	26.04
11	35 × .722420	25.28
12	35 × .701739	24.55
13	35 × .680950	23.83
14	35 × .661116	23.14
15	35 × .641861	22.47
16	35 × .623661	21.83
17	35 × .605015	21.17

18	35 × .587393	20.59
19	35 × .570285	19.96
20	1,035 × .553674	573.05
	Total:	$1,074.42

$1,074.42 – $1,000.00 =$74.42
$74.42/10 = $7.44
$70 – $7.44 = $62.56
($1,074.42 + $1,000)/2 = $1,037.21
$62.56/$1,037.21 = .0603156 or 6.03 percent

Duration and Convexity

Duration predicts a change in the bond's value caused by a change in interest rate. It is an abstract figure that tests the sensitivity to a change in interest rates. Bond convexity measures the sensitivity to a change in interest rates. It tracks where a bond price deviates from the expected move predicted by duration.

Macaulay Duration and Modified Duration

There are two forms of duration used to measure the effect of interest rate changes on process of yields. One is *Macaulay duration*, which measures the weighted average time until all the cash flows are received measured in years, and the other is *modified duration*, which measures price sensitivity. Both of these, but especially Macaulay, will tell how long it will take the investor to be repaid by the bond itself.

Here's an example of Macaulay duration:

A five-year zero-coupon bond will take five years to pay back its investor.

Bond Issue ⎯⎯⎯⎯⎯→ 5 Yrs ⎯⎯⎯⎯⎯→ Payment

As it took five years before the bond paid back its investment, the duration is five years.

Here's an example of modified duration:

Let's suppose a twenty-year bond that pays $35 interest semiannually. It is trading at 70 percent or $700, and the duration on the bond would be ten years ($70 per year × 10 yrs = $700).

Yr #1	Yr #2	Yr #3	Yr #4	Yr #5
$70	$70	$70	$70	$70
Yr #6	Yr #7	Yr #8	Yr #9	Yr #10
$70	$70	$70	$70	$70
Yr #11	Yr #12	Yr #13	Yr #14	Yr #15
$70	$70	$70	$70	$70
Yr #16	Yr #17	Yr #18	Yr #19	Yr #20
$70	$70	$70	$70	$1,070

Note: The last payment includes face amount of the bond plus the interest payment.

If the bond was acquired at a price of 77 percent of its face value or $770, the duration would be eleven years ($70 × 11 yrs = $770) without compounding the annual interest payments. A 10 percent rise in the bond's price would result in a one-year extension of its duration.

As interest rates rise, bond prices fall, and as interest rates fall, bond prices rise. Therefore as interest rates changed, the duration of the bond would change also. If interest rates in the market fell so that the market price of the aforementioned bond was par, or 100 percent of its face value, a buyer at that price would have to wait approximately 14½ years ($70 × 14.5 = $1,015) to get his or her money back.

• INTEREST ONLY/PRINCIPAL ONLY BONDS •

Earlier, we discussed the fact that issuers try to alter debt products from the basic bond structure to offer something slightly different that will attract investors. The basic bond structure in the United States is: Principal, name of issuer or issue, coupon rate, payment dates, and maturity date.

$10,000 ZAPPO *(issuing company)* 8% *(interest rate)*
Cl *(Callable)* 20XX *(First year call feature is alive)*
FA *(February/August)* 20ZZ *(Maturity year)*.

A bond issued for twenty years that pays interest twice a year
can be altered to become at least two other products. One is a
twenty-year zero-coupon bond and the other is a semiannual
interest-paying instrument. The forty interest payments
(twenty years x two) can then be broken down into near-term
and long-term payments, if a market exists for it. The zero-
coupon bond is known as the principal only portion, the
interest payment vehicle as the interest only portion.

• U.S. Treasury Bonds •

United States Treasury bonds lend themselves to this special treatment.
Bond dealers or other financial institutions would buy the bonds, put
them in escrow, and strip the interest payments away from the principal.
The principal became a zero-coupon bond (which the U.S. Treasury didn't
offer) and the interest payment would be sold apart from the core bonds.
The principal and each slice of the interest payments—now a zero coupon which maintains its original maturity date and with shorter maturi-
ties for the interest payments—each receive their own CUSIP numbers.

These products were originally sold under the names LIONs, TIGERs,
CATs, etc. Now, the government issues OID (original issue discount) zero-
discount bonds. As a result, a twenty-year U.S. Treasury bond that pays
interest every six months can, theoretically, be converted into as many as
forty coupon payment bonds and one twenty-year zero-coupon bond. Usually a buyer of the interest payments will buy a "strip" of payments.

Dominant Lending Rates

In the United States, U.S. Treasury bills, notes, and bonds are the benchmark instruments that longer-term and other debt instruments' interest is
based on. For short-term debt, as in overnight loans, the base rates used
are LIBOR, the federal funds rate, the U.S. Treasury rate, and Euribor.

LIBOR (*London Interbank Offered Rate*)

The LIBOR rate is set by London banks and is an average rate these banks charge one another. The rate is used to set mortgage rates and many of the derivative products discussed in this book.

Federal Funds Rate

This is similar to the LIBOR but is used as a basis for U.S. banks to charge one another for borrowing funds. It is sometimes referred to as the "overnight rate," but that term is generic to any rate used for lending purposes.

U.S. Treasury Rate

The U.S. Treasury rate is the base rate used to set the interest rate of U.S. Treasury instruments of different tenors; that is, the durations of the instrument. Many domestic debt instruments, corporate bonds, notes, etc., are priced off the Treasury rates.

Euribor (*Euro Interbank Offered Rate*)

Euribor is the rate set by a panel of European banks and represents the rate of interest charged by European Union banks for interbank borrowing. When it was determined that the LIBOR rates were being manipulated and that scandal broke, Euribor was one of the rates put forward to replace LIBOR as the primary source for funding.

These cash rates have many applications in both the derivative and nonderivative worlds. Besides being used to set interest rates or the resulting yields, these base rates play an integral part in many of the derivatives discussed in this book. A product user trying to get a better loan position may enter into a fixed or floating LIBOR rate swap. An owner of a collateralized mortgage obligation securitized instrument may want to hedge against interest rate changes that would negatively affect the value of the fixed-rate mortgage pools he or she owns. To do this, he or she would want to exchange that cash flow for one that is floating.

Now, let's turn our attention to the various forms of mutual funds.

CHAPTER 5

FORMS OF MUTUAL FUNDS

The term "mutual fund" covers a whole gamut of products. Defined as the pooling of money by participants in the attempt to accomplish a specific goal, "mutual funds" covers everything from a joint venture for a specific purpose to a multimillion-dollar investment fund that concentrates on a particular geographical area. Through shares, mutual funds allow investors to participate in a part of the trading world that otherwise would be closed to them because of cost, logistics, or regulations.

Technically, the amassing of capital to achieve a particular objective can be referred to as a mutual fund. Included in that general term are open-end mutual funds, closed-end investment companies, joint ventures, and unit investment trusts. We will look at open-end mutual funds first.

• OPEN-END MUTUAL FUNDS •

Mutual funds are a long-established product in the financial environment. When most people hear the term, they think of the open-end fund, which buys and sells its shares against the public. An open-end fund does not have a secondary market for trading purposes. When the shares of a mutual fund are acquired, they are bought from the fund and not from a third party, and when the shares are sold, they are sold back to the fund.

Many 401(k)s, 403s, and other retirement plans, which individuals control themselves or which are in the control of a money manager, have mutual funds in them. Many investment advisers use mutual funds as part of their investment decisions or to augment different strategies. The mutual fund segment is itself a crowded and very competitive part of the financial industry.

Open-end mutual fund companies have investment plans that come in all varieties. Some charge a fee known as a sales charge; that charge is reduced as more is invested. The mutual fund's sales charge is set up with "break points." These are the investment points that the total invested is required to pass for the sales charge to be reduced to the next lower level. Therefore, a mutual fund could have a sales charge that drops by one eighth of a percent for every $25,000 invested in the particular fund. A client investing $24,900 would pay a higher percentage sales charge than a client who invested $25,100. The Investment Company Act of 1940 mandates that clients be informed as their investment nears a break point.

Break Point Sales

Some mutual funds, known as no-loads, do not charge a fee, but generally have a higher operating cost than the load funds do. Funds that have load charges have different ways of applying them. These are known as A, B, and C investment plans, and here is what the different classes of plans entail:

Class A has a front-end sales charge. The sales charge is subtracted from every investment the owner makes. Break point sales charges are applicable here.

Class B has a back-end sales charge. This is a contingent deferred sales charge (CDSC), which is subtracted from what the investor was supposed to receive when he or she liquidated the shares if sold during the first six years. In the sixth year, the shares are converted to Class A shares.

Class C has higher operating fees and may be charged a fee as if it were Class A or Class B, but the shares are not converted and remain as Class C shares.

Some mutual funds are sold directly between the fund and the client; other funds are sold to clients through brokerage firms. Some of those brokerage firms maintain the clients' mutual fund position on their internal records along with other financial assets. The ownership records at the mutual fund do not reflect the beneficial owners' names but instead carry the nominee name of the broker-dealer. Other brokerage firms pass the transactions to the mutual fund so that the mutual fund knows the investor and not the broker-dealer. One reason behind a broker-dealer's decision is if the client was to use their fund shares to borrow money against (known as margin). The fund shares become the collateral for the loan and must remain in the broker-dealer's control and nominee name. It is a business decision made by the broker-dealer as part of its business plan.

Net Asset Value

Open-end mutual funds are priced once a day, at the end of the trading day, and they are priced at their net asset value (NAV). The net asset value, used to price mutual funds, is a computation made up of the value of the fund's portfolio, plus money awaiting investment, less expenses, divided by the shares outstanding.

Net Asset Value = (Value of the portfolio + Cash awaiting investment – Expenses) / Number of shares outstanding

Because an open-end fund stands ready to buy or sell its shares against the public, there isn't any need for a secondary market for trading open-end mutual fund shares. Therefore, orders being given to a mutual fund must be market orders; the mutual fund accumulates these orders and once a night executes buys and sells at the same clean price (not including sales charge or other fees) and sends responses back to the entering parties.

Here's an example:

Tom Katt owns shares of a mutual fund that was acquired at around $30.00 a share. One morning the fund's value increases during the day to $40.00 a share, and then the fund falls back to close at $30.00 a share. If Tom wanted to sell the shares during the day, when it was *at $40.00 per share, he could not, because open-end mutual funds are officially priced once a day after the close of business. If Tom wanted to sell it, he would receive the closing value of $30.00 per share, or the same price he paid for it. In the case of a different product, such as an exchange-traded fund (ETF), if it opened in the morning trading at $30.00 a share, and that was the price Tom had acquired it at, and during the day it reached $40.00 a share, Tom could sell it at $40.00 a share and not have to worry about where it is going to close.*

Another difference between exchange-traded products and mutual funds is that each share of an ETF or ETP is independent. Therefore the shares can be bought or sold as the client wishes. In the case of the mutual fund, since the shares are represented by a pool from the portfolio held by the fund, a sale by another person within the pool could require selling securities to pay that person. In the case of ETFs or ETPs, the buying and selling of shares is independent from the shares owned by others. Therefore there isn't a tax penalty when someone else sells securities.

The issuer of a mutual fund stands ready to sell open-end mutual funds to the public and buy back from the public. There isn't any secondary market. The price of the fund is determined by its net asset value, which means that the value of the portfolio plus money awaiting investment minus expenses divided by the number of shares outstanding will give you the net asset value per share. Closed-end funds are different, and we will discuss them next.

• CLOSED-END MUTUAL FUNDS •

Closed-end mutual funds begin their life in a similar fashion to open-end funds. The sponsor or the fund manager issues shares to potential investors. As the shares are sold, they accumulate the funds. Often, the participants have predetermined either the number of shares they want to have outstanding or the sum of money they are trying to accumulate. As with open-end mutual funds, they must establish ahead of time the products they are going to conduct business in and how they are going to use their portfolios. These choices would be controlled by the charter of the funds, by their prospectus, and in accordance with the Investment Company Act of 1940 and all subsequent rules and regulations.

Once the amount of shares have been issued or the amount of capital raised that meets their goal, the fund closes and trading is done based on supply and demand—either on an exchange or over-the-counter. Buyers and sellers trade among themselves without the mutual fund's participation. During the period of time the fund is being formed, as with all open-end mutual funds, the price per share is determined by net asset value.

Once the fund closes, it now trades by supply and demand, so the market price can be over or under the net asset value—or to put it another way, it can be a premium or a discount to the net asset value. The closed-end fund trades as if it were common stock going through the same operational processes to settlement. Closed-end fund trades settle in three days, the same as stock, whereas open-end fund trades settle on trade date.

Some Important Distinctions

Let's separate open-end funds from closed-end funds as required by the Securities and Exchange Commission (SEC). Closed-end funds should be called closed-end investment companies; this would distinguish them in type and form from the open-end mutual fund, which is simply called a mutual fund. Since open funds make a continuous investment as outside funds are received, and closed-end investment companies do not, if a customer who owns an open-end fund decides to sell his or her shares by liquidating some security positions, then holders who have nothing to do with this action wind up with a taxable event.

In a closed-end investment company, since the shares are traded among the public, the effect of one person's selling has no tax consequence for anyone else who owns shares in that fund. In addition, with a closed-end investment company, usually all the orders permitted in that marketplace are also permitted to be used by the closed-end investment company. Since the closed-end company is trading in an active, dynamic marketplace, you can buy and sell or sell and buy securities during the day—a feature you cannot do with mutual funds because of their pricing at night only. Closed-end investment companies offer their funds in a whole range of possible investment opportunities, similar to open-end mutual funds. They have taxable and tax-free bond funds, global issues, sector funds, and mortgage-backed security funds, to name but a few.

Next we'll look at joint ventures.

• JOINT VENTURES •

Joint ventures are usually one-time formal agreements aimed at achieving certain goals. Money or other assets are pooled together in an attempt to accomplish a nonreoccurring event, such as oil exploration. The venture itself may be an ongoing effort such as a real estate holding. It must have at least two parties, but there's no maximum limit on the number of participants. As corporations are legally recognized as individuals, one party may be a corporation, the other an individual.

If the effort is successful, other ventures may be formed. If the venture fails, it ceases to exist. If the parties want to continue their relationship after a venture fails, a new one must be formed. The participants all share in the profits or losses. The terms can be on a pro rata basis, service-performed basis, or any other arrangement the parties decide at the time of initial agreement.

Profits from a joint venture are usually taxed at the partnership level. Ownership in a joint venture does not lend itself to trading. Selling interests in the joint venture can be difficult, as it is basically an illiquid product and the disposing of the ownership may require approval from other members. The joint venture agreement may require the seller to sell its ownership back only to the venture, and the agreement may also require potential new owners to be approved by the other owners.

Members of the corporate world who participate in this segment of the market are referred to as venture capitalists.

• UNIT INVESTMENT TRUSTS (UITs) •

Unit investment trusts (UITs) are primarily composed of common stock or bonds, the portfolio of which is established by the offering date. Like a joint venture, the UIT is a one-time offering. A sponsor offers a set number of units (shares) to investors. These portfolios are not actively managed; therefore, their contents remain the same throughout the existence of the trust.

All trusts have a set expiration date. In the case of an equity trust, when that time comes, the equities are liquidated and the resulting funds proportionately distributed. In the expiration of a bond or other debt trusts, the contents of debt securities often will have matured by the expiration date. Those that have not matured are sold off, and all funds resulting from maturing bonds and sales of nonmatured bonds are distributed to the bondholders.

The process used for the dividend (equities) or interest (bonds) distributions is expressed in the trust's indenture. Other items covered in the indenture include the payout periods and the conditions or circumstances under which the management may alter the portfolio voluntarily. Remember, we are looking at three independent layers. There are the securities in the UIT that have their own life, the UIT that has its own modus operandi, and the client that invested in the UIT who is free to buy or sell the UIT. In equity UITs, corporate action taken by the issuer may be voluntary or involuntary. Voluntary action would include the dispensing of an issuer's rights offering. The trust agreement would state how the trust will respond. The UIT owner doesn't have a choice. In the involuntary corporate action, such as a bond maturing, the disposition of the proceeds are also covered in the trust agreement. In order to close out their positions in the UIT, the investors simply sell their units back to the sponsor. Some sponsors maintain a secondary market in the units. This permits the seller's investment to be paid for by the buyer and avoids the need for the sponsor to liquidate investments in the trust to honor the redemption.

CHAPTER 6

REAL ESTATE INVESTMENT TRUSTS

An always exciting aspect of the derivatives market is the sudden emergence of a dormant derivative product to the front page of the news. This can be observed by the recent rise in popularity and regulatory concern of Real Estate Investment Trust transactions.

• TYPES OF REITs •

An REIT is composed of either real estate mortgages or the tangible asset—the real estate itself. A few REITs may invest in both. The dominant REIT in the market is the one that is invested in the actual asset (the property). These are known as equity REITs; the other type is referred to as a mortgage REIT. The REIT product gives the general public an opportunity to "own" and participate in the real estate market. The REIT may invest in properties or the mortgages of heath care facilities, shopping malls, apartment complexes, office buildings, hotels, storage facilities, etc.

REITs earn revenue through one of two venues: one method, the equities REITs, obtains the majority of their income from rent on property owned by the REIT. The other method, mortgage REITs, derive their income from interest earned on investments in property mortgages and/or through the acquisition of mortgage-backed securities (this product is covered elsewhere in this book).

• INVESTING IN REITs •

Many REITs trade on stock exchanges while others are offered in the over-the-counter market and still others are privately placed. The first two, those that trade on exchanges, such as the New York Stock Exchange, and those that are distributed through the over-the-counter market must be registered with the Securities and Exchange Commission (SEC). Those that are privately placed are not so registered and are primarily offered to institutions and high net worth individuals who are supposed to be sophisticated enough to understand the risk/rewards scenario of the product.

The REITs that trade on exchanges trade as if they were common stock. Their market value is quoted, executions captured and reported to the public through pricing vendors, and transactions are processed from execution to settlement, through the same systems used by regular equity securities. Buyers and sellers trade ownership without any interference from the REIT issuer. SEC-registered REITs that do not trade on exchanges follow a similar type of issuance as open-end mutual funds, with shares issued through a distribution network. The terms for redeeming these shares are on an issuer by issuer basis. In addition, the individual REIT prospectus may contain a mandatory holding period. If at a later time the board of directors should decide that the registered REIT be listed on an exchange, the outstanding shares will become fully tradable once listed. Finally, the acquisition of a non-SEC–registered REIT constitutes a private transaction between the issuer and buyer. These are generally sold in rather large blocks of $100,000 or more and are therefore placed with institutions or high net worth individuals as mentioned previously. A private REIT can be a customized product (one off) or part of a larger block and its duration is set for a predetermined period of time (twelve years, for example). During that period withdrawals generally are not permitted. If an emergency should occur forcing the owner to sell, the share owner would pay a heavy penalty against the value of the REIT. Liquidation of non-SEC–registered REITs is issuer dependent and generally conducted under very limited conditions. One benefit of a private REIT is that it usually pays a higher rate of return than those that are publicly traded.

Owners of REITs can avoid long-term capital gains taxes on principal appreciation that may be due if they were to sell REITs, by using the REITs' value to invest in a new REIT called an umbrella partnership. Their participation (or contribution) in the new REIT is added to funds raised by an initial public offering of the new REIT. The original REIT owner becomes a limited partner in the new REIT. Along with the limited partnership, the original REIT owner receives put options that permit the limited partnership to be exchanged for cash or shares of the new REIT. The process is known as UPREIT. In a DownREIT, a property owner goes into a partnership with an existing REIT entity and forms a limited partnership. The newly formed limited partnership acts as a joint venture with the limited partnership's and the original property owner's acting independently of the original existing REIT. The value of the put options that the limited partners receive is based on joint venture property and not the total property of the limited partnership and the existing REIT.

• REGULATORY •

The SEC–registered REITs that trade on exchanges come under the rules and regulations of that exchange and FINRA (Financial Industry Regulatory Authority). SEC–registered REITs not traded on exchanges answer to the NASAA (North American Securities Administrators Association). NASAA is comprised mainly of state security regulators; non-SEC–registered REITs are not regulated. In addition, some may not be liquid or there may not be any liquidity when an owner may want to sell. BUYER BEWARE.

• ALTERNATIVE VEHICLES •

For diversification investors may acquire REITs through select mutual funds as well as through exchange-traded funds. Using the mutual fund or the exchange-traded fund vehicle allows the investor to own several REITs at one time. Options on REIT products trade on exchanges as well as on over-the-counter markets (mutual funds, exchange-traded funds, and option products are discussed elsewhere in this book).

• Income Tax Characteristics •

Under the Internal Revenue Code Section 856, an REIT is any trustor corporation or an association of participants that acts as a single investment agent specializing in real estate and or real estate mortgages. Under subchapter M (sections 856–59), Chapter 1 of the Internal Revenue Code, REITs are entitled to deduct dividends paid to its shareholders or investors from its earnings as an offset to income tax liabilities. Among the requirements for REITs to avoid certain income tax liabilities, they are required to distribute a minimum of 90 percent of their taxable income to the aforementioned participants. This same rule applies to mutual funds covered elsewhere in this book. The income tax owed on the revenue earned by the REIT is paid by the REIT owners. This is unlike the income tax obligations of other entities, such as corporations. In those cases, the entity earning the revenue has a liability to pay income tax on the earnings and the share owners pay income tax on the dividend distribution.

• Global Product •

Real estate investment trusts are truly a global product. They are offered in many countries of Africa (Ghana and Nigeria), Asia (Australia, Hong Kong, India, Japan, Pakistan, Philippines, Saudi Arabia, Singapore, and United Arab Emirates), Europe (Bulgaria, Finland, France, Germany, and the United Kingdom), North America (Canada, Mexico, United States), and South America (Brazil). Caution must be taken by the investor as the rules, regulations, and other restrictions differ from one country to another.

• Qualifications •

The formation of a real estate investment trust must be a fully taxable entity. It is operated through a management contingent who decides on investments and who oversees the day-to-day operation. The management answers to the board of directors or trustees. This senior group in turn answers to the shareholders. There must be at least one hundred shareholders of which no more than 50 percent of its shares are owned by five or fewer individuals. The REIT must have its investments gauges concentrated so that at least 75 percent of the entity's total invested portfolio is in real estate. The entity must have no more than 20 percent of its assets invested in taxable REIT subsidiaries. Finally, it must earn at least 75 percent of its gross income from real estate–related activities.

• TERMINATION •

Each REIT has its own termination point. In some cases the terms of the trust set the expiration. In some cases termination of the REIT is when the asset(s) is (are) sold or, in the case of mortgages, when the last mortgage is paid off. Any residual is disbursed to the remaining owners.

CHAPTER 7

EXCHANGE-TRADED
FUNDS

S uppose we took the global reach of some mutual fund's portfolio, which is priced once a day (and after the market closed) and made it resemble common stock that trades on an exchange and is priced moment to moment. That is basically what was done when the exchange-traded fund product was introduced. The product not only gave the investor a diversified investment with a single effort, it also gave the investor a product that trades daily in a liquid market.

Exchange-traded products (ETPs) track indexes or products in a similar way to a mutual fund, but there are major differences. *ETP* is the umbrella term used for these four exchange-traded products:

Exchange-Traded Commodities (ETC)

Exchange-Traded Currencies (also ETC)

Exchange-Traded Funds (ETF)

Exchange-Traded Notes (ETN)

Here are some quick facts about these products. ETPs trade during exchange hours and their share prices are disseminated frequently. The initial product of the group was exchange-traded funds, and then the others followed, with the group eventually being called exchange-traded products. Because ETFs were the first and as they are the dominant product, many refer to all the products as ETFs. In this chapter we will discuss ETFs exclusively, and move on to the remaining ETPs in the next chapter.

• EXCHANGE-TRADED FUNDS DEFINED •

An exchange-traded fund (ETF) is a unit that is backed by a basket of stocks. The stocks replicate an index. The index may be of the "passive" or "aggressive" type. The component parts of a passive index are adjusted periodically to stay true to the index's value, whereas the component parts of an aggressive index are traded regularly to take advantage of market opportunities. The component securities in the index can be broad based, covering industry in general, or they may be more focused by sector locally, by geographic area, by type of asset, by commodity, and so on.

Varieties of ETFs

The first ETF was Standard & Poor's Depositary Receipts, commonly referred to as Spiders or Spyders. The trading symbol is SPDR. The original SPDR was on the S&P 500 stock index. This ETF has the securities replicating the index maintained in a trust managed by State Street Global Advisors (SSGA). The trust is a unit investment trust (UIT) priced at one tenth of the index value. The index ETF pays cash dividends quarterly on the securities held in the trust, less any expenses.

  SPDR has grown into a family of ETPs that includes international and domestic, long- to short-term, stock and debt, income to growth, and many more types of ETPs. Another well-known issuer of ETPs is iShares, which are similar in nature. They were originally offered by Barclays Global Investors, and currently by BlackRock. They also trade in an exchange environment or through alternative trading systems, such as ECNs. iShares offers a wide range of ETPs encompassing both the domestic and international markets, with a wide range of products therein.

VIPERs are similar to the above and are issued by Vanguard. The term VIPER stands for Vanguard Index Participation Equity Receipts. Other popular ETPs are DIAMONDS, issued by State Street Global Advisors (ETF on the Dow Jones Industrial Average), and Cubes, which are issued by Invesco PowerShares (ETF on the NASDAQ 100 index). PowerShares issues aggressively managed ETFs. Some of the more familiar names issue whole families of ETPs. These names represent just a few of the issuers of ETFs and the list is growing. Charles Schwab, for example, has announced its intention of issuing its own ETFs.

The product, the ETF itself, is issued in one of two forms: one is structured like an open-end management investment company, which operates in the same manner as mutual funds and money market funds whereas the other one is structured as a unit investment trust. Most of the ETFs follow the management investment company format. Those that operate like management companies can alter their portfolio as they deem necessary, sell securities short, and participate in security lending programs, which can be beneficial to their management efforts. Those structured as unit investment trusts are mostly confined to what they can buy and sell. Generally market action is a result of a bond maturing or an instrument being called in. Those that are managed by investment companies can also use derivatives—such as options and futures—to augment and assist in achieving their goals.

• CREATION OF AN EXCHANGE-TRADED FUND •

The development of an ETF begins with the proposed ETF manager, who will sponsor the plan and present it to the Securities and Exchange Commission (SEC). Upon approval, the sponsor contacts a market maker or some other large financial trading firm that is qualified as an "authorized participant" to set up the supporting shares of stock in a trust. The trust is not part of the previously mentioned parties. The shares may be borrowed or owned. The authorized participant forms creation units using the shares to back the units. The trust then issues ETFs against the creation unit. The ETFs are a legal claim against the portfolio. The transaction is an "in kind" transaction (security for security) so there isn't any tax implication involved. The ETFs are then sold to the public and traded like shares of stock.

Note: If the "borrowed" stock pays a dividend, the authorized participant or trust must be sure the ETF owners and the borrowed stock owners *both* receive the payout. The corporation will only pay "one share owner"; the same is true with other "corporate actions."

Redemption of ETFs

If the owner of the ETF has amassed the required minimum of ETF shares as stated by the issuer at the registration of the ETF, he or she can take the accumulated shares to the authorized participant, who will redeem the ETF in exchange for the underlying securities.

Trading ETFs

The trading unit for ETFs is 100 shares, the same as for common stock. Trading is accomplished either on electronic platforms or by open outcry on the trading floor of an exchange. The quotes, the current bid and offers, as well as the size (amount of trading lots available at that price) are displayed on the same devices as listed common shares. Brokers service customer orders as they trade against market makers or other brokers. Orders to buy and sell ETFs are in line with equity orders such as market orders (buys accept the offer; sells accept the bid part of the current quote) and limit the types of orders. Those setting the maximum to be paid (buy limit) or the minimum to be received (sell limit) can be entered with an extended time period (GTC, or good till canceled) besides the day order that terminates at the end of the day if not executed. The order is either executed by electronic matching or through the assistance of a broker.

After execution, the terms of the trade, including the names (codes) of the buying and selling clearing firm, are reported to the entering firms and the clearing corporation, such as the National Securities Clearing Corporation, a subsidiary of the Depository Trust & Clearing Corporation (DTCC). Once comparison and unilateral netting has occurred, the positions move into the Depository Trust Company (DTC), another division of the DTCC for the electronic receipt and delivery of assets for final settlement.

On the customer side, the acquiring client operating under "T + 3" (trade date plus three) rules is going to pay the amount required for the purchase. Clients operating under "delivery versus payment" (DVP) rules will pay for the purchase when their broker-dealer delivers the newly acquired position to their custodian. (This last part is all accomplished through electronic entries between parties.) On the sell side, the seller must deliver the ETF to receive payment. If the sold ETF is in the client's account at the broker-dealer, the firm will make the necessary entries to settle the transaction. If the sold ETF is with a custodian, the selling client will have to give instructions to the custodian to deliver the ETF to their selling broker-dealer versus payment, and receive the proceeds from the sale.

Most of the popular ETFs track an index such as the S&P 500, as mentioned earlier. ETFs that are generally tracking a common stock index are the most popular of the groups we will discuss. Institutions such as Barclays Global Investors assemble the required amount of securities to replicate an index and issue ETF shares against it. ETFs trade very close to net asset value (explained earlier). These large institutional traders, market makers known as "authorized participants," buy and sell ETF shares directly in the marketplace. A financial institution, such as a bank, will take down (buy) a block of ETF securities and allocate (sell) them to its customers as well as to customers of other banks and other brokerage firms. Blocks of these ETFs that are owned or gathered by these large institutions can be surrendered and converted into the basket of the underlying securities.

Some of these large institutions actually become market makers for the securities; they have the ability to create shares when necessary and to decrease shares when necessary. Therefore they can maintain a fairly liquid market with fair pricing as a result. Traders are known to trade components of the ETF against one another or against the ETF itself. For example, say a trader named Bea Kwick believes that the price appreciation of a particular ETF is being retarded by shares of the Downer Corp., one of the component stocks in this ETF. Bea could buy shares of the ETF and short shares of the Downer Corp., thereby removing the impact of the Downer Corp. stock or neutralizing the effect on the index. If Bea's assessment is correct, she will profit from the short sale, and the appreciation of the ETF would be magnified.

• ETF STRATEGIES •

Exchange-traded funds offer the investor many of the strategies afforded them in their trading of stocks. Unlike mutual fund shares, which are limited to buying and then selling, the investor can sell ETFs short, due to the moment-by-moment pricing. They can also go in and out of positions on the same day at the then-current market prices, thereby incurring a profit or loss. Investors can enter more sophisticated orders, such as step orders, which are a series of limit orders to be filled if and when the index reaches specified price limits during the day or if the order is a good till canceled order over a period of days.

Another advantage to ETFs over mutual funds is that owners cannot be forced to accept taxable events because other shareholders are selling their ETF shares. With mutual fund shares, the fund stands ready to sell its shares (take in money to invest) or buy back its shares (sell investments to raise the cash need to pay out), which in turn forces the mutual fund managers to liquidate positions so that they can raise the cash necessary to pay the fund share sellers. In other words, mutual fund shareholders incur capital gains tax liabilities through the normal workings of the mutual fund's advisers, whereas the ETF shareholders' capital gains tax liability is limited to their buying and selling their own ETF shares, independent of the actions of other parties.

Exchange-traded funds also reveal their holdings late in the day. ETFs divulge this information so that hedge fund managers, traders, and anyone else using software programs that track the index can make the necessary adjustments to stay balanced with the index. The price of an ETF is determined by the net asset value of its contents. Therefore, any changes to the contents of the index must be duplicated by those entities that are using software to replicate the index value.

The buying and selling of the ETF is accomplished in the marketplace between public participants, so supply and demand could move the ETF price slightly over or under the net asset value. If, through the normal course of business, there is a discrepancy between the price of the ETF and the value price of the ETF index, arbitrageurs will take positions that will cause the market price to realign with the portfolio value. Remember, an ETF, given enough size, can be brought to the authorized participant, dissolved into its component parts, and the parts then sold. In the case of dividends and other cash distributions, both the mutual fund shareholders and the ETF holders pay income taxes. Some municipal bond funds and municipal bond ETFs are exempt, however.

As ETFs trade on an exchange or through electronic commerce networks (ECNs), buying and selling shares requires the use of a broker, which in turn causes the investor to incur a brokerage fee in the form of a commission. The commission fee is charged when the investor enters into the position and again when the position is closed out. In the case of mutual funds the fee, known as a load or sales charge, is a one-time charge per investment if the fund has a fee or sales charge at all. Those mutual funds that do not charge a fee are known as "no load" funds, but generally speaking, no-load funds charge higher operational fees. The total cost of owning a mutual fund versus the total cost of owning ETFs differs from fund to fund, from broker-dealer to broker-dealer, and is affected by the amount involved in the transaction.

Difference Between the UIT Form and the Mutual Fund Form

Exchange-traded products are issued in two different forms. Some replicate a unit investment trust, while others replicate a mutual fund. Though they have many similarities, the major difference is that a unit investment trust structure is built for the long haul. Many unit investment trusts are not managed at all. If a UIT is formed with a basket of thirty-year bonds, those bonds will remain in the basket for their duration. At the end of the thirty years the trust will end. Those ETFs or ETPs that are structured like a mutual fund are more actively managed. The portfolios they contain can change regularly, and the managers of the ETF are free to make changes as they deem necessary to seek better performance.

Another difference between the UIT form and the mutual fund form is that the unit investment trust will pay out to its investors periodically. This of course could affect the value of the index against the value of the ETF. It would depend on how and when the ETF is adjusted for the dividend. Mutual funds, on the other hand, reinvest all earnings and so the value of the ETF and the value of the index that was created for the ETF remain very close together. Spiders, DIAMONDS, and Cubes are three ETFs that use the unit investment trust form of management. The most common form of ETF, however, is the open-end fund. These funds are open in accordance with the rules set forth by the Investment Company Act of 1940. Some of the more common forms of ETFs that use the mutual fund structure are iShares, streetTRACKS, and PowerShares.

• LEVERAGED ETFs •

Leveraged ETFs are modified versions of regular ETFs. The modifications are aimed at either increasing the return of a basic ETF or losing the same amount. The basic ETF tracks an index. The idea behind it is consistency. It is expected to perform or accomplish what the index does. It is not supposed to outperform or underperform the index. The leveraged ETF must therefore use some other tool to "juice up" the return. To accomplish these returns, derivatives such as index options, equity swaps, or index futures are employed. However, nothing is guaranteed. This is one of the objections to the use of this product: that the concept is to replicate an index based on the index's component parts. The leveraged ETF adds another dimension of risk and expense, and these additional steps incur fees, which add to the cost and are deducted from any profit or added to any loss. The amount of the loss may be magnified by the same multiplier that was used in an effort to expand the profit.

Developing a Leveraged ETF

The leveraged ETF may be structured as bull (profits from upward price movement) or bear (profits from downward price movement), depending on the investors' outlook on the current and near-future market. To develop a leveraged ETF, the ETF manager is borrowing money to buy (or sell) the derivative instrument that will augment the investment's return. The management of the leveraged ETF must re-balance the leveraged ETF each day.

Here's an example:

An investor owns $1.00 worth of an ETF index and acquires through derivatives another $1.00 of index exposure for a total of $2.00 The leveraged ETF rises that day to $1.01 or 1 percent. The leveraged index position must rise by 2 percent also. If it is not exactly the same as a proper ratio, the management must rebalance the position, which means more market action, which means expense. The return being promised is a daily return, and the product is thought of as a tool of day traders and considered risky.

• GLOBAL ETFs •

Besides domestic ETFs that offer domestic securities, there are domestic-issued ones that may contain foreign issues. These are referred to as global ETFs and are available for trading on U.S. markets. ETFs are also issued in other countries, and these may contain that country's domestic issues and/or foreign issues (to them). The investor must differentiate between U.S.-issued, dollar-denominated ETFs that are composed of indexes made up of foreign stocks or other assets and the foreign-issued ETFs investing in their local securities or in foreign issues (to them) and settling in their local currency. With the U.S.-issued ETF, U.S. investors are given the opportunity to invest in financial issues of many countries. Through this vehicle investors can easily get involved with markets previously not easily accessible to them.

Until some of these U.S.-issued foreign ETFs were marketed, investment in foreign securities may have been prohibited due to foreign governments' regulations, especially when it came to an "outsider" using their currency. Some of the prohibitive factors included transaction cost, access to market, laws against foreigners' obtaining their currency or currency leaving their country, other regulatory issues, and timeliness of information. In some countries the cash used to make foreign investments is frozen for a period of time before it can be repatriated within the native country. ETFs did away with most of these hindrances, and the markets are huge. According to *Securities Technology Monitor*, the annual growth of ETFs has been 26.5 percent, with total assets reaching $1.7 trillion. The product gives both retail and institutional investors convenient access to markets around the world.

A sample of these concentrated ETF foreign shares are iShares' MSCI South Africa Index ETF or iShares' MSCI Switzerland Index ETF, which are country specific. There are product specific ETFs, such as S&P Global Clean Energy index fund, primarily composed of electric utilities industry and semiconductor industry, with the United States, China, and Japan being the dominant countries. iShares S&P Global Energy Sector Index Fund includes shares of Exxon Mobil Corp., Chevron Corp., BP PLC, Royal Dutch Shell PLC =A shares, TOTAL SA, ConocoPhillips, Occidental Petroleum Corp, BG Group PLC, plus others. The index is composed of 87.84 percent Oil Gas and Consumable Fuels, 11.57 percent Energy Equipment & Services, 0.31 percent S-T Securities. Then there is the iShares MSCI EAFE Index Fund comprising publicly traded securities in the European Australasian and Far Eastern markets, which include securities from the Financial, Industrial, Consumer Staples, Consumer Discretionary, Health Care, Materials, Energy, Telecommunications, Information Technology, and Utilities sectors.

These are randomly selected international ETFs and their appearance here is not meant to be a recommendation for purchase or sale. The point being made is that by entering one order into one trading market, the investor can own a "piece of the world." These ETFs all trade in U.S. markets, and after execution are processed through U.S.-based clearing entities, and settle in U.S. dollars.

• NONDOMESTIC-ISSUED ETFs •

ETFs are popular not only in the United States but in other counties also. In many cases, the same global banks that issue ETFs in America are issuing them in other countries. Even if the ETFs have the same name, they are different from the ones issued in America. The ETFs issued from the bank into the foreign market are denominated in their trading unit size, priced in their currency, settled in their currency, processed through their systems, and then come under foreign regulatory authority.

Transactions executed in the foreign market come under the rules and regulations of that country, which includes taxation and possible restrictions on foreign ownership. Trading strategies permitted in the United States, such as short sales, may not be permitted in the foreign markets. When thinking of employing certain strategies, make sure that all the component parts are traded and that the strategy is accepted in the same manner. For example, the strategy of buying an ETF on margin and selling a call against it in the United States necessitates, at a minimum, that the owner post 50 percent of the ETF purchase price. The option doesn't require margin because it is protected by the ETF. Before going into the strategy, the investor must check that options can be applied to the ETF. The margin requirements are the options of the American form and mark when payments are due. In the employment of a cross-border strategy that looks great on paper, many questions must first be asked before entering into it, such as:

1. Is the strategy permitted?
2. Can the required response be accomplished in the allotted time?
3. Are the required components easily obtained?
4. If the strategy involves cross-border products, are they as acceptable as the domestic variety?
5. Are there any restrictions on currency movement?

Finally, something that is always of concern when dealing with foreign currency, either the currency itself or a surrogate, is the exchange rate between the investor's currency and the one used in the strategy. Changes in that relationship affect the final outcome of the transaction.

• EXCHANGE-TRADED GRANTOR TRUSTS •

Besides open-end managed and unit investment trust–styled ETFs, there are exchange-traded grantor trusts. These ETFs (some question if they are ETFs) give the holders direct ownership of the assets comprising the unit. In the case of stocks, the holder receives dividends, if paid, that cannot be reinvested; voting rights; and in some cases, the ETF holder who is converting can ask for stock certificates. The trust has a limited life and is not managed. The components are locked in position and, in the case of mergers or acquisitions, the relationship of the components may change, with one security becoming the dominant one as the contents will not be rebalanced. One of the largest issuers of exchange-traded grantor trusts is Merrill Lynch HOLDRS.

• INVERSE EXCHANGE-TRADED FUNDS •

These ETFs are supposed to move contrary to the market. Thus if the market falls in value by 5 percent they are supposed to rise in value by a similar amount. Of course, should the market rise by 5 percent, they are to lose that amount. The main instrument employed to accomplish this is the short sale. One advantage is that an investor can "short the market" without the need of opening a margin account at a broker-dealer and posting margin. The investor is going long on the ETF that is going to short the positions.

Another name for inverse ETFs is short ETFs. For use of this product to be effective, the investor must have the downside, beginning to end, timed correctly to catch the "bottom" of the market, or else the strategy will backfire. In addition, the shorting of stock requires a careful investigation as to the availability of stocks needed to borrow, as well as compliance with recent regulations as detailed in the 1934 Securities Exchange Act's Regulation SHO. Failure to do either of these things would hamper the ability of the inverse ETF to perform as planned.

• LEVERAGED INVERSE EXCHANGE-TRADED FUNDS •

Products use derivatives to magnify the anticipated negative return of an underlying asset. Assuming that the underlying asset has been bullish in the market, and it is anticipated that a reversal is about to occur, besides short selling ETFs, one might use derivatives such as long put options, short calls, and short future positions. As mentioned under "Leveraged Exchange-Traded Funds," these added transactions incur additional expenses, which reduce profit or increase losses. The strategy itself may backfire and increase the loss by the applicable multiplier.

• MARGINING OF ETFS •

Let's take a look at the margining of ETFs, which is similar to stock margining. The buyer of an ETF can pay for it in full or borrow money to pay for up to 50 percent of it. The borrowing is referred to as "margin," which is leveraging. At 50 percent margin, the investor can buy twice as many ETFs as if the purchase was paid for in full. That means the investor can double his or her profit or losses. For this loan amount the investor pays interest. Financial institutions have the prerogative to mandate that investors deposit more than 50 percent against the purchase if the institution is uncomfortable with the risk, but never less. Broker-dealers and other financial institutions will want equity in the account before they allow the investor to utilize margin.

If the value of the ETF that was acquired increases, the client's equity will grow. If the ETF loses value, the equity will shrink. Should the equity shrink below a certain percentage of the account's value (regulation has it at 25 percent, financial institutions have it higher, at 30 to 35 percent), the client must provide more equity in the form of cash or valued equities.

Here's an example:

The MUD ETF is trading at $94. Salvatore Amanda buys 100 MUD ETF for a cost of $9,400. Sal acquires the ETF in his margin account and must deposit 50 percent. He deposits the $4,700 and the firm Stone, Forrest and Rivers, where Sal has his account, lends Sal the difference.

KEY:

CMV = Current Market Value

Equity = Monetary portion belonging to client

Debit Balance = owed by client to firm

Loan Value = Maximum that can be lent

Excess = the amount remaining that can be borrowed

SAL'S ACCOUNT:

Long 100 MUD ETF @ 94 =	**$9,400**
Equity =	**−$4,700**
Debit =	**$4,700**

THE MUD ETFS DOUBLE IN PRICE TO 188 PER SHARE. SAL'S ACCOUNT NOW HAS THE FOLLOWING VALUES:

Long 100 MUD ETF @ 188 =	**$18,800**
Equity =	**−$14,100 (75%)**
Debit =	**$4,700 (25%)**

NOTE: THE DEBIT BALANCE HASN'T CHANGED AS CASH HAS NOT ENTERED OR LEFT THE ACCOUNT.

Current Loan Value = 50% of Market Value =	**$9,400**
Less the Debit Balance = what Sal has borrowed =	**−$4,700**
Excess = Sal can borrow an additional	**$4,700**

Sal can also do nothing.

Sal decides to borrow the $4,700 and buy a ZIP ETF that is currently trading at 100.

On the $10,000 purchase, Stone, Forrest and Rivers can lend 50 percent, or $5,000.

Sal takes the $4,700 excess in his account and applies it to the ZIP purchase.

Between what Stone, Forrest and Rivers can lend, $5,000, and the $4,700 excess in Sal's account, Sal has $9,700 to apply to the new purchase of $10,000. Sal is still short $300. He will get a T call for $300 from Stone, Forrest and Rivers, which he meets.

Sal's account now looks like this:

Long 100 MUD ETF @ 188 =	**$18,800**
Long 100 ZIP ETF @ 100 =	**+ $10,000**
Total market value in the account =	**$28,800**
Total Debit Balance ($4,700 original debit + $4,700 additional loan on the MUD ETF + $5,000 lent on the ZIP ETF) =	**$14,400 (50%)**
Sal's Equity	**$14,400 (50%)**

We have seen what happens when the account moves in favor of Sal. What happens if it moves in the opposite direction and the value of the ETF falls? According to FINRA (Financial Industry Regulatory Authority), the equity in the account can fall until it hits 25 percent of the market value. As equity and debit balance are the two components of the account, they are complementary. As we have seen, when the equity was 50 percent, the debit balance was 50 percent. Therefore, if the equity cannot fall below 25 percent, the debit cannot increase above 75 percent. In addition, as equity fluctuates with market value and those moves do not affect the debit balance, we will use the debit balance to determine the level the value of the account could fall to.

What figure is $14,400 75 percent of? The answer is $19,200. If the market value in the account was $19,200, the equity would be $4,800, which is 25 percent. The account cannot fall below this amount. If it does, Sal will be called for more equity.

Concerns about ETFs are surfacing from two different areas. The first, from the sales side, is saturation: there may be too many originators offering the same products in the marketplace. The second is from an investors' and trading viewpoint, that the creating and disassembling of ETF units may upset the normal market pricing mechanisms. Thus regulators and industry organizations are watching the impact to determine if any limiting actions may be necessary.

Now that we have a fuller understanding of ETFs, let's take a look at the remaining ETPs.

CHAPTER 8

OTHER EXCHANGE-TRADED PRODUCTS

The concept introduced by exchange-traded funds has carried over to other products. However, due to the nature of these exchange-traded products' (ETPs') underlying products, the deliverables and some other features found in ETFs are treated differently.

• EXCHANGE-TRADED COMMODITIES (ETCs) •

Exchange-traded commodities are offered either as a single commodity or in the form of index tracking. Unlike ETFs, which track a basket of equities or equity indices, ETCs are debt securities that may or may not be collateralized. In some cases, the commodity itself determines whether or not the ETC is collateralized. Those that track hard commodities such as gold and silver, which are easy to store and require little if any maintenance, are more likely to be collateralized than those tracking cattle and live hogs.

The ETC may invest directly in and track the performance of a commodity or an index that is designed to track the product. Some of the process for deciding whether to track the product's values or use an index depends on the ease or difficulty of obtaining accurate and timely information. The London Stock Exchange offers ETCs on the following individual products: natural gas, crude oils, gasoline, heating oil, aluminum, zinc, copper, nickel, gold, silver, live cattle, lean hogs, wheat, corn, soybeans, sugar, cotton, coffee, and soybean oil. They also offer various commodity index ETCs. ETC shares are traded on an exchange, just like an ETF, where there is a basket of securities forming an index that the ETF will trade against. An ETC could be a product with only one commodity or, like an ETF, one that has multiple products. These products can be bought and sold on a stock exchange in the same manner as if you were trading exchange funds. The ETCs track an index in the same manner that an ETF does. The index generally indicates total return, which means it's exposed to three sources of returns.

The most obvious source of the index's returns is the change in the future price, which is a result of the change of the spot or cash price. The second, which is more of an adjustment, occurs when the front month of the future product "rolls out" into delivery and the near month "rolls in." There usually is a price difference that must be accounted for, a gain or loss, and it becomes part of the index value. The third source is interest or other income earned on the collateral being used in margining the position. The ETC and ETF trade the same way; they share a format, and they go through the clearing corporation the same as stock. The essential difference is the underlying assets.

ETCs that trade as a single product include aluminum, Brent oil, coffee, crude oil, gasoline, heating oil, soybean oil, soybeans, sugar, wheat, zinc, and others. As with the shares of an ETF, those of an ETC on a commodity are all equal.

Here's an example:

In silver, the trading lot is one unit, and as of March 1, 2013, the last price in U.S. dollars was $28.58. The ETCs are backed by silver bars which are maintained and serviced by a trust. The silver currently backing each share is .9910722 ounces per share. It would require 99,107.22 ounces to create a basket that would represent 100,000 shares of this product. In dollars, it will cost $2,883,745 to create this basket.

The above works for ETCs of physical silver shares and for ETCs of physical Swiss gold shares.

• Exchange-Traded Currency (ETC) •

Another variation on the theme, exchange-traded currencies track a currency or group of currencies against another currency. It is a helpful product for those looking for an easy way to hedge a position. Unlike currency options and currency futures, they do not force an action. Options expire, futures become deliverable, but these do neither. The issuer of the ETC deposits either the foreign currency or futures to back the ETC.

An ETC may be an exchange-traded fund or an exchange-traded note. When it's an ETF, it's supported by cash deposits of future contracts. ETNs, on the other hand, have non-interest-bearing debt obligations tied into them. Therefore, the ETN is tied to the existence of the issuer.

There are single-currency ETFs or ETNs, as well as multicurrency, inverse currency, and leveraged currency. It is the multicurrency ETF, though, that affords the investor exposure to the widest geographical area.

This product has little use in long-term investment portfolios. Currency ETFs tend to track either the foreign deposits of another currency or futures contracts on that currency. They trade in a very small window moving up or down gradually over time, in step with the global economy. Also, there is always the possibility of government intervention. Recently, we have seen more volatility in certain currencies caused by the financial crisis. As an income-producing asset, on the scale of income-producing products, currency is among the lowest.

• Exchange-Traded Notes (ETNs) •

An ETN or exchange-traded note is a debt security that is a senior and perhaps unsecured instrument. Senior debt means that there isn't any debt that has a priority over it in the case of payments, or problems such as default. The term "unsecured" relates to the fact that there may not be any assets backing the note except for the intangible good name of the issuer, which is usually a bank. Other derivative products have some sort of assets behind them via securities, or in the case of commodities, the commodity itself; perhaps the assets could even be in the form of cash or some other asset. Not with ETNs, however.

Risks

In the last ten years, the percentages of exchange-traded notes that are collateralized have grown. Even though they are a debt instrument, they do not pay interest periodically and the returns are based on the performance of a benchmark, another market index, or whatever is used to set the value of the note as a benchmark. FINRA has issued warnings about this product, calling the following risks to investors' attention:

- Credit Risk—Whether or not ETNs are backed by any type of asset, they may not have fully secured debt obligation of the issuer.

- Market Risk—As with all products, ETNs are open to market risk in the form of losses due to price changes in the underlying asset. As the benchmark or index value changes due to market forces, the value of the ETN can result in a loss of principal to investors. This is basically the same as with any instrument and any investment.

- Liquidity Risk—Because ETNs are exchange traded, the trading in this particular product may not have developed to where it has a "firm" market. In other words, there might not be enough activity in the market with this particular product to make the price being quoted a solid one.

After the demise of Lehman Brothers, issuers of ETNs began to place assets underlying the notes so that they would have a resiliency, or value, in case the bank itself got into financial trouble. The value of the asset as a percentage of the note's value must be understood by the potential investor. An investor thinking of acquiring an ETN should read the prospectus, offering circular, term sheet, or other official document and determine where the asset is and how obtainable it is should the need be to either liquidate it or convert it into cash by some other means.

There have also been several articles written about hidden fees on ETNs. These articles do not appear to include ETCs or ETFs. As a matter of fact, several articles have been published recently calling ETFs a very good investment idea but mentioning that some of the products following after are not as good an investment and should be examined very carefully. ETPs allow individuals, hedge funds, and other investors to gain access to a wide range of diversified portfolios without owning the underlying products, which would cost considerably more. Take care in investing in these products as there are differences. Some of them, if an entity or individual owns a large enough position, can send the product to the issuer and have the assets that are behind the ETF delivered in its place. This is a service that other products, such as mutual funds, do not offer.

• TRACKERS •

Tracker certificates resemble ETFs, but they are not permitted to be sold in the United States. They are offered in two forms: total return trackers and excess return trackers. The total return tracker will track an index or group of assets that is underlying the certificate. The value includes dividends and other payouts, which are added back. The excess return tracker excludes dividends and other payouts, and therefore may sell at a discount to the total return tracker. Since total return trackers usually sell at a premium to the index they are not as popular as the excess return, which is usually issued at a discount. There is also the actively managed certificate (AMC). This type of tracker is flexible and can have many different attributes. It can be structured to resemble a mutual fund, without the regulatory concerns, or even a hedge fund. The cost is a fraction of the underlying index value, yet depending on its structure, may give the investor full benefits.

Deutsche Bank issues its db X-trackers for trading in Europe and Asia, for instance. These are compliant with the Undertakings for

Collective Investment in Transferable Securities, otherwise known as UCITS. The UCITS is a set of European directives which permits open-end funds to operate freely between the member states. SICAV (Société d'Investissement à Capita), for example, operates under UCITS and is an open-end collective investment scheme operating across Western Europe.

CHAPTER 9

OPTIONS PRODUCTS

The term "option" has the same meaning in the financial industry as it does anywhere else. It gives its owner the privilege of taking some predetermined action, at a price, for a period of time. Individuals who are interested in acquiring a home may take an option on a home, prohibiting the seller from selling the home to anyone else while the option is enforced. During that time, the prospective buyers can see about securing a mortgage or continue looking at other available properties. In order to secure this option, the prospective buyer pays the would-be seller a fee. The option gives its owner the privilege of exercising the option according to the terms of the contract. At the end of the contract's life the prospective buyer must either buy the house or let the option contract expire. At a nanosecond after the option expires the seller is free to sell the home to anyone else and at any price they negotiate. Options are tools, and as with any good tool, the value shows only when it's properly used.

In this chapter, we'll discuss the variations of options.

• CALL OPTIONS AND PUT OPTIONS •

There are two types of options in the financial industry: the call option, which gives its owner the privilege to acquire the underlying product;

and the put option, which permits its owner to sell or dispose of the underlying product. The basic structure of an option is very straightforward. The option owner controls the action; the seller of the option has to do nothing until a buyer exercises the option. After the buyer does so, the seller must perform the terms of the option contract.

In the case of a call option, let's suppose that it is on 100 shares of ZOW common stock, where the owner of the call option has the privilege to buy the shares at a price, $60 a share, for a period of three months. If the options owner decides to exercise the option, the seller of the call option must deliver 100 shares of ZOW to the option owner, who will pay $6,000 for the stock. If the owner doesn't exercise the option at the end of the three months, the option will expire worthless. If this was a put option, the owner would have the privilege to sell 100 shares of ZOW at $60 per share. Should the put owner decide to put (sell) the stock, the seller of the put would be obligated to receive 100 shares of ZOW and pay the put owner $6,000. As with the call option, failure to exercise would result in the option expiring.

• POSITION TERMINOLOGY •

There are several different ways you can refer to option buyers and sellers, depending on the situation. The buyer can be referred to simply as the buyer, long the option, the holder, or the taker. The seller of the option is referred to as the seller, short the option, the writer, or the grantor. The usage of the different terms is derived from where and when a particular individual was introduced to the product and the environment they are operating in. The terms "buyer" and "seller" can get to be confusing because the buyer of an option may want to sell it at a later time, to close the position, whereas the option seller at a later time may be looking to buy, in order to close out that position.

The initial action sets the correct term. The terms "long" and "short" have their confusing aspects also. The term "long" is industry jargon for owner, but the term "short" denotes that in many cases, another action must occur. For example: "The short security position was covered with borrowed securities," or "They sold more than they bought so they had a short position that had to be bought close to the position." In the case of an option short position, the seller doesn't have to do a thing unless an option owner exercised his or her privilege against it.

The short option position comes into being when an option contract granting the privilege to exercise is sold to another party—the option buyer. Generally, the seller wants the option to expire because that would mean it is worthless and the seller would keep the difference between the price the option was originally sold at and zero. The price an option is traded at is known as the premium. Therefore the seller or writer of the option wants the option to expire so that they may keep the premium.

The terms "holder" and "writer" go back ages to when the option seller actually wrote a paper contract and sent it to the buyer, who held it until they exercised the option or it expired. The option was initiated by presenting the paper document to the writer and surrendering it to be exercised. If the holder decided to do nothing, the writer would be free of any responsibility after the cutoff time at option expiration. The terms "taker" and "grantor" are not used in the United States, but they are used in other countries. The most common terms used in the United States to differentiate the option position are:

Sales personnel = Buying and Selling
Operations and accounting personnel = Long and Short

Owner	*Seller*
Buyer owns the option, has the privilege to: exercise it or sell it.	Writer either: honors the contract if exercised, or buys it.

All options expire. Listed options, those traded on an exchange, enjoy an active secondary market where they are traded in and out of positions much easier than options traded in an over-the-counter market.

Underlying Issue

The product or issue underlying the option can be just about anything. For example: As I said earlier an individual interested in buying a home, who is also concerned about arranging financing, can "take an option" on the house that would restrict the seller from selling it during a pre-determined time period. The word "option" appears when you acquire a new automobile. It comes with standard features and the other features that you can add on are optional. You will also see the word "option" on restaurant menus, where accompaniments to what you order are optional, in vacation packages, in your telephone contract package, apps on your mobile phone, and on and on. The financial industry uses the option products as part of many different types of strategies. From being a surrogate for the underlying product, where the buying of call options on the ZAP common stocks are used instead of buying the actual stock, or to being used as primary exposure reduction vehicle, by establishing offsetting options positions against it.

Among the underlying financial products used for options are stocks, baskets of stocks, indexes, debt instruments of all types, interest rates, currencies, commodities, and futures. One option contract usually supports one trading unit of the underlying product. For equity options in the United States, one option covers 100 shares of the underlying stock priced in dollars; in the United Kingdom, one equity option covers 1,000 shares priced in pence.

In the futures product, one option covers one future contract. In the case of those underlying products that do not have set underlying trading sizes, the contract size is determined by the exchange on which it initially trades, or in absence of the exchange (i.e., over-the-counter), the contract sizes are stipulated in the option's specification document. This document, known as the confirmation, or terms sheet, is especially important in certain over-the-counter options where the contract size is negotiated between parties.

Option Structure

We've already discussed the types of options available and the underlying product. Now, let's talk about structure. In option jargon, the term "class" refers to the underlying issue. All Loster Corporation common stock options are from the same class, and all index options are from the same class, etc. Put or call options are referred to by the "type" of option. Index-based call options on a particular index are of one class and one type;

index-based put options on the same particular index are of the same class but a different type. Currency-based call options on a particular currency are of one class; put options on the same currency are the same class but a different type. Therefore if we were looking at equity options on two different stocks, we would be looking at two "classes" (each stock) and four types (each of the underlying stocks would have a call type and a put type).

Next is the term "series." The series is made up of the strike price (the transaction price should the option be exercised) and the expiration date of the option. A call on ZAP common stock with a strike price (or "exercise price") of 40 would cost the call owner $40 per share to call in (buy) the shares, should the call be exercised. As 100 shares is a trading lot in the United States, the exercise of the call would necessitate the asset exchange of $4,000 for 100 shares of stock to settle the exercise (plus applicable commissions and fees). The strike price of the option was $40, which would be the price used for settlement of the exercise regardless of what price the stock is actually trading at at that time. The same holds true for a put option. If it was a $40 strike price put that was exercised, the exerciser of the put would be exchanging 100 shares of ZAP for the receipt of $4,000 less applicable commissions and fees.

The strike price of an option is either negotiated between parties (over-the-counter options) or set by the issuing authority (listed options). Listed options are issued under a set regimen with strike prices issued at varying levels, such as five-point intervals for options whose underlying securities are trading at a price between $X and $Y. (There are special exceptions to the regimen, such as stock dividends, for example.)

The description of an option includes the expiration date. Many option products that trade on exchanges have set expiration dates. For example, standard equity options that trade on U.S. exchanges expire the Saturday after the third Friday of the expiration month. The expiration date for over-the-counter options is negotiated. Options Clearing Corporation, the industry organization responsible for issuing all exchange (listed) traded options, also issues weekly options on selected equity and ETF issues.

In listed options, call or put options on the same underlying security that have the same expiration month and the same strike price are considered to be from the same series. Because listed options have set strike prices and expiration dates comprising the series, they trade in fairly liquid

| OPTION STRUCTURE
  HIERARCHY |

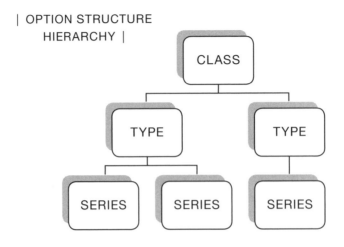

| PUT / CALL HIERARCHY |

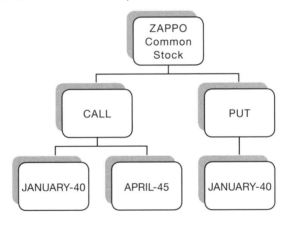

markets. Therefore the basic structure of an option is: Type (put or call), Class (underlying issue), Series (expiration month or week and strike price).

Let's say, for example, that it's a call on the common stock ZAP with an expiration of April and a strike price of $40. The basic structure would be Call ZAP Oct 40 call (owner has privilege to buy) on 100 shares of ZAPPO Corporation common stock expiring the Saturday after the third Friday of the expiration month at a price of $40 per share.

Option Symbology

When listed option trading began, a pattern was established to identify the option. The options in question were all based on common stock. The strike price internal was 5 points assigned to letters A through T, and expiration months were divided between calls and puts. As calls were traded, first the letters A through L were used to designate call options, and M through X were used to designate put options. So a call on Pipper Company common stock with a strike price of 40, expiring in April, would be coded PIP (stock symbol) D (4th letter = 4th month) H (5 pt interval × 8 = 8th letter). This identification methodology held for a while, but as there was a proliferation of products the coding became more and more difficult to apply.

Long-term Equity AnticiPation Securities (LEAPS), for example, which are issued for more than a year, required special accommodations for the year of expiration. Prior to their introduction, the year the option expired was not important as the longest listed option issued was for nine months. Another problem occurred when any security rose or fell 100 points during the duration of an option contract. Though rare, a stock could rise from $40 per share to $140 per share, which would require a change to its symbol. If, for example, the above-mentioned PIP was trading at 40, the symbol D was used to designate 40, 140, 240, etc. What if PIP rose in price to 140 while the 40 calls were still trading? As the designation PIP D H was already being used for the $40 option, the convention was to change the stock symbol. The more the old methodology was manipulated, the more confusing it became. In the year 2010, a new methodology was introduced.

The new symbology contains 21 bytes, divided as follows:

Symbol	6 bytes
Year	2
Month	2
Day	2
C/P	1
Strike Price	5
SP Fraction	3
Total	21

An equity option would be as follows:

OPIP	12	8	23	C	0040	250

A call on PIP common stock with a strike price of 40.25 (1/4) expiring August 23, 2012

Premium

The term "premium," as most commonly used, refers to the option's price, which is made up of two component parts. One part is "intrinsic" value (or "in the money" value), the other is "time" value. Intrinsic value is a value that must be in the option price. A call option with a strike price of $30 which is on a security whose current market value is $34 has an intrinsic value of 4 points or $4. If a person was given the option for free, that person could "call in" the stock at $30 per share and sell it at $34 per share, earning a profit of $4 per share or $400 on the 100-share lot. Therefore, the cost of the option must be at least 4 points.

A put with a strike price of $60, which has an underlying security with the value of $54, has 6 points intrinsic value. If the option owner was given the option for free and exercised it, the put owner would be acquiring the stock at $54 per share or would have already owned the stock which has current market value of $54 per share and would be "putting it out" at the strike price of $60 per share, thus earning a 6-point profit. Again, "intrinsic value" is synonymous with the term "in the money."

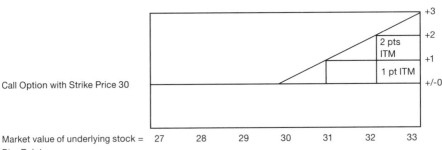

| CALL OPTION STRIKE PRICE |

Call Option with Strike Price 30

2 pts ITM

1 pt ITM

+3
+2
+1
+/-0

Market value of underlying stock = 27 28 29 30 31 32 33

Pt = Point
ITM = In the money

The relationship between the option's strike price and the underlying issue market value reveals how much of the premium price is intrinsic value and how close the option is to being executable.

An option can be "in the money," as in the example above, or "at the money," meaning the strike price of the option and the value of the underlying issue are equal, or "out of the money," which means that if the option was exercised, the option owner would have a loss. As option products span time, from issuance to expiration, the value of the underlying issue exists in a dynamic environment being changed by market forces. It is therefore possible that the option can swing from being in the money to being out of the money and back several times during its life.

It must be noted that the relationship being discussed is between the strike price of the option and the underlying issue's value. This is not to be confused with trading profit or loss, which includes the price of the option that was paid at the time of purchase and the price of the option received at the time of sale. This is why the example above mentions that the option was given to the owner for free, like a gift.

• EXERCISE CAPABILITIES •

One item that all option products share in common is that they expire. When they are about to expire, the underlying products that support the various products become the focus of attention. At expiration, out-of-the-money options expire. At-the-money options are usually allowed to expire also. The term "expire" is valid in this terminology because the option ceases to exist. Options that are in the money and still in position will either be traded away or exercised.

Those that are "traded out" close the option and the position ceases to exist. Once an option is exercised, it ceases to exist and the owner has to either receive, in the case of a call, or deliver, in the case of a put, the underlying security, issue, or equivalent against payment. The writer is on the opposite side. In the case of a call, the writer must deliver against payment; in the case of a put the writer must receive against payment. An exception to this pattern is cash settling options where, on exercise, the owner of the option receives payment and the writer pays regardless if it is a put or a call. Therefore, with options that are cash settlers, the owner of an IND index call option with a strike price of 350 will receive 6 points if the index is at 356 on exercise and the owner of an IND 350 put option will receive 8 points if the index is at 342. Assuming the value of the index is times $100, the call owner would receive $600, and the put owner would receive $800. It must be noted, though, that for every long or owner position there must be an offsetting short or writer position.

Exercise Privilege Factors

The exercise privilege that goes to the owner of the option is dependent on one of two factors. First, the option may be the American form of option, which can be exercised any time during its life, but only in the money options. The other popular form of option is the European form. It is exercisable only at the end of its life, again only if it is in the money. The American form of option is found in equity options that are listed for trading on option exchanges and for many over-the-counter transactions (as in the stock options). The European form of option can be found in many of the listed index options that are traded because of their trading relationship to another product called futures. The European form is also popular in over-the-counter options where the terms are negotiated.

Exercise Price

In either case, once the option is exercised, the participants in the contract must perform their respective duties. In the case of a call equity option, the buyer must be prepared to pay for the receipt of one unit per option (100 shares of common stock) of the underlying security. The writer of that option must be prepared to deliver 100 shares of the underlying security. Payment will be the strike price agreed to between the buyer and seller, also known as the exercise price. Therefore, the owner of a ZAP call with a strike price of 50 who exercises the option must be prepared to receive 100 shares of ZAP common stock and pay the exercise price of $5,000 (100 × $50 = $5,000). In a similar vein, the owner of a put option on a stock called, let's say, WOW, with a strike price of 30 upon exercise, must deliver 100 shares and receive payment of $3,000.

In both of the previous events, while the customers' accounts are adjusted to accommodate the exercise of the option, the actual securities and cash involved become part of the firm's daily operating systems and flow with other securities transactions into that day's settlement cycle.

• THE CUSTOMER'S STRATEGY •

One of the questions that always surfaces is: what makes customers decide at expiration to either exercise the option, trade it out, or let it expire? The answer will depend on the customer's strategy.

> *For example, if Ms. Jenna Raite owns stock for a good period of time, she could take the profit she currently has in that security if she sells it today. On the other hand, she is concerned that the price may go higher, thereby increasing her profit. Then again, the stock may fall in value and she would give up some of her profit. She might consider buying a put, which gives her the right to sell the stock at the current price. While this would cost Jenna some of her potential profit on the option premium, it would protect her from losing more, and the preset price is guaranteed to her as long as the option is outstanding. Jenna would simply exercise the option.*
>
> *If, on the other hand, the stock has risen in value over the period of the option's life, the increase in stock value would be used to offset the cost of the put option, and once that is neutralized, further increases in the stock's price only add to the profit. If it's an out-of-the-money put, and it had a long time to go before expiration, and if Jenna was more confident that her stock profit was quite secure, she could sell the put option as it neared expiration and, if the value of the underlying stock hadn't changed, she could sell the put out for less than it was acquired out, thereby recouping some of the cost. The premium on an out-of-the-money option is always time value, which dissipates as the option ages and nears expiration. Time value is a wasting asset.*
>
> *A call option on equities at expiration is another tool. Let's suppose a customer, Della Whear, thought that RIP was a good security to buy. As Della does not have a lot of money, she cautiously bought a call option going out for eight months on RIP with a strike price of 30. When she bought the option, RIP was at $27 a share, so the option was out of the money. The call cost Della 2 points. Over the eight-month period of time, Della's assessment of the stock proved to be correct. The stock*

rose, and at expiration, it's trading at $40 a share. Della's option, with a strike price of $30, has 10 points of intrinsic value. As we are at the option's expiration, there isn't any time value left in the premium. Della has a choice: take her 8-point profit (10 points intrinsic value minus the 2 points cost of the call = 8 points) and sell the option, or exercise the option and buy a $40 stock at a price of $30 a share, hoping that RIP increases in value even more. Of course there is a downside. With the option Della could only lose $200 plus expenses. If she converts it to stock through exercise, she can lose as much as $3,000 for the stock purchase, plus $200, the cost of the option, plus commissions paid the broker-dealer, plus other expenses if the stock went bankrupt.

• INDEX OPTIONS •

The next product we will look at is index options. These are options that trade on a multitude of indexes such as the S&P 500. The distinguishing feature of these option products is that they are cash settlers. On exercise, securities are *not* delivered or received. Instead the owner of the exercised option will receive the cash difference between the option strike price and the closing or assigned value of the index. On exercise, the determining price for settlement is the closing or adjusted price for the index, which means that during the trading day, the index value at any moment cannot be used for exercising purposes. The owner of an index option cannot exercise an index option the way an owner would a stock option or one that has a deliverable as a result of the exercise.

For example, Mr. Carl Lee buys a stock call option on 100 shares of SAW common stock, a call option that has a strike price of $40 per share when the stock's price is at or below $40, so it is out of the money. Let's assume further that one day the stock opens for trading at $40, then suddenly rises to $50 a share, and closes that day at $40 per share. Carl can give instructions to call the stock in at $40 per share and sell the optioned stock during the day at $50 per share versus the exercise the same day. In the case of an index option, since its value is computed at the end of the day, Carl could not do that type of transaction because he has nothing to sell.

For another example, if Ms. Ivy Green owns an index option with a strike price of 500, and one day the index opened at 500 and rose to 550 during the day, then fell back to 500 at the end of the trading day, there isn't any exercise action Ivy can take because the closing value of the index determines the index's value. Let's continue with our make-believe index at 500. Let's suppose the client, Ivy Green, owns a call option on the index with a strike price of 500. At the end of a period of time, the index is trading at 550. That is the closing price on a given day. Ivy decides to exercise the option. The next day her account will be credited the 50 points × $100 difference or $5,000. The writer's account would be charged that amount.

In the case of a put option that is a cash settler, let's suppose that Ivy owned a put with a strike price of 500 and at the end of the trading day the index closed at 490. Ivy would exercise the option and receive the 10-point difference. In either case, with a cash option, put or call, the exerciser receives the currency. The writer pays for the exercise.

• CURRENCY OPTIONS •

The last variation of an option for settlement will be a currency option that is a put or call using currency as the underlying security. Most of the currency options traded on the exchanges in America are dollar denominated, meaning the currency you are going to settle the trade in is the U.S. dollar. You're going to pay the premium in U.S. dollars and profit or loss will also be in U.S. dollars. However, when you go into the over-the-counter market, that exchange changes. You could buy a currency option denominated in British pounds, in the euro, Japanese yen, etc.

The payment currency will be determined by the structure of the option and its specifications. Currency options are usually quoted or displayed as follows: first currency divided by the second currency. For example, in a GBP/USD option, how many U.S. dollars do you need to buy one British pound?

The U.S. dollar is trading at $1.50 to the British Pound. Ms. Lilly White is planning to vacation in England in a few months. From *what she has read, she believes that the dollar will weaken against the pound. If that is true, the cost of the vacation will escalate. One currency is the commodity that is being bought or sold, the other is the currency that is used to pay for the transaction. While in the United Kingdom, Lilly spends £10,000. If the conversion rate is $1.50 to £1.00, it will cost Lilly $15,000. If the dollar strengthened against the pound so that the conversion rate was $1.30 to the £1.00 it would cost Lilly $13,000, a savings of $2,000 for the same vacation. If the dollar weakened against the pound so the conversion rate was $1.70 to the £1.00, the same vacation would cost Lilly $17,000, or $2,000 more.*

While Lilly knows there are several products that would "lock" in the rate, Lilly decides to buy a six-month call with the strike price of $1.50. If after her vacation and the options are due to expire, the U.S. dollar is $1.65 to £1.00, she calls in her option and uses the profit to offset the extra cost of her vacation.

• FUTURES OPTIONS •

The final version of options we will mention in this chapter are options on futures, which we will discuss more in a later chapter. As we have stated previously, futures are another derivative with their own underlying product. Therefore, an option on the future gives you the privilege, not the obligation, to buy or sell the underlying future. The future itself will have a delivery date, the delivery date will then determine when the product must be delivered, and of course the future itself determines what must be delivered. We have options on futures on indexes and not a real tangible product in any of the three—so can they even be assumed to be real? That is something to think about.

In the next chapter, we will go deeper into option strategies.

CHAPTER 10

OPTION STRATEGIES

As we've discussed already, options are tools. What follows in this chapter are different strategies and their intended purposes. As with any tool, the wrong tool at the wrong time won't do the job. Let's get right into it.

• BUY/WRITES •

The first strategy we will look at is called a buy/write or buy and write. Its purpose is to generate income. An investor, William Fold, purchases a stock for its income purposes, not for capital appreciation. Bill buys a stock, say, ZAP at $38 a share. The stock pays a dollar a share dividend annually, or a $0.25 dividend quarterly. Bill checks the quote for options and sees there is a three-month option with a strike price of 40, which means it is out of the money, and selling for a dollar ($1.00 × 100 shares = $100). Bill writes the option against the stock owned, and the short call position is known as a "covered call." The broker-dealer is not exposed to any risk as Bill's stock would be used to satisfy the short call should it be assigned, so all margin requirements, if they exist, flow to the stock. Provided the stock does not rise to over $40 a share over the next three months, the customer has just earned a hundred dollars from the premium, the dividend for the stock for a year, literally overnight.

If the stock does not trade above $40 per share for the next three months, the option will expire worthless. At that point, the client keeps the premium and does not have any further obligation, and the client can enter into a new buy/write strategy. This can be done over and over, as long as the relationship between the price of the underlying stock and the option premium makes it advantageous to do.

Buy/Write Risks

During this time Bill faces two risks with the buy/write positions. One is that should something good happen to the company and the stock rises above $40 per share, then Bill is left with a hundred dollars earned from the short call, plus any dividends that may have been paid, plus the 2 points when the stock gets called away at $40 a share. Bill made a total of 3 points on the entire transaction. If the stock goes from $38 per share to more than $40 per share, the customer has lost the opportunity of earning a greater profit. But remember, Bill did not think the stock was going to appreciate in terms of capital. Therefore, the option is doing exactly what it should be doing.

The other downside to a buy/write occurs when the stock starts to lose value. If it fell from 38 to 36 to 34, the customer still would have a call option outstanding, which is protected by the stock. Should they decide to liquidate the stock and limit their loss, they would have an uncovered out-of-the-money call for the duration of the option's life. Maybe the stock would not turn around and run up in value, but maybe it would. If the client sells the stock, the short call option becomes "uncovered." The client must post margin for the uncovered position, which is "marked to the market" daily and exposes the client to unlimited risk should the stock have a strong rally. If the stock price does turn around and begin to run up, the short call would be in the money once the stock was above $40 per share. Upon being exercised against, the client would have to go into the market and buy the stock at whatever price it is trading at. Then the client would have to deliver the newly acquired stock against the call at $40 per share.

Of course, while this was going on, the client could buy in the short call, closing out the option position, or buy back the sold stock to cover the option, or even do both, thereby developing an option-free long stock position. With commissions and other costs included, this last part could be very expensive.

• SPREADS •

The next strategy we will look at is a spread, which is both the purchase and sale of equal numbers of puts or calls, having the same underlying security but different series. Remember, the series is made up of the option's expiration month and the strike price. The spread position can also be obtained if the missing "leg" enters the position through trading. In other words, if the client is long a call option on ZAP Oct 50, the long position would become a spread position automatically if the client sold a call on ZAP with some other series besides the one that is owned.

In a case of a spread, one option is the main option, or the driver, and the other option is either a premium reducer or used as a risk reducer. Let's examine this distinction more closely.

Supposing a client, Nicole Endyme, believes ZAP, which is currently trading at $51 per share, may rise in value as high as $55 per share in the next three or four months. Nicole calls her broker and discovers that a $50 per share strike price call option with a tenor of six months is selling for 5 points. If she buys that option and she is correct and the stock does go to 55, at expiration she will just about cover the cost of the option. She then inquires as to the current premium of the next higher strike price option with the same tenor. She is told that there is a call with a strike price of $55 selling for 2 points. Nicole gives the order to buy the $50 strike price call option with a premium of 5 points and at the same time sell the $55 call with a premium of 2 points for a net difference of 3 points.

In these examples we ignore commissions; therefore, the position has cost Nicole 3 points, of which 1 point is already intrinsic value. (Long a call with a strike price of $50, the underlying stock is trading at $51.) If she is correct and the stock does rise to 55 and goes no higher, her long option with a strike price of 50 will be worth 5 points at expiration. The short option with a strike price of 55, which she sold, will be worthless. The position cost Nicole 3 points; it is worth 5 points, giving Nicole a

2-point profit. No matter how high the underlying stock price was to climb, the position that currently exists, she will have a 5-point window between the $50 and $55 options and a 2-point profit at $55. If the stock rose to $100 per share at the options' expiration, Nicole would be ahead by 50 points on the $50 strike price option, but behind by 45 points on the $55 strike price option, for a gross profit of 5 points, less the 3-point cost for a net profit of 2 points. Therefore, for an investment of 3 points for six months, she is going to make 5 points for a net profit of 2 points, which is a return of 66⅔ percent on her investment. This is an example of an option being used as a premium reducer.

Risk Reducer Spreads

Let's look at a spread where the secondary option is a risk reducer.

> Ms. Randi Miles has been watching the common stock of Craig Incorporated for several months. The stock was dropping in value but has started to turn around and come back. Randi believes she has seen the bottom of the run. She wishes to sell puts and therefore as the stock continues to rise, the puts will go out of the money, leaving her with the premium received. The stock is currently at $62 a share. Randi searches with her iPad for a three-month put option and sees that, with a strike price of $60, it's trading for 5 points. She decides to sell ten puts and deposit the margin required by her security account. If she is correct and the stock does not fall below $60 per share in the next three months, she will walk away with a $5,000 profit. However, what if she is wrong and the stock turns from $62 per share and starts to run down again? She could face a huge loss.
>
> If Craig Inc. falls and reaches 55, her profit is wiped out, and after that, she will start to lose her money. So Randi goes into the market, looks at the $55 strike price put, which is trading at 1½ points, and buys ten puts. She now has a box of a 5-point loss. For Randi's short $60 strike price put options she received $5,000 (5 points × 100 shares = $500 × 10 options = $5,000). For her $55 long put options, she paid $1,500 for a net of $3,500. If the stock value remains above $60 per share, she will keep $3,500 ($5,000 received from the puts she sold with the $60 strike price, less the $1,500 she paid for the puts she bought

with the $55 strike price). However, if the stock starts to fall below 60, the picture changes rapidly. If the stock was to fall below $60 per share, let's say to $57 at option expiration, those short puts with the $60 strike price would be assigned (exercised against) by holders of the 60 puts buying the stock at $57 per share and "putting" it out at $60. That is a 3-point loss to Randi per exercise ($3,000 – 10 puts 3 points each).

Randi will see her profit shrinking as the stock continues to fall. Once it goes below $55 per share, Randi can sustain no greater loss than the 5-point spread between the $60 and $55 per share. As she sold ten of the $60 strike price puts for 5 points = $5,000, and she bought ten of the $55 strike puts at a price of 1½ for a cost of $1,500, the net difference is $3,500, which she received. However, the 5-point difference ($5,000 loss) between the $60 and $55 strike price options could leave her with a $1,500 loss even if the stock went to zero. Without the purchase of the $55 strike price put option, Randi faced a potential loss of $55,000 ($60,000 from the $60 strike price put, less the $5,000 that she received from selling the ten puts). Randi would have to pay $60 per share for the 1,000 shares of worthless stock represented by the ten short $60 strike price puts.

Both this example and the previous one demonstrate how, in a spread, a secondary option is used either to reduce the premium or as a risk reducer. We will now go on to bull and bear spreads.

• BULL AND BEAR SPREADS •

A bull spread is industry terminology for any spread where the benefit occurs if the stock rises. A bear spread is any spread where the benefit occurs if the price falls.

Bull Spread

Here's an example of a bull spread using calls.

Ruth Lest buys a six-month call on KOW with a strike price of $30. KOW is currently trading at $28 per share. The option premium is

4 points. Therefore, Ruth has bought an out-of-the-money call option that has 4 points of time value. Ruth believes that the underlying stock, which is currently at $28, may rise to $34 or $35 a share within six months. To reduce the premium cost, Ruth sells a $35 strike price call on KOW for 1 point, bringing the net cost to 3 points. At this point in the transaction, Ruth can sell a $35 call that goes farther out in time so that the premium received may be greater.

For the first six months, the short call is covered by the long call, but going long with the program as presented, Ruth would have to post margin now for the longer period short calls even though the long calls cover them for the next six months. If someone was able to exercise the $35 strike price call against Ruth, Ruth would call in the long $30 strike price call. However, after the long calls expire, Ruth is left with uncovered short calls. The margin rules mandate that she post margin for all the short calls now and not when the long calls expire.

Ruth has bought a $30 strike price call for 4 points and sold a $35 call for 1 point for a net cost of 3 points. The stock is out of the money by 2 points. If Ruth's assessment of the situation is correct, the stock near expiration of the options will be at $34 or $35, or even higher. Ruth's short $35 call position will kick in, value-wise, when the stock crosses $35. If the stock doesn't reach $35 per share, the $35 strike price option will be worthless. Ruth's main call is the $30 strike price call, which will be worth 4 or 5 points or more at expiration, if the stock is selling at $34 or $35.

If the stock was at $35 at option expiration, the $35 strike price call minus the $30 strike price call will leave Ruth with a maximum of a 5-point spread. Since it cost her 3 points to do this, her net return would be 2 points for a return of 150 percent on her investment. If the stock fell and was below $30 per share when the options expired, Ruth would have lost her investment. As the only way Ruth could have benefited from this position was if the stock rose in market value, it is considered a bull spread.

A Note on Having Multiple Options

The previous example highlights a very important point. The spreads as we have presented them exist as long as there are two options, a long and a short option, and as long as the long option expires on or after the short option. Should the short option go out longer than the long option, there is a period of exposure when the long option no longer exists. For margin purposes, once a spread is composed of a short option that is out for a longer period of time than the long option, it is treated as an uncovered position from day one. Therefore, those investors who have spreads where the short option goes out longer than the long option have to post margin on the uncovered option, even though it is covered temporarily by the long option. As far as margin goes, any time the short option has more value than the long option, the person whose account it is must post margin; I will go into the margin computations later on.

Let's see an example of a bull option, using puts. Remember that a bull spread is one that anticipates an increase in the value of the underlying security. Therefore, if Ms. Lest sold a three-month put on KOW with a strike price of $60 when the stock was trading at $62, she would be writing an out-of-the-money put option because no one would buy the stock at $62 and put it out at $60 per share. However, if for the other leg of the spread, she bought a KOW three-month put with a strike price of $55, that would act to protect the position should the stock fall in value instead of rise. Should the stock fall below $55 per share, Ruth would incur a 5-point loss, because she would have to receive the stock at $60 on the exercise of the $60 strike price put, but turn around and exercise her long put at $55, losing 5 points on the turnaround. That figure would also be less whatever she collected for the sale of the $60 put, it being more valuable than the buy of the $55 put.

Exhibit A

1. Stock @ $62 per share
2. Short put option with strike price @ 60, out of the money by 2 points
3. Long put option with strike price @ 55, out of the money by 7 points
4. Short 60 strike price put's value > Long 55 strike price value
5. Position owner collects the difference

Exhibit B

1. Stock at $50 per share
2. Short put option with strike price 60, in the money by 10 points
3. Long put option with strike price 55, in the money by 5 points
4. Short put option with strike price 60 value > Long put option with strike price 55 value
5. Position loses 5 points on every turnaround option exercise

However, if the stock did not drop below $60 per share, and instead increased in value, both options would expire, worthless, and Ruth would keep the difference between the premium she received for the $60 put and the premium she paid for the $55 put. Therefore, she would want the stock to go up to be profitable in that position, which is the hallmark of a bull spread.

Bear Spreads

We will now design spreads that expect the stock to go down. This type of spread is known as a bear spread.

Let's suppose that RAM common stock is trading at $48 per share. Randi Miles sells a six-month RAM call with a strike price of $50. That option is out of the money by 2 points, as no one will call a stock in at $50 that is trading at $48. However, if the RAM stock should rise, Randi could have a rather extensive exposure once the underlying RAM stock crosses over $50 per share and the call option is in the money. Therefore, to protect her option position, she buys a six-month call with a strike price of $55. That move limits Randi's loss to the difference between the premium she received when she sold the $50 strike price call option and the premium she paid when she bought the $55 strike price call option, subtracted from the 5-point loss Randi would occur if the stock rose above $55 per share. At that price or above, Randi would have to respond to option exercises. She had *to deliver stock at $50 per share when the short call was exercised against her and receive stock at $55 per share as she exercised her long option. If, however, the stock never reaches $50, both options will expire out of the money and Randi will keep the difference between the $50 strike price option and the $55 strike price option premiums.*

Given the time until expiration, the lower strike price call option will always have more value than the higher strike price call because it would be the one that goes from out of the money to in the money first. Likewise, the higher strike price put would have more value than a lower strike price put because it would go from out of the money to in the money first.

Bear Spreads Using Puts

We will now look at a bear spread using puts. Again, long put options want the stock to go down in value.

With the stock at $62, Nicole Endyme buys a six-month put with the strike price of $60 for 3 points. That put is currently out of the money, as no one is going to pay $62 per share and put the stock out at $60. To lower her premium, Nicole sells a six-month $55 strike price put for ½ point as that put option is out of the money. The premium received from the $55 put reduces the cost of the $60 put.

As the stock loses value, from $62 down to $55, Nicole's long put is increasing in value—intrinsic value—and the short put is currently at the money. Therefore, this is the maximum Nicole can earn on this position. What the put cost when it was out of the money by 2 points was 3 points. At expiration, it is worth 5 points. Nicole is now profiting on the $60 strike price put, because it is 5 points in the money at expiration and the premium on the $55 put is now zero; that option is now out of time and it is at the money. Nicole then keeps the 5-point profit from the $60 strike price put, less the 3 points she paid for it, plus the ½ point received when Nicole sold the $55 strike price for a net of 2½ points profit. This is a bear put spread.

Other Spreads

The relationships and purpose of a spread are further defined where the difference between the long and short options, whether calls or puts, is the strike price. This type of spread is known as a vertical spread, a price spread, or a money spread. In the case where the options in a spread, whether puts or calls, have a difference in the expiration month, this type of spread is known as a horizontal spread, a time spread, or a calendar spread. Spreads in which the expiration month and the strike price are different are known as diagonal spreads.

• STRADDLE •

We will now look at a strategy known as a "straddle." This is accurately named because the individual is buying a put and buying a call or selling a put and selling a call on the same underlying product for the same period. Therefore, it appears that this investor is straddling the fence. To be accurate, if the description of the call series and the description of the put series are the same, it is called a straddle. If the series are different from each other, either in strike price, expiration month, or both, it is called a combination.

> *Assume a client, James Nasium, is buying a put and a call on the same underlying—either that, or he is selling a put and a call on the same underlying. The reason for this strategy has to do with the premiums received or the premiums paid. If the straddle is being purchased, then the expectations are that the premiums will increase either through volatility or movement of the underlying issues in one of the two directions. Whether the underlying issue goes up and the call increases in value and the put decreases in value, or the underlying issue goes down and the put increases in value and the call decreases in value, remember: the decreasing option, the one whose premium is decreasing, cannot go below zero.*

The "leg" that is increasing on a call is limitless; if it's the put that is increasing, the maximum is the difference between the strike price of the put and the underlying stock at zero. If the straddle is being sold the seller wants the premiums to decrease. The position seller would want the total premium to decrease. If it is volatility of the underlying issue that is causing the high option premiums, the straddle seller would want the volatility to decrease, causing the option premiums to decrease so that the position can be bought back at a lower price. If the rise in premiums in the options was caused by an anticipated event, should the event not occur the premiums would decrease, allowing the position to be bought in at a lower overall price. Also, if what is causing the current option premium to be inflated doesn't happen during the life of the options, the time value that is in either or both of the options will dissipate, allowing the closing out of the position at a profit.

Here's another example:

Ron Rin Inc. is rumored to be in talks with Ann Publishing about a possible merger. The common stock of Ron Rin is showing increased volatility and has risen 4 points since the rumors began. Research analysts are of the opinion that the combined companies could benefit. Thomas Aytto is of the opinion that if the merger goes through, Ron Rin will be worth 12 to 15 points more. If talks fall apart, the stock would lose the 4 points it gained and, perhaps, even more. Tom decides to buy a six-month call on Ron Rin with a strike price of $60 for 5 points and to buy a six-month put on Ron Rin with a strike price of $60 for 4 points. Ron Rin is currently trading at $60 per share. Tom is hoping to cover the 9-point cost as the talks develop. Tom can cover the cost if the stock rises or falls by 9 points, or experiences a combination of rising and falling a span of 9 points from high to low.

To Tom's delight, two more companies enter the scene and the volatility of the stock rises and falls as each event unfolds or doesn't. The underlying stock is now trading at $120 per share. Tom closes out the straddle with a nice profit. Meanwhile, Charles "Chuck" Staik has been following the events and thinks the wild times are calming down and that the put and call options on Ron Rin are overpriced. One or both of the options is due for a consolidation of its premium. He sells a six-month call on Ron Rin with a strike price of $120 for 15 points and sells a six-month put on Ron Rin with a strike price of $120 for 17 points. Now Chuck just sits there and hopes the situation *stabilizes and things get back to normal. This would cause the time value in the options to decrease, and Chuck can now buy in the short options for less than he sold them for, taking a profit. If Chuck is wrong and the stocks continue to rise or fall, the 32 points Chuck received as a premium would be in jeopardy.*

CHAPTER 11

GREEK TERMS FOR OPTION STRATEGIES

There are six primary Greek terms that are used to measure the effect the underlying product price movements have on the premium, and the time remaining in the option. Understanding these Greek letters permits traders, speculators, and investors to alter their portfolios to meet current conditions. It is possible for the application of different option strategies on a security position to use the respective Greek-letter concepts to change a portfolio that is long 50,000 shares of stock into one that is short 50,000 shares of stock. This is one of the many aspects of options that you might find interesting.

• BETA •

"Beta" is the relationship of a stock or portfolio to a broad market index such as the Standard & Poor's 500 stock index. The securities can be negative or positive beta. Beta is expressed as a ratio, with the index being classified as 1. A stock with a beta of 1 replicates the selected index value volatility. Some exchange-traded funds refer to their relationship to an index as how close their movements are to the movements of the index. If the target index is the S&P 500, an ETF claiming to replicate it should have a beta of 1:1, or over or under that return by an insignificant amount. If the index has a return of 5 percent, the referenced securities should also have a return of 5 percent.

The more positive the number is, the more volatile the security's price movements will be to the index movements. A stock with a 2:1 ratio has a high beta. A security with a beta of 2 should have a return of 10 percent if the index has a return of 5 percent. Whether the index goes up or down in value, one can expect the security's price to fluctuate similarly, and the return will justify its beta. If the beta is less than 1, but still a positive number, it means that the security will track the index but its price volatility will be less than that of the index. With a negative beta, the security moves in the opposite direction to the index. However, the volatility of many stocks has no relationship to an index, their beta being zero.

The tracking of the time value of an options premium reflects the effect of its beta. While a high beta reflects exaggerated price movements, the high beta also means high volatility, which in turn means more time value, all other things being equal. An at-the-money six-month call option with a strike price of $60 and a beta of positive .80 would have less time value than an at-the-money six-month call option with a strike price of $60 and a beta of positive 2.

• DELTA •

Delta measures the movement of an option premium versus the underlying issue's price movement. It is presented in ratio form from 0.0 to 1.0. An option premium with a delta of .50 will move ½ point to the underlying issue's 1-point move. The delta of an option premium increases as the option goes from far out of the money to way into the money. In other words, a deep-in-the-money option premium will closely follow the underlying stock's price. A long deep-in-the-money call may prove to be a less expensive way to own the underlying stock. Buying one hundred shares of stock at 80 would cost $8,000. Buying a six-month call on that same stock that has a strike price of 60 when the stock is trading at 80 would cost around 20 points or $2,000. If during the six months the stock rose to $90, the stock owner earned $1,000 while risking $8,000, the option owner earned $1,000 while risking only $2,000.

Delta in Action

Let's take a look below at a mockup of a pie chart showing the percentage of premium made up of the time value of a three-month call option with a strike price of $30 at different underlying price points and different deltas.

| OPTIONS |

 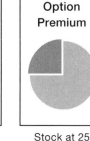 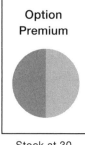 

| Stock at 20 | Stock at 25 | Stock at 30 | Stock at 40 |

From a probability standpoint, what are the chances the stock option will finish in the money?

Using the strike price of $30, what would the effect on the premium be if the stock moved from $19½ to $20½ with a couple of weeks remaining? The option premium probably wouldn't change. Delta is 0.

With the stock moving from $24½ to $25½ with a couple of weeks to go, the option premium may increase by ¼ of a point. Delta is .25.

At $29½ to $30½, the stock option may or may not be in the money: the premium may change by ½ point. The delta therefore is .50.

At $39½ to $40½, the option premium, which now carries a 10-point intrinsic value, may increase just under dollar for dollar. The premium is so rich at this point, the stock itself could almost be purchased at margin. The premium price would almost move point for point, so that would make the delta approximately .90. As this is a listed option, there would be call options on this stock with higher strike prices trading at lower premiums that would be a more attractive choice to most investors.

• Gamma •

Gamma is the degree to which the delta changes in relation to the underlying issues.

If a portfolio comprising a security and several different option positions has a net synthetic position, that position can and will change as the underlying security's price changes. Option delta changes as the underlying price changes, and gamma measures that change. If the change in the deltas is small, there will be little if any gamma and no need to make adjustments to the synthetic position. Should the change in the delta be high so that the gammas are high, the position definitely will change and it will require constant monitoring.

For instance, Eve Day owns 10,000 shares of stock and wants to sell deep out-of-the-money calls while keeping the position delta neutral. The options selected have a delta of .10. She sells 1,000 calls (1,000 calls × 100 shares each = 100,000 × .10 = 10,000) share equivalent. The position is delta neutral. A 1-point move in the stock will have a slight offsetting effect on the option's price. The underlying stock moves up in value, causing the options to inch their way closer to being at the money. Because of this price change, the delta changed to .15 (1,000 calls × 100 shares each = 100,000 × .15 = 15,000). Eve is now long 10,000 shares of stock and short the equivalent of 15,000 shares. To get back to delta neutral, Eve would have to buy in 333 calls, leaving the short option position with 666 options (666 calls × 100 shares each = 66,600 × .15 = 9,990 shares). Should the stock fall in price, Eve may have to short more options to maintain the delta-neutral position on the 10,000 shares. From day to day, the gamma would have to be checked to ensure the delta-neutral status.

• Rho •

Rho measures the change in time value due to interest rate changes. The risk-free interest rate is factored into the option premium. It affects the time value portion of the premium as the in-the-money portion is based on the intrinsic value. As the risk-free interest rate changes, it has an effect on option premiums, and rho measures that effect.

A 1 percent change in the general interest rate would have what effect on the option premiums? The answer depends on what percentage of the option premium is made up of time value.

• TAU •

Tau measures the change in premium as volatility changes. The more volatile an underlying asset becomes, the more the option premium will increase. The reverse is true as well, however. The effect of volatility changes on a premium would be particularly important with straddle positions. The long or short positions of equal numbers of puts and calls having the same underlying and the same or similar series are based on an event's happening or not. In anticipation of the event, the volatility will change and so will the value of the position. Tau measures that change.

• THETA •

Theta measures the decay of time value over the life of the option. It measures the decay on a day-to-day basis. The time value of an option will not decay at a consistent rate. In an option with 182 days remaining, the daily decay rate will not be 1/182 until expiration, charting in a straight-line downward curve. Instead, the decay will be calculated each day as 1/182, then the next day 1/181, the next day 1/180, etc., resulting in an arc-shaped downward curve.

• THE OPTION PREMIUM •

The option premium does not move in lockstep with the underlying security's price. If it did, then it would be very simple—an option that is 5 points in the money would be selling at 5 points. An option that is at the money and options that are out of the money would be trading at nothing. One of the key factors involved in the option premium is the expectation of what the underlying can do over a period of time. Naturally, the more time an option has before it expires, the more possibilities can influence the premium of that option, and that part is called time value.

The part of the option that is in the money, which must be there, is called intrinsic value. Besides the expectation of what the underlying security, or currency, or index, can do over the time of the option's life, there is also the actual price of the option. As an option goes deeper and deeper into the money, it becomes very expensive to own. And as it becomes more expensive to own, it will have less and less time value as a percentage of the total option premium. This can be referred to as "bang for the buck," and it is best explained by the following example.

Call Option Example

The underlying stock of an option that is out of the money is trading at $26 and the option has a strike price of $30. If it is a call option, it is out of the money, as no one is going to call the $26 stock in at $30 a share. Therefore, the option is virtually worthless. There are some variables, though. What would the option be worth if it had one week to go until expiration? What would the option be worth if it had three months to go until expiration? What would the option be worth if it had six months to go until expiration? The time element changes the view of the option premium. What has the stock's activity been in the last couple of months? How volatile has it been? What is the possibility or probability that the stock could be at $30 or higher at the end of the option's life?

Let's suppose the stock has not been very volatile over the last few months and this option is now 4 points out of the money. With a week to go, there is a very, very slim chance of the stock's gaining the 4 points to close at or in the money. Therefore, that option is virtually worthless. However, with three months to go, the screen changes based on what we have discussed so far. Maybe there is a 10 percent chance of the option's crossing the $30 mark and closing out in the money. With six months to go, maybe there is 25 percent chance of the option's crossing in the money. Therefore, should the stock move from $26 to $27 in the case of the option with one week to go, there would be a very small change in the option premium because it still has 3 more points to go before it goes in the money. However, for the option with three months to go that had a one-in-ten chance of crossing in the money, that option premium would change more, maybe by an eighth of a point. For the option that was six months out that had a 25 percent chance of crossing in the money, the option premium would change by a quarter of a point. Therefore, a trader could buy 100 shares of the stock at $26 a share and sell four calls with a strike price of $30 and six months to go. If the stock rose by 1 point, the four calls would increase by a quarter of a point each for a total of 1 point. The trader would thus have a delta-neutral position.

There are two factors working against this position. First, should the stock's value continue to rise, the difference between the market price of the stock, which was $26, and the strike price of the option, which is $30, diminishes. As the stock rises in price, so would the correlation of the option premium change to the underlying security's price change. Therefore, should the stock rise to $28 a share, there is a very strong possibility that the premium would change by more than a quarter of a point, perhaps half a point to compensate. So the trader would have to buy back two of the four options that he or she sold.

The other factor working against the position is time. With six months to go and the option out of the money by 4 points, it's a completely different picture from the same stock and the same option with the same prices with three months to go. Therefore, the premium of the option would change accordingly because of the effect of time on it. As we said earlier, if an option is 4 points out of the money with three months to go, its premium would change by maybe an eighth. An option that had one month to go at 4 points out of the money would change even less.

Put Option Example

Let's look at the same relationship from the put side of the equation. The stock is trading at $26 and there is a six-month put with a strike price of $30. That put is in the money by 4 points. Therefore, the premium, at a minimum, would be 4 points. That is called intrinsic value. Let's suppose someone had previously sold 100 shares of the stock short when it was trading at $40 a share. The stock is now trading at $26. They have a 14-point profit in the short sale. The aforementioned put option has six months of time remaining, so they can sell the put and make at a minimum $400, plus time value, per put based on the amount of stock they are holding. Since the option is in the money by 4 points, it will probably carry, at the price of $26, very little time value. Six months is a long time, though, so it will have some time value adding to the amount of money the short seller would receive if he or she sold the puts.

Our client is now short 100 shares and short one put with a strike price of $30. The stock is at $26. Even if anybody exercises against the client right now, remember that these are American options, exercisable at any time during their life, and they would still lock in the 14-point profit because they would have to take the stock in at $30 a share, and pay for it at $30 a share. They sold short at $40, they are taking the stock back in to close out their short sale at $30, plus the 4 points they made on the premium of the option. If the stock continues to fall, then this customer basically is locked in because the further down it goes, it will not increase with any further decline of the stock. What they are making on the short sale they are losing on the short put. People who own the $30 put will be definitely buying the stock as long as it is below $30 per share, and exercising the put at $30 a share. This client who sold that put for at least 4 points will have to take the stock at $30 a share regardless of how far below $30 the stock is actually trading at.

What if the stock should start to rise? If it went from $26 to $28, the option premium in the market would definitely decrease. But the client has made 400 points plus time value. Therefore, when someone exercises the client at $30 a share, they will simply take the stock in, close out their short position, pay the $3,000 per 100 shares, and be left with a 14-point profit. It would be 10 points from the short sale, from $40 to $30, and 4 points from the option premium they made, plus any time value that was in that option premium.

To expand on a previous example, when the client sold the stock short, the firm had to borrow the stock from someplace. They then used that borrowed stock to deliver against the short sale, because the buyer of the stock couldn't care less whether it was a short sale or a long sale—they want their stock. From this point on, the short seller is responsible for all corporate events that take place, including dividends, rights, and any other types of corporate actions. When the client decides to close the short sale out, he will have to buy it back and deliver the stock that he just purchased to the lender. However, since the client has puts against the short sale and those puts are in the money, chances are that at expiration, someone will exercise their puts against him.

He is short the put, so therefore whoever is long the put is going to put the stock to him at the strike price of $30 a share. He will take the stock after paying for the stock itself, $3,000, and return it to whoever it was borrowed from. Actually, *he* will not do this; rather, the brokerage firm he uses for trading will. Therefore, his short position is now closed out. His option has been exercised. He is left with nothing but a $1,400 per 100 share option position, profit less commissions and taxes, of course.

With the option deep in the money, 4 points, on a $26 stock, there would be little time value in the option premium. As the option got closer and closer to expiration, that time value would dissipate. Therefore, at expiration, there would be an in-the-money option that will be exercised against the short seller. If the puts were out of the money, we would have the same situation with the amount of time to go before the options expire and the relationship between the strike price of the option and the underlying stock value. Its movement against the underlying stock price changes would also be a delta.

Hedge funds and other institutions that use options in many different ways are very concerned about the deltas they are carrying. It is the deltas that they are watching. Among their concerns is the change of the premium from one point to another. Earlier, we established a matrix with the option changing its price from hardly anything to an eighth to a quarter, and as the option got closer and closer to its expiration, that delta would change. People who deal with options and get involved with deltas are also curious as to the amount of change that the delta will go through, giving a different price to the underlying security. The measuring of the delta's change is called the gamma, as discussed already.

CHAPTER 12

NONSTANDARD OPTIONS

The basic structure of an option contract can be applied to a host of different products. Like standard options, these products involve placing a put or call on a quantity of an underlying product, have expiration dates, and have exercise (strike) prices. However, as the terms of these contracts are negotiated, there isn't a fixed protocol that has to be followed. Included in this group of nonstandardized options are options that are not listed for trading on exchanges and are commonly known as over-the-counter (OTC) options.

• OVER-THE-COUNTER OPTIONS •

As alluded to before, over-the-counter options are custom made. The transactions are accomplished between options dealers and clients, or clients being represented by broker-dealers. The terms are negotiated and confirmations are sent between the broker-dealer and the client, and between the broker-dealer and the options dealer. Neither Options Clearing Corporation nor any other clearing corporation is involved with these transactions. Therefore, the transactions are not guaranteed, and there are no corporate action notifications or other services that clearing corporations offer. In case of default of one of the two parties, the remaining party must seek legal action to recover the loss.

On exercise, it is one on one, between the original participants or the designees, which enter the required information into the underlying issue's regular processing stream. For example, exercise of an over-the-counter equity option would be sent to National Securities Clearing Corporation (NSCC), and exercise of an option on U.S. Treasury bonds would be sent to Fixed Income Clearing Corporation (FICC).

Options that are not listed to trade on an exchange are referred to as over-the-counter options. While there are still puts and calls, the underlying issue, underlying quantity in some underlying products may not be the standard unit, and the expiration day and/or strike price will not be standardized as they are in listed options and the currency used to settle an exercise is also negotiated. These are customized options or one offs without any secondary market such as the Chicago Board Options Exchange (CBOE) or the New York Stock Exchange (NYSE); therefore the secondary trading that occurs in "listed" options is a nonoccurrence with this product. Options in this market are negotiated between the initiator, who is attempting to achieve some strategy, and a put and call dealer. It is usual in this market for the dealer who was used to get the principal into the position to be the same dealer used to close out the position. In addition, the dealer who was used to get into the position is the contra side to any option exercise. As there isn't a clearing corporation involved in the processing stream with this type of option, the contract remains between the originator and the dealer. The dealer may refer an option exercise to be against another financial institution but the dealer remains responsible as the contra party. If the dealer defaults or ceases as a business entity, the contract ceases to exist.

In case of exercise, the one triggering the action notifies the counterparty of the intention and then submits the underlying transaction into its processing stream. For example, if it is an FX (foreign exchange option), the terms of the option contract would be sent to the clearing banks of both parties and the currency exchanged.

• CAPPED OPTIONS •

The capped option is generally an out-of-the-money long option position with an embedded feature that states that if the market price of the underlying issue should reach or pass the option's strike price, thereby changing the option status from out of the money to at the money or in the money, it is to be automatically exercised. In the case of a call option, the underlying security would have to close at or above the strike price of the option. In the case of a put, the underlying security price would have to close at or below the option's capped price.

One use of a capped option is to protect a short security position. Let's suppose a client went short 10,000 shares of WIP $66 per share. The stock is now $49 per share. The client is concerned as to whether this is the "bottom" or the stock will lose even more value. If it is the bottom, the stock may start to rise in value, dissolving same of the paper profit. The client can see if the near-term option is inexpensive enough for the client to buy 100 near-term calls with a strike price of $50. For that cost, the client is attempting to lock in a 16-point profit (less expenses). If the stock continues to fall in value, the short-term call options will expire worthless. If the stock begins to rise and closes at $50 per share or above, the options will be exercised and the short position will be closed out.

· LEAPS ·

LEAPS stands for Long-term Equity AnticiPation Securities, which are options with longer terms for expiration than the standard option. A LEAPS option, which trades as a put or a call, can exist for up to three years with an expiration in January. Whereas a standard option is not marginable, LEAPS generally are. As the LEAPS's life dissipates when it matches the standard option, it ceases to exist as a LEAPS and takes on the role and settlement cycle of the standard nine-month option. LEAPS are primarily used by long-term investors and can be used as a surrogate for the underlying stock itself. As with all options that are owned, you can never lose more than the price you paid for it. In the case of LEAPS, you don't have to buy the stock if you think whatever event is going to happen will happen within the next two years. If you buy the stock you are tying up a considerable amount of money. If you buy a LEAPS on the same security, you're tying up less money and your downside risk is only the cost of the option.

• Flex Option •

The next option we will look at is a flex option. The standard equity and index option has a fixed expiration date; it expires the Saturday after the third Friday of the appointed expiration month. With flex options, the terms of the contract are negotiated, and that includes the strike price and the expiration date. Because of the uniqueness of each option, they do not trade in a continuous market. They are, however, cleared through a central clearing corporation, Options Clearing Corporation. Therefore the structure of a flex option is very similar to that of the standard over-the-counter option as all terms are negotiated. The major difference, a very important one, is that the flex option clears through a clearing corporation, which guarantees performance.

• Options Clearing Corporation •

Options Clearing Corporation (OCC) is the issuer and guarantor of all listed option products, and it also provides price transparency. Regular over-the-counter options, those not traded on an exchange, are between the buyer and the seller of the option. They are also generally illiquid. If something should happen to the buyer or seller in an over-the-counter option transaction, the counterparty must work any problems out by themselves. This includes absorbing any losses and reinstating their clients to their true positions. On listed options, standard options, LEAPS options, or flex options, should a counterparty default, the clearing corporation stands up for the terms of that contract and makes the transaction valid, along with the exercises and other terms.

The products Options Clearing Corporation offers options on are equity, interest rate, debt, index, dollar-based currency, ETFs, ELX futures, futures on the VIX index, and others that are pending. Unlike standard equity products, options go on for a second life. Therefore, OCC not only settles trades, but maintains the record of outstanding or open positions. This is known as the options' open or products' open interest. Because of the second life, clearing firms must tell OCC what effect the option trade has on the overall position. By federal law, clearing firms must separate client trades from their own, known as proprietary trades. Orders going to the options exchanges must carry the designation *C* for customer or *F* for firm. OCC doesn't care or want to know what effect the trade will have on a particular customer's account—that is the broker-dealer's responsibility—but they do want to know what effect it has on the overall customers' position. The instruction as to what effect the trade will have on the position are *B o* for "Buy to open," as in opening a long or owner's position; *S o* for "Sell to open," as in establishing a writer or short position; *B c* for "Buy to close," which closes out a previous *S o* position; and *S c* for "Sell to close," which closes the previous *B o* position.

Most listed options, including all equity options, expire the Saturday after the third Friday of the expiration month. Therefore, the third Friday of the month is the last day of trading. Equity options that are in the money by $0.75 or more will automatically be exercised. To prevent an unwanted exercise, clients should use "Ex by EX," a process that stops the exercise. Investors should be mindful that an option close to being at the money and qualifying for exercise on "expiration Friday" may be, based on the expired option's strike price, theoretically out of the money by Monday.

• BINARY OPTIONS •

A binary option, which is traded over the counter and on the NYSE Amex, is considered high risk and illiquid as there is very little, if any, trading between the time it originates and the time it expires. Recently, binary option trading platforms have been developed to encourage trading of these products. The binary options that trade on the NYSE Amex exchange are known as fixed return options or FROs. They are offered in two versions: "cash or nothing" and "asset or nothing." These options are binary in practice as there are only two outcomes. Either they pay a preestablished value or, if the option is not in the money at expiration, it is terminated.

Let's say the option will be in the money at expiration. If it is, the option owner will receive $5,000. If the option is out of the money, the option owner receives nothing. This is an example of a cash-or-nothing binary option. If it was an asset-or-nothing binary option, the option owner would receive the value of an asset, perhaps the market value of the underlying stock, if the option finished in the money at expiration—and nothing if it is out of the money. There are cash-or-nothing puts, and cash-or-nothing calls, as well as asset-or-nothing calls and asset-or-nothing puts. Notice that in this product, the amount by which the option is in the money is unimportant, as a fixed amount or the current value of a chosen asset will be paid.

• KNOCK-IN OR KNOCK-OUT OPTIONS •

Quite often, there is a security position backing the option.

For example, a client buys 1,000 shares of Whipper Corporation currently trading at $50 a share. The client sells ten calls on Whipper Corp. with a strike price of $55 per share. This strategy is called "income writing." The client wants the options to expire out of the money so that the premium received from the sale of the options becomes income to the client. If the stock rises from $50 per share to just below $55 per share, the client is still in a good position as the options have a $55 strike price and are still out of the money. If the stock should rise above $55, the client will risk losing the securities. In doing so, though, the client picks up the premium from the options that were sold and the 5 points gained from the rise in the underlying stock's price increase. However, if the stock begins to fall in value instead of rise, the client has a problem.

If the client decides to liquidate the stock, and limit the loss, the client would have ten naked (uncovered) call options in the account, which, even though they are out of the money, must be margined. If the stock should turn upward and start to run up in value, the client could face a major loss, especially if the stock surprisingly opened for trading one day to a price way above $55 per share. However, the whole sequence changes if the position was originally structured as follows: The client buys 1,000 shares of stock at $50 per share and proceeds to sell ten three-month call options with a strike price of $55 per share. Also built into the option transaction is the premise that if *the stock falls in value below a certain price, the options contract is canceled. This protects the client from the stock's turning around after it went down in value and the client sold the shares to limit its loss. Therefore the aforementioned transactions could be: buy 1,000 shares at $50 per share, sell ten knock-out call three-month options with a strike price of $55 and a knock-out provision if and when the stock falls and reaches $45 per share. The $45 is the safe zone where the client can close out the stock position without concern about exposure to the uncovered option. All of this will be factored into the premium paid and negotiated between the buyer and seller of the options.*

Four Types of Knock-out Options

The "knock out, knock in" option is more complicated than it presents itself. It is part of a group called "barrier options." There are actually four types of knock-out options: an up-and-out call option, a down-and-out call option, an up-and-out put option, and a down-and-out put option. An up-and-out call option would have a limited upside value.

For example, suppose the stock is trading at $30 per share and the knock-out option contract reads that if the stock rises to $40 per share, the option is canceled. That means that the writer of the option faces a 10-point loss, maximum. Whatever value the stock may have going forward, no matter how high in value it rises, once it reaches $40 per share the option is dead. The buyer of the option must think that the stock will not rise to $40 and therefore is not going to rise more than 10 points, so the buyer can buy this option at a much lower premium than if the upside potential were unlimited.

A down-and-out call option would be a very good protection should someone own a large block of stock and have sold calls against it, as reviewed in the previous paragraph. As the stock loses value, the owner of that position is losing money and the options are going further and further out of the money. However, liquidating the security position would leave the client with uncovered options. The down-and-out call option would automatically terminate the option obligation when the stock fell to a certain price. This type of thought process could also be used in put option strategies. Supposing a client believes that a stock is going to fall in value by about 6 or 7 points. The client can reduce the cost of that put by making it a down-and-out put option at 10 points. The writer of that option knows that the maximum risk is 10 points. The buyer of that put option is looking for less than a 10-point downswing; therefore, the put will cost much less as the writer's risk is contained.

Let's assume, for a knock-in option, that the current market price of an underlying security is at $30 per share and the strike price of an option with that underlying is $30. The option is selling at 5 points, which means that underlying security must rise 5 points before the purchase of the option becomes profitable. The buyer of that over-the-counter option will be paying 5 points time value for no reason other than to hope that the underlying stock rises above those 5 points to cover that cost. If the buyer of the option was of the opinion that the stock was worth more than $35 per share, the buyer would be better served if an "up and in" call option was negotiated, stating that the option does not become alive until the stock has reached the 5-point level. The writer of the $30 strike price option does not have any obligation during the time the stock moves from $30 to $35 and the option goes into the money. Therefore, the 5 points of the $30 strike price option's premium is a throwaway. The option can be negotiated for a much lower cost to the buyer than it would be if it were just a straight over-the-counter option with a strike price of $30. A down-and-in would work in the same fashion for an over-the-counter put option.

> The Worsco Company is in financial trouble and its common stock is falling in price. Its common stock is presently trading at $47 per share, down from $80 per share. Mr. Theodore Bear believes that the company will fail and file for bankruptcy. A six-month put with a strike price of $45 is trading for 7 points. That means that $38 is the break-even point. Bear negotiates a down-and-in six-month option with a "kick-in" at $38. With the writer of the option getting the next 7 points down, obligation free, the premium Bear would be charged is significantly less.

Part of the negotiation that goes on with these barrier options is what constitutes a barrier event. For example, on an up-and-in call option, if the stock rises to that barrier price one time over the life of the option, does that trigger an event? Or does the price have to be sustained over a period of time? Must the event happen at a given time during the day? That's all part of the negotiation that goes into the barrier option contract between the writer and the holder, the seller and the buyer.

• COMPOUND OPTIONS •

The last form of options we will look at is options on options. Another name for these compound options is "mother and daughter options." If the holder of one of this type of options exercises it, the former holder will either own or write another option. So what we have here is a three-tier situation. There is the underlying asset, over which is the first option, and over that option is the second option. There are four variations of this form of option: There is a call on a call, a call on a put, a put on a put, or a put on a call.

Pricing this form of option is naturally more complicated. As with the standard or regular option, the premium consists of time value, which was explained earlier, and the intrinsic value or in-the-money sum of the option, should it exist. Starting with the price of the underlying security, apply the strike price of the option that covers it and then the exercise price of the secondary option that covers the first option. What also must be taken into consideration in determining the premium are three factors: dividends, as dividends affect the price of the underlying securities (though not the value of the option directly); the risk-free interest rate, or the Treasury bill rate, which would be earned if the money was simply invested in U.S. Treasury bills; and the time remaining to the expiration of the first option and time remaining to the expiration of the second option. Naturally, the second option has to expire on or before the first option.

Here's an example:

Let's assume there is a very volatile stock that Steve Adore has a long American-style put option on. The option has a duration of two years, and the premium is very expensive. The owner of that position is willing to "sell" a slice of the time remaining for a fee. Izzy Smart is interested and negotiates a call contract with the put holder, Steve, for three months, which gives the call buyer, Izzy, the right to "call in" the put position for the next three months, starting today. If the underlying stock should drop in value to a point allowed in the negotiated agreement, the call holder can call in the put option and exercise it.

Previously, we looked at the rationale behind buying calls or buying puts or selling calls or selling puts. As stated in the opening, options are a tool, and therefore there are many different ways they can be applied.

• SYNTHETIC OPTIONS •

The following exercises involve the use of an underlying product and a call option and a put option. Each of these has the ability to be long or short, owned or owed. The three products, therefore, offer a total of six possibilities for use. In a spread position, for example, the participant is long and short equal numbers of calls or puts on the same underlying product but different series. One of the two options is the main option; the other option is there to either reduce the premium cost of the main option, or act as an insurance policy, to curtail further losses. In a straddle position the participant can have long equal numbers of puts and calls, or short equal numbers of puts and calls on the same underlying product having the same series designation (straddle) or different series designation (combination). In the above cases, we used options but left the stock position out. Now let's include it.

Elsewhere in the book we mentioned a buy/write—the buying of stock and writing of an out-of-the-money call against it as a way to enhance income. If the long stock position increases in value, that's good. If the short call position increases in value that's bad, because once the call is in the money the underlying stock will be called by an option's owner, or if not, the short call increases in value as the underlying stock increases in value, making it more expensive to buy the short call back and close out the short option position. Therefore the long stock and the short call cancel each other out as the stock rises.

For every dollar the long stock rises, which is a good thing for the owner of the stock, the in-the-money or intrinsic part of the short option premium increases too, which is bad for the short options writer. If the long stock loses value, that is bad for the stock owner but good for the short call position because it becomes less expensive to buy it in, and once the stock's value falls below the option's strike price, the option is out of the money. The problem is that the long stock can continue to lose value after the option is worthless. Therefore, what put option position has a negative impact on its owner the more the underlying security or index value decreases?

ANSWER: A short put position. This is an example of a synthetic short put position.

Here's another example:

Let's suppose Dynaflow (DYN) common stock index has a value of 50. If a client was long a call on the DYN index with a strike price of 50 and short a put option on the DYN with a strike price of 50, what index position would that replicate? Hint: What stock position develops a profit when the price increases and creates loss when the value falls?

ANSWER: A long stock position. A rise in price would benefit the long call owner, but a drop in value would be bad for the short put writer.

Staying with DYN common stock, what position is replicated if the position comprised a short DYN stock at 50 and a short put option with a strike price of 50?

ANSWER: A short DYN call position. An increase in value of DYN would have a negative impact on short DYN stock, which would be offset by the loss in value of the short put to a point. The position is bad for the short stock, but good for the short put. Once the short put is worthless, should the stock continue to rise, the short stock sale would be working against the position.

What if a client's position was short DYN stock position long a DYN call? What put position would be replicated?

ANSWER: *A long put. If the stock rose, the loss on the short stock position would be offset by gain on the long call, a zero-sum game. If the value of the stock fell, the short stock position would benefit and the long call would lose value and eventually become worthless. A long put position benefits from a drop in the underlying's value.*

If a client is long DYN stock and long a DYN put, this would replicate what position?

ANSWER: *A long call. As the stock lost value, the long put would gain value, offsetting the loss in the long stock position. As the stock gained value, the long put would become worthless and the stock would benefit.*

Finally, what does a long DYN put and a short DYN call equate to?

ANSWER: *A short stock position. As the value of DYN rises, the short call gains value and the put loses value until it becomes worthless. This is bad for the position holder. As the value of the stock falls, the short call loses value until it becomes worthless and the long put gains value, which benefits the position owner as would a short stock position.*

• RAINBOW OPTIONS •

The options we have discussed thus far are focused on one product. For instance, a call on PIP common stock or a put on IND index option is only interested in the performance of that underlying. A rainbow option is focused on multiple events happening. It is as if the option were on a basket of independent, unrelated items. Using a sports example, you're not just selecting a baseball team to win the World Series; rather, you are selecting a baseball team to win the World Series, a football team to win the Super Bowl, and a car and driver to win the Daytona 500 NASCAR race. All three selections must be successful or the selection option is worthless. A rainbow option is based on assets, and each asset has a color—hence the rainbow. In addition, there should be some correlation between the components.

An example of the use of this type of product could be the number of successful oil wells that will be dug and the quantity of oil that will be discovered. Alternatively, one might ask what the interest rate will be on a floating-rate note at its maturity, and which currency the client will choose to be paid in. The components can have different expiration dates and/or different exercise terms. The important factor is that there is a correlation of the components' all moving the same way. In the first example, the number or percentage of successful wells must be reached and the estimate as to the amount of oil pumped must still be valid.

There are multiple payoff types depending on the assets making up the rainbow option. If there are two deliverable assets, the payoff may be one of the two assets or cash. If option payout is in cash, the currency that it is to be paid in is the choice.

• CURRENCY OPTIONS •

To understand currency options, one must first understand foreign exchange. Let's assume that ZOW common stock was trading at $25 per share. The stock increases in price to $40. We can say the dollar fell against the value of the ZOW stock, because formerly $25 was needed to buy one share of ZOW stock, and now $40 is needed. In this example, the common stock is the commodity and the dollar is the currency. Now let's assume one British pound sterling costs $1.46. If the U.S. dollar rose and got stronger against the British pound sterling, the dollar figure would decrease because now you would need fewer dollars to buy one British pound.

If a British pound sterling option is denominated in dollars, the British pound is the commodity and the dollar is the currency. If the U.S. dollar rose against the British pound, the value of the call would decrease, and put options would increase in value. If the option has a strike price of USD $1.50 and the conversion rate was USD $1.50 per British pound, the option would be at the money. If the U.S. dollar rose against the British pound to where it was USD $1.40, a put would have 10 points intrinsic value. The owner of the USD $1.50 British pound put would purchase the British pound at $1.40 per pound and exercise the long put to receive $1.50 per British pound.

Currency options are European-style and dollar-denominated options. They are traded on the PHLX and the International Securities Exchange. The PHLX trades the Australian dollar, British pound, Canadian dollar, euro, Japanese yen, New Zealand dollar, and Swiss franc. The International Securities Exchange trades those plus the Brazilian real, Mexican peso, and Swedish krona. These too are dollar denominated.

The options are denominated in dollars. The British pound and the euro are always quoted in dollars; the others are converted into dollars for trading purposes. In other words, the natural quote for the New Zealand dollar is NZ $1.23 to the U.S. dollar. The exchange rate is USD $0.7991 per NZ dollar, which is the complementary side.

• Option Margin •

The formula for an uncovered written equity call option is 20 percent of the underlying market value plus the premium, less the out-of-the-money sum, or 10 percent of the underlying market value plus the premium, whichever is greater, with a minimum of $250 per option contract, also whichever is greater.

An uncovered put is almost the same, except it's 20 percent of the underlying market value plus the premium, less the out-of-the-money sum, or 10 percent of the option exercise price plus the premium, whichever is greater, with a minimum of $250 per option contract, whichever is greater.

Ms. Mary Land sells one Call PUP Apr 50 @ 2. PUP is now trading at $47 per share. Therefore, PUP is out of the money by 3 points. The margin calculation for this uncovered call is:

20% of the underlying value − $4,700 × 20% = $ 940.00

Plus the premium + 200.00 $1,140.00

Less the out-of-the-money sum   − 300.00 $ 840.00

OR

10% of the underlying value – $4,700 × 10% = $470.00

Plus the premium + $200.00 $670.00

with a minimum of $250 per contract
   The margin requirement is   *$840*

Ms. Della Ware sells one Put BOW Jul 60 @ 1 with BOW trading at $62 per share. The option is out of the money by 2 points. The margin calculations for this uncovered put are:

20% of the underlying value – $6,200 × 20% = $1,240.00

Plus the premium + $100.00 $1,340.00

Less the out-of-the-money sum   – $200.00 $1,140.00

OR

10% of the exercise price – $6,000 × 10% = $ 600.00

Plus the premium + $100.00 $ 700.00

with a minimum of $250 per contract
   The margin requirement is   *$1,140*

• OPTION SPREADS •

Spread option margins are more intricate. A spread is defined as having equal numbers of long and short options of the same type (put or call), but different series.

If the long option expires on or after the short option and is the more valuable one, no margin is required; the account's principal pays the required difference between the two premiums.

If the option that was sold expires after the long option, opening the firm to risk for the period after the long option expired, the client pays the difference or receives the difference in the premium price between the two and must post margin on the short (sold) option as if the sold were an uncovered option.

Ms. Minnie Soto buys 1 Put DOG Nov 50 @ 2 and sells 1 Put DOG Nov 55 @ 4. DOG is trading at 53.

The short (sold) option position has the most value, but as the long (bought) options expire with or after the short option, spread margin is applied. Spread margin is the difference between strike prices of the two positions, or the margin required on the short option as if it were an uncovered position—whichever is less.

Difference between strike prices
55 − 50 × 100 shares = $500

Calculation for an uncovered option:

20% of the underlying value − $5,300 × 20% = $1,060.00

Plus the premium	**+ $400.00**
	$1,460.00

Less the out-of-the-money sum = 0   *$1,460.00*

The option with the strike price of $55 is in the money as the stock can be acquired by the put owner at $53 per share and put to the put seller at $55 per share. In other words, the $50 strike price put is out of the money but is reducing risk of the $55 written (sold) put to only 5 points. The current price of DOG has the $55 put at a 2 point disadvantage.

OR

10% of the exercise price − $5,500 × 10% =	**$550.00**
Plus the premium	**+ $400.00**
	$950.00

Whichever is greater, with a minimum of $250 per contract.

In spread margin, either the lower difference between strike prices or the calculation for an uncovered margin is used, as it represents *the minimum necessary margin to cover the risk to the firm. Therefore the margin required for this position is $500 because it represents the maximum the firm and customer have at risk.*

A Straddle Example

Miss Zori buys 1 Call ZIP Aug 50 @ 5 and buys 1 Put ZIP Aug 50 @ 2 for a total cost of 7 points. As this straddle covers a long position call and a long position put, the client pays for both in full. Another client, Miss Azipi, sells 1 Call WIP Mar 60 @ 3 and sells 1 Put WIP Mar 60 @ 2. WIP common stock is trading at $62. As this straddle contains a short put and a short call, the margin requirement is the uncovered margin from the greater side plus the premium from the other side.

	Call	Put
20% of underlying value =	$1,240	$1,240
Plus the premium	+ $300	+ $200
	$1,540	$1,440
Less the out-of-the-money sum	0	$200
	$1,540	$1,240

OR

	Call	Put
10% of underlying value =	exercise price = $600 $620	
Plus the premium	+ $300	+ $200
	$920	$800

With a $250 per option minimum

Take the requirement from the greater side ($1,540) plus the premium from the other side ($200) to arrive at the requirement ($1,740).

CHAPTER 13

FUTURES AND COMMODITY PRODUCTS

A future product is one that trades on an exchange, where participants with different agendas meet to set a price today for the delivery of a product that will occur at a later time. Among the participants are those that are actively involved with the underlying product and want to "lock in" prices and those who are trading in and out of positions for profits. Among the products offered for trading are contracts on agricultural products, precious metals, base metals, foreign exchange, interest rates, debt products, lumber, petroleum, and indexes. A seller of a future product knows today the price that will be received when his or her product is delivered at a specific date in the future. The buyer of the future knows what will have to be paid upon receipt of the product at that time. For example:

Ms. Lena Board contracts with Ms. June Budds for 1,000 widgets that Lena will make and deliver at the end of six months. June is to pay $1.00 per widget upon receipt. Lena and June have entered into a future contract.

The future product is multifaceted. It is one of the most misunderstood products by the public, as well as by some professionals, and yet it affects our lives more directly than the vast majority of other products that we trade. The product, and its underlying products, is in the news on a daily basis. What is interesting is that when clients have a position on the profitable side of a transaction and they are part of the profit, you will hear that the product is "overregulated." Conversely, when their position is on the losing side of the market, they might say, "Well, the government ought to do something about this manipulated, out-of-control product."

• FUTURES •

As stated above, the future product sets a price today at which a delivery will occur at a later date. The price is based on a projection from today's market price and on current wisdom about the product and its near- or long-term environment. Often the deliverable underlying product doesn't even exist at the time the parties enter into the agreement, especially in agriculture products. It is also possible that during the future product's existence there can be more open contracts outstanding on a particular product than can possibly come to market within the delivery period, and yet no one seems to be overly concerned.

For example, there can be more wheat contracts outstanding in a given month than it is possible to grow, store, or deliver. In addition, some of the products being traded will not actually be received or delivered. Still in other products, it is impossible to deliver the actual product that is underlying the future contract. An interesting feature of some of these products that make up the futures market is that their value increases as their underlying faces adversity. An event happening that affects one product could have an effect on another, completely disassociated product.

Finally, some of the largest positioned traders, who have millions of dollars on the line, may never have actually seen, touched, or eaten the product they are trading—or if they did, they didn't know it. With some products, a new market begins at the time the futures become deliverable with other products. The deliverable product blends into an existing market and is indistinguishable from the mass.

Future Pricing

How do traders know what a price will be six months from now? Actually, they don't. They try to estimate the value based on the current (spot) market price, augmented by relevant and applicable data such as interest rate costs for carrying the position, storage charges for maintaining it, spoilage (using average past experiences), transportation charges, current economic conditions (globally and locally), trends affecting consumers' choices, industrial and agricultural trends, governmental programs, economic and weather forecasts—and that's just to name a few. Many future products are truly global and their value is affected by currency exchange rate changes, foreign government stability, and economic conditions in the far reaches of the earth.

How is future pricing applicable?

Let's take farming as an example. The farmer must grow crops to sell in a market to earn income. The crops take months to grow from seed to harvest and then to market. The farmer would have an idea as to what the direct expenses and indirect costs should be, but is not sure what price the market would be willing to pay for the product at the later time. The futures market would provide that future price information today. Traders and speculators are using their best assessments to set a price for that month's future contract. At a minimum, the current spot (cash) price is known, and from there, the assumed futures price can be extrapolated.

The farmer may have a choice of which products to grow during this season and must analyze each one. Based on this factual and projected information, the farmer would then decide which products to grow. If the farmer wanted, he or she could sell contracts on the product selected to plant today, and lock in the selling price that would be received when the product is delivered. Knowing the selling price is locked in, the farmer would then be concerned with the expense side of the equation. If the farmer held the future position until delivery, the price contracted for would be the price the farmer would receive. If the product is selling for more than the contracted amount, the farmer missed out on additional revenue. If the market price is below the contracted price, the farmer is better off financially. The farmer has hedged the value of the actual crop.

As the future contract trades on an exchange, there is a liquid market that affords the farmer the ability to trade in and out of positions, or simply to monitor and adjust the positions during the product's growing and delivery process. There are other factors affecting the farmer's decision besides price, though, such as the amount that will actually be grown. Is the farmer concerned about a bumper crop or a thin one? Aside from the amount actually grown, what is the crop's quality? Many of the products that futures trade on are graded, such as coffee and soybeans. The final price that the farmer would receive is based on the grade the product received. What is actually being traded during the "futures" phase of the cycle is a generic product whose price will be adjusted to reflect its grade. Knowing all of this, the question remains: what percentage of the expected crop does the farmer want to hedge with the futures contracts and how much remains not hedged?

If the farmer doesn't hedge the crop at all, he or she could face financial ruin if the market price at delivery is far below the growing cost. If the entire expected crop is hedged, the farmer has traded away the possibility of greater profit for protection from earning less. If the total crop grown is less than the amount required by the future contract sold, the farmer must cover the shortage, which may mean acquiring the shortfall in the open market or buying in the short contracts or paying cash for the shortage. Regardless, this action would probably be at a loss.

Each provider or user in the future market faces similar choices and possible results. The above example illustrates the concerns of a farmer, but if assessing the near-term unknown is a problem, what is the impact of all the other viewpoints on the segments of the market? Some participants look at the future long-term, others for less time, still others for seconds or less. All these opinions collectively are what make up the futures market, and through that, price discovery.

Besides the product providers and product users, there are speculators. These people trade for their own accounts and at their own risk. They usually maintain positions for short periods of time, sometimes less than an hour, hoping to profit from their trading prowess. They do not take delivery of the product they are trading the future on, with the exception being when the underlying product is part of the trading strategy. The trading activity they generate adds liquidity to the marketplace. This is reflected not only in tighter spreads (the difference between bids and offers) but also in the depth of the market, which allows it to absorb trades of larger quantities.

Some authors lump the product provider and the product user into one name: "hedgers." In the above example, the farmer is hedging the value of the crop against unknown risk. The user is doing the same thing by locking in the price of the product against the unknown. The speculators are trading in and out of positions based on the futures' price trend or anticipation of some data being released. In some markets speculators are known as "scalpers," because they buy and sell or sell and buy on minimum price movements for short-term gains.

• DETERMINING THE NEED FOR A FUTURE PRODUCT •

For a future product to exist there must be market risk. The risk can be either real or perceived, or degrees of both. The risk takes the form of market value volatility. Volatility can be caused by the product underlying the future, or its relationship to another product. It can also be caused by pressure from competitive products or some indirect event happening. An example of volatility caused by the product itself is the fluctuation of oil contracts. An oil contract's price is affected by production, demand, weather, the global economy, the economy of emerging countries, and, most recently, speculators.

For an example of a product that is affected by relationships, look at soybeans. Besides the soybean futures themselves, soybean oil and soybean meal futures are also traded. A fourth product, soybean crush, is also part of the group. About sixty tons of soybeans will produce forty-seven tons of soybean meal and eleven tons of soybean oil. The rest is soybean crush or mash. This is an example of products that have a direct effect on other products. All four products are used for different purposes. Therefore, a change in demand for one affects the other three.

If the growth in the popularity of edamame (soybeans cooked in their pods) continues, the demand will eventually affect the soybean market itself. Theoretically, this would cause fewer soybeans to be processed, which in turn would cause less soybean oil, meal, and crush to be processed, and so on and so forth. What would happen to the prices of the individual soybean products if some respected periodical printed an article stating that tests are under way which are intended to prove that a teaspoon of soybean oil each morning could possibly deter and/or assist in the cure of some dread disease? Do you think the current balance between the soybean products would be affected?

First, the volatility of the soybeans group would increase because of the unknown change in demand on soybeans and soybean oil. It is anyone's guess how much this news would impact the current supply of soybeans and soybean oil. What would be the degree of shift away from soybeans to soybean oil? Would the impact on soybean meal be positive or negative? If soybean processors start crushing more soybeans to make more soybean oil, what happens to the additional soybean meal that is being produced as a result?

Wheat, rice, corn, and potatoes compete with one another both in the futures market as well as in the spot or cash market. If the price of wheat were to increase to the point where the price of bread and other wheat products became prohibitive, the public would turn to bread made of rice, corn, or potatoes. Producers would gear up to meet the new demand, and the demand for wheat bread would become stagnant, or it would even fall as the demand for the other products increased. We may be witnessing this at present. The increase in the number of people with allergies to wheat and wheat products is growing and at some point may be causing a switch in the demand for wheat. An example of this is the demand for gluten-free products, which use rice, corn, or potatoes as a substitute for wheat.

As summers get hotter, prices on many of the products we eat and/or feed to animals have been increasing already. Some believe the recent summer heat may be an effect of global warming and be permanent. Others believe it is part of a normal cycle. Given the reality of the situation, would you buy or sell long-term agricultural products futures?

The Shared Need

As mentioned previously, there must be a strong need, shared by many, to hedge or offload risk. The more diverse the need, the more diverse the interest in the future product will be, the stronger the market in that new product will be. This need will drive the idea for a new product, its purpose, proposed nomenclature, specifications, etc. In other words, those proposing the product must make their case before the Commodity Futures Trading Commission (CFTC) and the case must be strong enough that it will receive approval. The CFTC is an independent federal regulator of the futures market, whose mission is to "protect market users and the public from fraud, manipulations, abusive practices and systemic risk related to derivatives that are subject to the Commodity Exchange Act, and to foster open competitive and financially sound markets." Besides product approval, the CFTC oversees the futures exchanges, commodity pool operators, commodity trading advisors, commodity futures merchants, and approved persons operating in the industry.

As future products trade on exchanges (either in physical locations, electronic, or both), an exchange that is interested in listing and trading the product will put the proposal forward to the Commodity Futures Trading Commission (CFTC). However, we are getting ahead of ourselves. For a product to be considered, there must be a multiuser need and sufficient interest to support the trading of the product. The size or quantity of the contract must be married to the volatility in such a way that the contract size is large enough to serve the need of many users, and be volatile enough to attract traders and speculators who add liquidity to the market. The volatility, which translates into dollars and cents, must be high enough to be attractive to traders, but not so high that it becomes too expensive for the traders to trade. The relationship between contract size and volatility is a balancing act.

Here's an example:

The coffee contract is for 37,500 lbs. The minimum trading "tick," the minimum allowable price movement, is $0.05 or $18.75 per contract (37,500 lbs × $0.05 = $18.75). The wheat contract is for 5,000 bushels of #2 soft red winter, #1 soft red winter at a $0.03 premium, other grades according the exchange rules, minimum tick $0.0025 or $12.50 per contract (5,000 bu. × $0.0025 = $12.50). The S&P 500 index, when originally launched by the Chicago Mercantile Exchange (CME), was set at $500 a point. It grew to become too expensive to trade, though, and was subsequently split 2 for 1 or $250 a point. In

1997, the CME launched the E-mini contract, which is valued at $50 times the index value and has been very successful.

Futures on agricultural products usually have delivery months that co-incide with the delivery of the physical product. The delivery destinations are also the same as those of the physical product. Currency futures, which trade in pairs, are settled through financial institutions, such as banks, and their delivery is calendar controlled and set by the marketplace on which they trade. The currency pairs are the "commodity" currency and the "payment" currencies (i.e., EUR/USD, the euro denominated in U.S. dollars).

Not all products that are launched become successful. Years ago a Government National Mortgage Association (GNMA, or Ginnie Mae) future product was launched on the GNMA mortgage-backed pass-through securities. The GNMA product comprises unique pools of government-guaranteed or -insured mortgages. The pools operate as "pass-through" instruments; that is, something that pays interest and pays down mortgage principal monthly. Unlike a corporate bond which pays interest periodically, according to a preset schedule, and pays its principal (the face or amount of the loan) at the end of the loan's life, the GNMA, as do some other mortgage- and asset-backed securities, periodically pays down the loan or mortgage principal to the loan owner as the borrower pays the loan back to the lender. The underlying principal of the loan is depleting over time. Therefore, each periodic interest payment is based on the principal remaining at that time of the payment. The practitioners of the GNMA future product found the delivery process of the GNMA's pass-throughs due for settlement cumbersome and awkward, as they had to mix and match mortgage pools. Reacting to the same stimulus in a very similar way was another product that was much easier to work with—the future on U.S. Treasury instruments. The delivery of U.S. Treasury bonds against the Treasury bond future was far simpler, and both products—the GNMA future and the Treasury bond future—traded in similar patterns and served the same hedging purpose. Ultimately, the GNMA future disappeared and is no longer being traded.

It is common lingo to say that futures expire. They do not! If the future position is not closed out when its contracted delivery time has arrived, it transforms from being a future to becoming its underlying product or a cash representation of the same.

• STRUCTURE OF A FUTURES CONTRACT •

The futures contract consists of the components of the following examples:

1. The underlying product and quantity
   a. Gold—100 troy ounces
   b. Soybeans—5,000 bushels of #2 yellow grown in Indiana, Ohio, Michigan, Iowa, Illinois, and Wisconsin
   c. Wheat—5,000 bushels of #2 Soft Red Winter
   d. Light crude oil—1,000 barrels
   e. Euro—125,000 euros U.S. dollar denominated

2. Trading symbol
   a. C—Corn (open outcry)
   b. ZC—Corn (CME Globex [Electronic])
   c. GC—Gold

3. Pricing unit
   a. Cents per bushel
   b. U.S. dollars per ounce

4. Tick size (minimum price movement)
   a. ¼ of a cent per bushel
   b. $0.10 per ounce

5. Delivery month
   a. Dependent on the product (agriculture coincides with the product's delivery cycle)

6. Method of trading
   a. Electronic via computer-based trading programs
   b. Open outcry on an exchange floor

(continued on next page)

(continued from previous page)

7. Trading hours

    a. Different times per product group as it is product dependent

8. Daily price limit

    a. Some products permit unlimited price swings

    b. Allowable price move during a one-day period

    c. Trading ceases when exceeded

9. Settlement procedure for:

    a. Domestic currency settlers

    b. Foreign exchange settlers

    c. Product (physical) settlers

    d. Produced, adjusted for quality, settlers

10. Last trade date

    a. Last opportunity to unwind position

11. Last delivery date

    a. Dependent on product

    b. Dependent on convention

• EXAMPLE OF A FUTURES CONTRACT SPECIFICATION •

Here's an example of a soybean futures contract from the CME Group:

SOYBEAN FUTURES

CONTRACT SIZE

5,000 bushels (136 metric tons)

DELIVERABLE GRADE

#2 Yellow @ contract price

#1 Yellow @ a $0.06/bushel premium

#3 Yellow @ a $0.06/bushel discount

PRICING UNIT

Cents per bushel

TICK SIZE

¼ of a cent per bushel ($12.50 per contract)

CONTRACT MONTHS/SYMBOLS

January (F), March (H), May (K), July (N), August (Q), September (U), and November (X)

TRADING HOURS

CME Globex 5:00 p.m.–2:00 p.m. CT, Sunday–Friday; Open Outcry (floor) 9:30 a.m.–2:00 p.m. CT, Monday–Friday; (opens @ 7:20 a.m.) CT for major USDA crop reports

DAILY PRICE LIMIT

$0.70 per bushel expandable to $1.05 and to $1.60 when the market closes at limit bid or limit offer. There shall be no price limits on the current month contract on or after the second business day preceding the first day of the delivery month.

SETTLEMENT PROCEDURE

Daily Grains Settlement Procedure

LAST TRADE DATE

The business day prior to the 15th calendar day of the contract month

LAST DELIVERY DATE

Second business day following the last trading day of the delivery month

(continued on next page)

(continued from previous page)

TICKER SYMBOL

CME Globex

ZS

S = Clearing

Open outcry S

EXCHANGE RULE

These contracts are listed with and subject to the rules and regulations of the Chicago Board of Trade (CBOT).

....

Notice: There are the grades acceptable for delivery, and there are daily trading price limits. The limits, which widen each day, are to allow the futures commission merchants (FCMs) to contact their clients and call for more collateral.

• FUTURE PRODUCTS[1] •

The following is a list of the products on which futures contracts are traded:

1. Foreign Exchange
   a. Australian dollar
   b. British pound
   c. Canadian dollar
   d. Eurocurrency
   e. Japanese yen
   f. Mexican peso
   g. New Zealand dollar
   h. Swiss franc
   i. U.S. dollar

---

[1] List accumulated from various future exchanges.

2. Precious metals
   a. Gold
   b. Palladium
   c. Platinum
   d. Silver

3. Nonferrous metals
   a. Aluminum
   b. Copper
   c. Lead
   d. Nickel
   e. Tin
   f. Zinc

4. Interest rates
   a. Eurodollar
   b. Euroyen
   c. U.S. Treasury 13-week bills
   d. U.S. Treasury 5-year notes
   e. U.S. Treasury 10-year notes
   f. U.S. Treasury 30-year bonds

5. Indices (A-Domestic)
   a. Dow
   b. S&P
   c. NASDAQ 100
   d. Hard Red Spring Index
   e. Goldman Sachs Commodity
   f. National Corn Index
   g. National Soybean Index
   h. RJ/CRB
   i. Russell

(continued on next page)

(continued from previous page)

6. Indices (B-Foreign)
   a. S&P CNX Nifty Fifty
   b. Nikkei

7. Animal
   a. Feeder cattle
   b. Live cattle
   c. Lean hogs
   d. Pork bellies

8. Agriculture
   a. Apple juice concentrate
   b. Cocoa
   c. Coffee
   d. Cotton
   e. Orange juice
   f. Sugar
   g. Wool

9. Dairy
   a. Milk
   b. International skimmed milk
   c. Powder
   d. Nonfat dry milk
   e. Dry whey
   f. Butter
   g. Cheese

10. Grain
    a. Barley
    b. Canola
    c. Corn
    d. Distillers dried grain
    e. Oats

    f. Rough rice

    g. Soybeans

    h. Soybean oil

    i. Soybean meal

    j. Sugar

    k. Wheat

    l. Wheat (Black Sea)

    m. Wheat (Red Spring)

11. Fuel

    a. Brent crude

    b. Carbon

    c. Crude oil

    d. Electricity

    e. Heating oil

    f. Emissions

    g. European Gasoil

    h. Gulf Coast Sour Crude

    i. Light Sweet Crude

    j. Natural Gas

    k. RBOB Gasoline

    l. Russian Export Blend Crude

12. Lumber

    a. Random length lumber

    b. Softwood pulp

13. Exchange-traded products

    a. Numerous ETFs are listed

    b. Largest in capitalization being PowerShares DB Commodity Index Tracking Fund

14. SWAPs

• THE U.S. FUTURES MARKETS •

1. CBOE Futures Exchange (CFE) (owned by Chicago Board Options Exchange)

2. Chicago Mercantile Exchange (CME) (Since 2007 a Designated Contract Market owned by the CME Group)

3. Chicago Board of Trade (CBOT) (Since 2007 a Designated Contract Market owned by the CME Group)

4. Chicago Climate Exchange (CCE)

5. ELX Futures (Electronic Liquidity Exchange)

6. ICE Futures U.S. (formerly New York Board of Trade or NYBOT and now part of Intercontinental Exchange)

7. Kansas City Board of Trade (KCBT)

8. Minneapolis Grain Exchange (MGEX)

9. Nadex (formerly Hedge Street)

10. NASDAQ OMX Futures Exchange (NFX) (formerly Philadelphia Board of Trade or PBOT)

11. New York Mercantile Exchange (NYMEX) and (COMEX) (Since 2008 a Designated Contract Markets owned by the CME Group)

12. NYSE Liffe US

13. OneChicago, LLC (single-stock futures [SSFs] and futures on ETFs)

CHAPTER 14

THE FUTURES MARKET

The futures market comprises its own special types of members and processes due to the uniqueness of the products. For example, in this market agricultural producers come to the market to lock in a price of their future deliverable products or hedge their positions and manufacturers and other users come to lock in their purchase prices or hedge the prices that they will eventually pay. In between the two are speculators and traders, thereby developing active markets.

• MARKET MEMBERS •

First, let's take a look at commodity pool operators.

Commodity Pool Operators (CPOs)

A commodity pool operator is an entity or organization that solicits and pools clients' funds, and trades futures contracts, options on futures, and foreign exchange contracts or invests in other commodity pools. Unless exempted from registration, commodity pool operators must be registered with the Commodity Futures Trading Commission. All registered CPOs must be members of the National Futures Association.

Exemption from registration would occur for the following reasons: 1) the entity is under the jurisdiction of another approved authority; 2) it operates small pools with less than $400,000 of capital *and* has fifteen or fewer participants in each pool; 3) operators do not commit more than 10 percent of the current market value of their assets to establish a commodity position and their trading is independent of their security positions; and 4) the pools are open only to sophisticated participants who are restrained by preestablished position limits.

Commodity Trading Advisors (CTAs)

A commodity trading advisor is an organization or individual who, for compensation, will advise others on the buying and selling of futures contracts, options on futures, or retail non-exchange-traded foreign exchange contracts. Agreements with clients may include discretionary trading authorization besides the giving of trading and strategy advice.

Futures Commission Merchants (FCMs)

A futures commission merchant is a person or an entity that is registered with and approved by the CFTC, and is permitted to buy and sell future contracts with public (retail) and professional (institutional) clients. Besides FCMs' being permitted to carry clients' accounts and enter into trades for them, they are also allowed to extend credit (margin) for those clients.

Leverage Transaction Merchants (LTMs)

A leverage transaction merchant specializes in the trading of margined or leveraged contracts for themselves and/or their clients. At all times, the leverage transaction merchant must stay leveraged between long and short leveraged customers. The equity in the leverage transaction merchant's account is the difference between the market value and the amount owed on the carrying loan. The market value consists of the equity and the leveraged amount that is owed. The greater the loan portion is to the equity portion, the greater the loss in the case of default. As the value of the position changes in the marketplace, the loan amount in the account remains the same and the equity changes dollar for dollar.

Associated Persons (APs)

An associated person is any person associated with a futures commission merchant, commodity pool operator, commodity trading advisor, or leverage transaction merchant, who operates in the capacity of solicitation of commodity futures orders or commodity option orders. An associated person would also cover the unsolicited acceptance of commodity futures orders or commodity option orders or the supervision of same, and he or she must be registered. Excluded from this designation are those solely employed in a clerical-level position.

Hedgers

Hedgers are clients, usually professional, that use futures contracts to offset market risk on products that they are involved with. The farmers who "hedge" the price their crops will bring in at market months from now by selling contracts today are hedgers.

Speculators and Customers

Speculators are clients or traders that buy and sell futures contracts over a short term, trying to profit from their trading prowess. They are an integral part of the market as they add liquidity. Customers are classified as either hedgers or speculators, as mentioned elsewhere.

• MAKING ORDERS IN THE MARKET •

A quote is made up of a bid and offers. Bids reflect the highest price that has been announced to acquire for the future; offers represent the lowest price that has been announced for sale of the product. It is against the rules for floor members (those who are registered with the exchange to transact business in the trading area) to announce a bid below the current bid or an offer above the current offer.

Types of Orders

Different marketplaces have specialized orders that suit the needs of the particular underlying product. The following are the standard orders that fit all marketplaces.

Time Constraints

Orders are assumed to be "day" orders unless other instructions are appended to them. A day order is one that expires at the end of the day if not executed. The majority of orders that are entered into the market are day orders. At the other end of the time spectrum is the good till canceled (GTC) order that remains in force until it is either executed in the marketplace or canceled by the originator. As the future product has a built-in clock as part of the contract, orders are canceled automatically when the future contract goes into the delivery phase.

Market Order

A market order is one that accepts the current market. Buy orders accept the current offer; sell orders accept the current bid. Here's an example: Coney Island Sand six-month future contract is quoted bid $124.75—offered $125.00. A seller would receive $124.75 per contract; a buyer would pay $125.00.

Limit Orders

These are orders that set the maximum to be paid on a buy order and the minimum to be received from a sell order. The rules prohibit buy orders to be executed at a price above their limit and sell orders to be sold at a price below their limit. However, a buy order can be executed below its limit price and sell orders can be executed above their limit price. Orders are executed at the limit "or better." It is the way market participants can control the price that they receive.

Stop Orders and Stop Limit Orders

These orders are memorandum orders that become live orders when their price is reached or passed.

Let's suppose that Betty Wont acquired a future contract on Coney Island Sand at $125 per contract. The contract has been falling in $0.10 increments and is now @ $123.40. She decides that if it reaches $123 she wants to sell it. Betty wants to convey that message to the broker on the exchange trading floor. With the market now trading around $123.40, if she enters an order to simply sell the future contract at $123, it would be executed immediately at $123.40 on a $123.00 limit. The broker who has the order would read the order as "sell 1 contract and don't accept less than $123," which is not what Betty wanted to do. So Betty enters a stop order at $123. The broker on the floor reads the order as "sell 1 contract of Coney Island if the market reaches $123 or goes below." If the contract doesn't reach $123, the order will not be elected. If the market does reach $123, the order becomes a market order or a limit order, depending on the type of order Betty entered.

Market if Touched

Another variation of an order is called "market if touched."

Let's assume Betty wants to buy another contract of Coney Island Sand, which is currently trading at $123.40. She is interested only if she can see a positive trend in the market prices. The market has been trading aimlessly around $123.50 for weeks. She enters an order to buy 1 contract at $125 MIT (market if touched). If the market reaches $125, Betty is assuming that this is the positive sign that she has been looking for, and the order will become a market order.

• THE MARKETPLACE •

Futures trade either by open outcry on a trading floor of an exchange or electronically via trading platforms or both. Those products that trade on exchange trading floors are assigned to trading pits. The pits are usually encircled by steps, with the top steps inhabited by brokers representing futures commission merchants. These FCMs, in turn, are representing their clients. The brokers stand on the top steps so that they can receive orders from and send back reports to their respective firms. On the middle steps are usually the traders who are trading for the proprietary accounts of their firms and carrying out strategy instructions. On the bottom of the pit are the floor traders who trade for their own accounts or for the accounts of their employer firm.

Floor members call out their bids or offers with a certain discipline. The members bid for the contract and they sell at a price. The key words here are "for" and "at." Instead of the floor members' saying "I want to buy ten contracts of near month future contract of the British pound future at $1.5825," they simply say "Twenty-five for ten." If they were selling, it would be "Ten at twenty-five." The members are forbidden to announce bids below the current bid or to announce an offer higher than the current offer. They can do the reverse, though. A floor member can bid higher than the current bid or make an offer lower than the current offer. The only time the floor members would call out the delivery month would be if it was not the current month. Trades are gathered and reported to the exchanges' respective clearing corporations as well as to the member firms.

Electronic

Systems such as CME Group's Globex, LIFFE CONNECT, and others are trading platforms. Member firms have agreements with interface vendors, such as Thomson Reuters or SunGard, or have their own developed software. In selecting a vendor, one must take care to choose one that not only interfaces with the marketplace the member is currently trading in but can also accommodate further expansion into other markets. Once connected to the marketplace, members carry on "business as usual" with the matching of buying and selling being performed electronically.

Floor Trading

We obviously cannot look at all of the exchanges, but we will look at two. The first exchange we will discuss is the CME Group, which offers two types of trading. There is electronic trading through a product called Globex and there is floor trading, in which members trade in pits. The pits are a separate area in which one or more products trade. There are brokers, market makers, and floor traders "in the pit." Anyone trading in the pit must be employed by a member firm and approved as a trader floor person.

Members operating on the floor as traders or brokers must put the trades they execute through their clearing firm unless they have special permission and clearance from the CME to do so. In other words, if SF&R is a clearing firm and you are a broker for SF&R or a market maker for your own account clearing a trade through SF&R, all the trades you execute must be on SF&R's books at the clearing corporation.

Trading in the pit is performed by a process known as "open outcry." The participant making the bid and/or offer announces it to the crowd, giving the quantity and the price of the bid or the offer. If it is a different product from the current trading month or months, it is up to the member making the announcement to include the fact. It is the responsibility of both participants in the trade, be they brokers or traders, to confirm their trades as to the price, quantity, commodity, contract month, and respective clearing members, and for options the strike price, put or call, and expiration month. It is their responsibility to confirm the trades as soon as possible, but in no event can it be longer than fifteen minutes after the trade.

The bid or offer itself is established in a way where the member firms that represent the public as well as the clearing firms have phone booths around the pit. The orders are sent to the members on the floor either electronically or by hand signals. In both the electronic and open-outcry trading methods, while a quote, bid, or offer is outstanding, it is subject to immediate acceptance by any trader on the floor. Members are required to honor all bids or offers that have not been withdrawn from the market, and the prices at which the execution took place are binding.

There is a special type of order traded on the floor known as an "all or none" transaction. The member requesting a quote, either a bid or an offer, on an all-or-none order must be able to satisfy the threshold amount of the order before it can be executed. The amount responded to can be equal to or greater than the amount of the threshold orders amount. Example: An order arrives to buy one hundred contracts all or none at the market. Sellers must be able to fill the quantity of the buy order before it can be executed. Many times the execution price for the buy order is slightly higher than the best offer because the quantity to fill the order is not at the best offer so the buyer will have to pay up to entice sellers to trade. One or more floor members or electronic members may respond to the request for a bid or offer, but the entire amount must be satisfied at one price. Another service offered by CME Group is called CME ClearPort. This service initiates a process that clears over-the-counter derivative products. It is used by banks, hedge funds, and trading entities, as well as FCMs (futures commission merchants) and IDBs (Interdealer brokers).

After the trade has been negotiated and executed, the transmission is submitted to the clearinghouse. CME Clearing is a central counter-party clearinghouse, which means that once the trade is compared, CME Clearing intercedes between the buyer and the seller. Therefore, the buyer has now acquired the future or option from the CME and the seller has sold the future or option to the CME. Through this process, since the CME is acting as a central counterparty, should either par-ticipant go into default, the CME counterparty will make good to the surviving firm for any damages they may incur. The following are among the products that the CME Group clears in over-the-counter (OTC) programs: default swaps, OTC energy contracts, OTC foreign exchange, OTC interest rate swaps, OTC metals, and OTC agricultural swaps.

Another exchange is the ICE (IntercontinentalExchange). Like the CME Group, it offers a variety of different products including energy futures, agricultural credit derivatives, and the Russell indexes—both options and futures. The ICE is a global market, operating markets in Europe, the United States, and Canada, with over-the-counter energy and over-the-counter credit markets. Among the services offered by the ICE is Creditex. It is a wholly owned subsidiary of the ICE, an inter-dealer broker for credit default swaps and bonds. The ICE operates a hybrid model, which includes voice transactions as well as electronic execution. The hybrid model facilitates trading of index derivatives, single-name credit default swaps, emerging market securities, liquid structured products, and corporate bonds. The voice trading allows participants to trade according to specific requirements and preferences.

• VARIANCE IN DELIVERABLES •

Coffee

One of the products that the ICE offers for trading is a Coffee C contract. Its symbol is KC, and its contract size is 37,500 pounds quoted in cents and hundredths of a cent up to two decimal places. The contract's listings are March, May, July, September, and December. The minimum price movement is $18.75 per contract, and delivery is physical. A notice or certification is issued based on testing the beans and by cup testing for flavor. The exchange uses certain coffees as a base and from this base judges which coffees are superior and should go for a premium and which coffees are inferior and should trade at a discount.

The following coffees generally trade at par or basis: coffees of Mexico, El Salvador, Guatemala, Costa Rica, Nicaragua, Kenya, New Guinea, Panama, Tanzania, Uganda, Honduras, and Peru. Colombia is at a 200-point premium; Burundi, Venezuela, and India are at a 100-point discount, Rwanda is at a 300-point discount, and the Dominican Republic and Ecuador are at 400-point discounts.

What is also interesting is that effective March 2013, for coffee being delivered for the March 2013 contract, the discount for Rwanda became 100 points instead of 300 points and Brazilian coffee was to be delivered at a discount of 900 points. The coffee contract specifications then go on to talk about acceptable delivery. Coffee can be delivered at exchange license warehouses in the Port of New York district, the Port of New Orleans, the Port of Houston, the Port of Bremen Hamburg, the Port of Antwerp, the Port of Miami, and the Port of Barcelona at discounts of up to $1.25 a pound.

Deliveries will be accepted seven business days prior to the first business day of the delivery month. The last notice day is seven business days prior to the last business day of the delivery month. Therefore, deliveries can be made anytime between those two dates. The last day of trading is one business day prior to the last notice day. The type of coffee traded is Arabica, which also trades on the NYMEX and the Tokyo Grain Exchange. The Tokyo Grain Exchange also trades Robusta coffee, as does the NYSE Euronext marketplace.

Fuel Futures

To see how complex some of the products that we trade in the futures market are, take a look at the energy or fuel futures. The CME Group trades light, sweet, crude oil, natural gas, reformulated gas, heating oil, and ethanol. CME also has a crude oil volatility index that measures the amount of movement of oil contracts. The ICE futures and options market trades Brent crude, Brent NX Crude for New Expiration, WTI West Texas Crude, ASCI, the Argus Sour Crude Index, Galo Sulphur Gas Oil, Gas Oil, UK Natural Gas, Title Transfer Fund Natural Gas, and UK Power, which covers the delivery of electricity on a continuous base load basis, plus emissions and coal futures.

Brent crude is extracted from the North Sea. This type of oil is a benchmark to price European, African, and Middle Eastern oil that is exported to the West and all over the world. It is now sourced primarily by the United Kingdom, Norway, Denmark, the Netherlands, and Germany. While it is a major oil in the economy, it is not as light as its counterpart, West Texas Intermediate Oil. The lightness of oil has an important impact as it goes through the refinery process. The lighter the crude oil is, the more of it will be converted into gasoline for use by automobiles and other vehicles.

The best example of this is motor oil, as currently used in automobiles and trucks. If the oil container reads 5W20, it means that the colder the oil is, the more easily it will flow. The warmer or hotter the oil is, the slower it will flow. When your engine is cold, you want the oil to quickly lubricate all the parts; however, as the engine gets hotter, you want the oil to thicken so that it continues to cover necessary operating parts. If the oil is running too quickly, it will not form a film that is needed to minimize the friction in the engine. West Texas Intermediate, known as WTI, is also a very high-quality oil, and because it is lighter than Brent, more of it is converted into gasoline.

The Brent blend actually comes from fifteen different oil fields located in the North Sea. It contains about .37 percent sulfur, whereas

West Texas Intermediate is about .24 percent sulfur. Because of the fact that WTI has less sulfur than Brent crude, it is generally the more expensive of the two.

Coal Futures

The coal future we will be studying here is the Central Appalachian Coal Future. This one trades on the CME Globex and ClearPort electronic markets.

The contract size is 1,550 tons, and the minimal fluctuation is a penny per ton. The future becomes deliverable on the fourth-from-last business day of the month prior to the delivery month. Trading is conducted in the current year and the next four years, making this one of the longer futures that is offered. Contracts for each new year are added following the termination of trading in the December contract of the current year. Settlement of the contracts is of course physical. The delivery period may be the first calendar day, but not later than seven days before the end of the calendar delivery month. The seller may not complete the delivery of coal later than the last calendar day of the delivery month. In other words, sellers have up until seven days before the end of the delivery month to begin delivery, but they cannot deliver the rest or the remaining portions after the last calendar day of the delivery month.

Coal has very specific grade and quality specifications that must be met before it can be accepted as good delivery. The various tests it goes through are part of a group of criteria covering many products established by the American Society for Testing and Materials. Among the qualifications is the test for moisture in the coal. Other tests include measuring volatile matter and the grindability of coal—the ability to grind it into fine particles that will instantly combust. There are also size requirements.

The ICE also trades coal futures, but these futures are settled in cash, not with physical delivery. The Central Appalachian coal future trades as an electronic futures product. Another product traded on the ICE is the CSX coal future. This contract is also financially sold based on the price of coal delivered via the Eastern Rail network from the Central Appalachian mining area. The prices are set by the Platts

CAPP Rail (CSX) OTC assessment. Platts provides pricing for many of the energy products that we use every day.

Another product that is traded on the ICE is Richards Bay coal futures. The prices of these contracts are determined by the price of the coal loaded at the Richards Bay Coal Terminal in South Africa. The contract is cash settled against the price determined by the American Petroleum Institute No. 4 index (API 4), which appears in Argus/ McCloskey's Coal Price Index Service. Yet another product traded is the contracts on Newcastle coal, delivered to the Newcastle Terminal in Australia. This is also a cash-settled product.

As you can see from the above, coal is a global product, and the different markets and different depositories where coal is delivered, and its prices, are set according to local convention. The ICE also offers options on many of these products. The options expire at the same time futures come in for delivery. If you exercise the option, you get involved with the underlying, which is the future, which then gets you involved with the underlying product, which as we said above is either a physical delivery or a financial or cash delivery.

Emissions Contract

One of the more interesting or exotic products that trade on the ICE is the emissions contract. This contract permits firms that are below the permissible amount of carbon dioxide emissions to sell the permissible amounts that they are under to those firms that are over the allowable amount. In other words, those firms that have incurred the expense to be in compliance are rewarded by those who haven't. Because the weather plays such an important part in the emissions world, there is risk, and because there is risk, the ICE produces futures that can trade on this product.

The ICE offers four types of contracts that trade on this carbon problem or in carbon units: EU Allowable, EU Aviation, Certified Emission Reductions, and Emission. The futures allow those who are involved in this market, either as direct participants or as speculators, to buy and sell futures contracts, which therefore keep the market liquid so that firms' participants can take advantage of it. Those firms that adhere to strict standards and keep their emissions below the allowable limits are rewarded by being able to sell the difference between what they are at and what they are allowed to be to those firms that are over the limit. Those firms are therefore paying a penalty for not being more conservative and more careful in their use of fossil fuels. The hedgers and speculators who deal in the emissions futures are either protecting their positions or trading on the expectations of what the newest product is.

• FUTURES ORDER AND REPORT REQUIREMENT •

As an order for trading assets is time critical, there are requirements that must be satisfied and formats followed before an order arrives in a marketplace for execution. These instructions and the format that they follow are designed to make sure that critical information is not omitted or overlooked and that data can be easily and quickly identified by the broker or trader. This organization of facts allows for the execution and reporting of the order in an efficient and expedient manner. This regimen may differ from one marketplace to another but is found in all markets in some form.

1. THE ORDER BEING ENTERED
   FOR EXECUTION MUST CONTAIN:

   a. Date and time of entry. Some orders are "clocked" several times on their way to the point of execution. This way any delay in entering can be tracked.

   b. Entering firm (clearing member). Necessary for the contra party to know and important for trade processing later on in the operation process and in settlement of the transaction.

   c. Buy/Sell long/Sell short. Besides knowing what the order enterer wants to do, certain markets have conditions or restrictions on selling short.

   d. Quantity. Must be for a specific number and lot size so that the contra party can respond to the proper quantity.

e. Product symbol. Most products that are traded either use symbols or approved abbreviations.

f. Limit price or market price. As the execution is a verbal commitment, any order execution restriction must be adhered to.

g. Special execution instruction.

2. REPORT

a. Executing party's identification code. Must identify who the actual parties to the trade were.

b. Contra executing party identification code. Mandatory information for exchanging of assets when the transaction settles.

c. Quantity and execution price. Must be agreed to by both parties for settlement to occur.

d. Date and time of execution. Required for verification purposes.

e. Contra firm (clearing member). May be the same as "C" or different if contra firm is not a member of a clearing corporation.

Quality Requirements

Some products' descriptions include quality requirements. As detailed previously, a certain grade of soybeans is deliverable against the soybean contract before adjustments are made for settlement price. Gold must be assayed at 99.5 percent pure before it is acceptable as good delivery.

The coffee contract calls for the delivery of a specific grade, based on which all other grades are priced. The traded grade sets the settlement price of the coffee contract. At the time of delivery, samples of the coffee are submitted for taste testing. Professional tasters taste the brewed coffee and rate the lot. After the rating process has been completed, the now graded coffees that have been deemed to have better qualities will have their settlement price adjusted upward. Those that are inferior will have their settlement price adjusted downward.

The amount of the adjustment is determined by guidelines established in the contract's specifications. Therefore, as with some other future contracts, the coffee future contract trades as one product until settlement, at which time the physical deliverable is tested for quality. Those who were long (owned the position) going into delivery receive delivery receipts that state the grade they are to receive. If it is not the grade they can use, they trade away that receipt for one they can use. Another example of this delivery process is the gold future, which has a quality delivery requirement as to the purity of the gold bars. These must be assayed before the recipients will accept them.

CHAPTER 15

FUTURE MARGIN PAGE RATINGS

To understand the workings of the futures market, the reader should remember that in many cases the product under consideration doesn't physically exist. In agricultural products, such as wheat, the provider or farmer is selling bushels that may currently be in seed form. The user or miller is buying a product that they can't claim for months. There is also an active market that permits participants to update their opinions moment to moment and, when they think it is advisable, change the position they may have. During this period of time, between the "taking down" of a position and delivery of the product, prices will change.

A simple but realistic way of comprehending a futures price is to look at the price today, add to it the applicable expenses, such as storage and interest costs—commonly known as "cost of carry"—and that should be the future contract's price. However, we have excluded all the variables that could happen between today and delivery, such as, in the case of wheat, the size and quality of the crop coming to market when the future becomes deliverable.

• INITIAL MARGIN •

As prices fluctuate, buyers and sellers are asked to deposit collateral into their accounts to protect the futures commission merchant (FCM), or whichever entity they are trading through, from loss. The amount, which is known as "initial margin," differs from product to product, but it averages about 5 percent for most products. It is set at a fixed per contract rate. We will use dollar amounts for explanatory reasons. The amount is fixed by the futures exchange on which the product trades, and is determined by the marriage of quantity and underlying product volatility that we spoke of earlier. The amount must be large enough to protect the futures commission merchant from at least a major one-day price move, and yet not be so large as to be prohibitive to trade.

To explain this process, let's assume that a product that sells for about $1.00 per unit today also has a contract size of 100,000 units. Over the last year, one particular day the price fluctuated $0.09, and another day it fluctuated $0.07 in a day. For the remainder of the year, it fluctuated between $0.01 and $0.03 per day with the price fluctuating around $0.01 for the majority of the days. If the initial margin was set so that all cases were covered, participants would have to deposit $9,000 per contract for a product that usually trades at a range of $3,000 per contract or less. What the futures market employs here is known as "value at risk." The assumption would be that over 95 percent of the time an initial margin of about $5,000 per contract would be sufficient to cover the majority of daily movements. If that boundary was broken, the exchange would stop trading for that day to give member firms the ability to contact their clients, who must deposit more collateral.

Besides setting initial margin, the exchange will also set a minimum per contract equity amount that is required to be in the account at all times. When equity falls below this amount, the client must deposit more. Normal business practice dictates that the client must deposit at least the amount that is required to bring the account's equity up to initial per contract margin. If the maintenance margin was set at $2,000 per contract, it would give the account an operating range of $3,000, which is the range the product trades in for the majority of the time.

Each day the value of the contracts in the account is adjusted to reflect the current market price. This process is called "mark to the market." The mark is added to or subtracted from the futures equity in the account, depending on whether the position made or lost money. The adjustment is called "variation margin," and it is what is used to honor the contract. It is most important that the terms of the contract always be honored.

• FUTURE MARGIN EXAMPLES •

Here's an example from the buyer's perspective:

Client Stan Tahl bought one of the above contracts at $1.00. As there are 100,000 units in the contract, Stan could become the owner of 100,000 units at a cost of $100,000 ($1.00 × 100,000 = $100,000). Regardless of what prices the "units" are trading at when the future becomes deliverable, it is going to cost Stan $100,000. Stan would deposit the $5,000 initial margin in his account and owe the FCM $95,000 to be paid when the units are delivered.

STAN TAHL'S ACCOUNT:

Long 1 Contract (100,000 units) @ $1.00

Initial Margin =	**$5,000**
Account balance =	**$5,000**

Let's assume the market price of the unit rises from $1.00 to $1.02. The accounting system at Tahl's FCM will credit Tahl's account $2,000 ($0.02 profit in 100,000 units = $2,000).

STAN'S ACCOUNT WOULD THEN HAVE THE FOLLOWING BALANCES:

Initial margin =	**$5,000**
Variation margin =	**+$2,000**
Account balance =	**$7,000**

If the futures became deliverable with the units still trading $1.02, the market representative for Stan's FCM would accept the units and pay $102,000. The FCM would collect the $95,000 owed by Stan and *add to it Stan's original $5,000 for a total of $100,000 (exactly what Stan owes) plus the $2,000 variation margin, paying the representative a total of $102,000.*

Let's suppose the price of the unit dropped by $0.03 from $1.02 to $0.99. Stan's account would be charged $3,000 and the variation margin would drop from plus $2,000 to minus $1,000.

Initial margin =	**$5,000**
Variation margin =	**−$1,000**
Account balance =	**$4,000**

If at delivery the price was still $0.99 per unit, the market representative would receive the units and pay the deliverer $99,000, and Stan would have to pay the $95,000 still owed. The FCM would add the $95,000 to the $4,000 that is in Stan's account for a total of $99,000. Stan still paid $100,000 ($5,000 original margin + $95,000 = $100,000) for $99,000 worth of units.

In the first case Stan paid $100,000 for units worth $102,000. In the second case, Stan paid $100,000 for units worth $99,000. He paid exactly what his contract called for.

Unlike in the stock market, it is as easy to sell (go short) a futures contract as it is to buy (go long) a contract. In the stock market, going short stock requires a margin account and the ability to borrow the stock being sold. The borrowed stock is delivered to the new buyer (the contra side to the short sale), who pays for it as any buyer would. The proceeds of the short sale (cash) are given to the stock lender as collateral against the borrowed stock. When the short sale is closed out, the short seller buys the stock in the market and it is returned to the security lender. The collateral (cash) is released to the short seller, who uses it to pay for the closeout purchase. All of this activity is processed through a broker-dealer. Any money difference is the profit or loss to the short seller.

In futures, as in other derivative products such as options, selling or going short a position is as natural as buying. Therefore a buyer of a future contract could be establishing a new open long position, adding to an existing long position, reducing a short position, or closing out a short position. Similarly, the seller of a future contract could be opening a new short position, adding to an existing short position, reducing a previous long position, or closing out the previous long position. The net effect of all this activity is reported to the clearing corporation, where the activity becomes part of "open interest" computation for that product.

As every buyer has a seller and vice versa, let's introduce the contra party, Ms. Ann Tenna, to provide an example from the seller's perspective. Ann is selling 100,000 units for $100,000. She must deposit $5,000 initial margin, which is the requirement per contract, set by the exchange. Upon delivery, Ann is to receive $105,000, made up of $100,000 received for the delivery of the units and her margin deposit of $5,000 returned.

STAN TAHL'S ACCOUNT		ANN TENNA'S ACCOUNT	
Long 1 Contract (100,000 units) @ $1.00		**Short 1 Contract (100,000 units) @ $1.00**	
Initial margin =	$5,000	Initial margin =	$5,000
Account balance =	$5,000	Account balance =	$5,000

Let's assume the market price of the unit rises from $1.00 to $1.02. The accounting system at Tahl's FCM will credit Tahl's account $2,000 ($0.02 profit in 100,000 units = $2,000). At the same time, the accounting system is charging Ann's account the $2,000.

STAN'S ACCOUNT WOULD HAVE THE FOLLOWING BALANCES:		ANN'S ACCOUNT WOULD REFLECT:	
Initial margin =	$5,000	Initial margin =	$5,000
Variation margin =	+$2,000	Variation margin =	−$2,000
Account balance =	$7,000	Account balance =	$3,000

If the futures became deliverable with the units still trading at $1.02, the market representative for Stan's FCM would accept the units in the marketplace and pay $102,000. The FCM would collect *the $95,000 owed by Stan and add to it Stan's original $5,000, for a total of $100,000 (exactly what Stan owes). Afterward, the FCM would add the $2,000 variation margin and pay the representative a total of $102,000 for the 100,000 units. Ann's market representative would deliver 100,000 units and receive $102,000. The market representative would pay Ann's FCM $102,000. The FCM, upon delivery notification, would release to Ann the $3,000 balance remaining in her account, which when added to the $102,000 received when the units were delivered would total $105,000—exactly what she is owed. Based on the terms of the contract, Ann was to receive $100,000 and her margin deposit of $5,000 for a total of $105,000.*

Let's suppose the price of the unit dropped by $0.03 from $1.02 to $0.99. Stan's account would be charged $3,000 and the variation margin would drop from plus $2,000 to minus $1,000. Ann's variation margin would be credited $3,000 and would change from a minus $2,000 to a plus $1,000.

STAN'S ACCOUNT WOULD HAVE THE FOLLOWING BALANCES:		ANN'S ACCOUNT WOULD REFLECT:	
Initial margin =	$5,000	Initial margin =	$5,000
Variation margin =	−$1,000	Variation margin =	+$1,000
Account balance =	$4,000	Account balance =	$6,000

If at delivery the price was still $0.99 per unit, Stan's market representative would receive the units and pay the deliverer $99,000. Stan would still have to pay the FCM the $95,000 still owed. The FCM would add the $95,000 to the $4,000 that is in Stan's account for a total of $99,000 and pay that to his market representative. Stan still paid $100,000 ($5,000 original margin + $95,000 = $100,000). Ann's agent would deliver the units for $99,000. Upon notification of the delivery, the FCM would release the $6,000, which when added to the $99,000 received for the units gives Ann a total of $105,000, which is exactly what she is due.

In the prior example Stan paid $100,000 for units worth $102,000. In the second case, Stan paid $100,000 for units worth $99,000. In Ann's case, she received $100,000 for units worth $102,000, and in the second case, Ann received $100,000 for units that were worth $99,000. Adding in the variation margin, Ann has a total of $105,000.

As stated above, the initial margin was set at $5,000 and maintenance margin was set at $2,000, giving a $3,000 spread. What would happen if the product value was to move up $.05 in a day, from $.99 to $1.04? Stan's variation margin would change from minus $1,000 to plus $4,000, and Ann's variation margin would change from plus $1,000 to minus $4,000.

STAN'S ACCOUNT:		ANN'S ACCOUNT:	
Initial margin	$5,000	Initial margin	$5,000
Variation margin	+$4,000	Variation margin	+$4,000
	$9,000		$1,000

As Ann's account is below the $2,000 maintenance requirement, Ann would be "called" for $4,000 to bring the account back up to initial margin. With the $4,000 that Ann deposited in her account, Stan's and Ann's accounts have these balances:

Initial margin	$5,000	Initial margin	$9,000
Variation margin	+$4,000	Variation margin	−$4,000
	$9,000		$5,000

You'll notice that Ann's account balance has now returned to initial, or standard, margin.

Let's assume delivery occurred at $1.04. Stan would deposit the $95,000 still owed. That amount plus Stan's initial $5,000 = $100,000 + $4,000 variation margin = $104,000. Ann's agent delivered the units for $104,000. Ann is entitled to receive $100,000 for the units and her initial margin deposits returned ($5,000 initially + $4,000 from the call) for a total of $109,000. The 100,000 units are delivered and Ann receives $104,000 for them, plus the $5,000 balance from her account = $109,000.

• LEVERAGE •

Leverage, in this case, refers to the fact that Stan and Ann are depositing around 5 percent of the value of what they control. If the asset price changed by around 5 percent, one of them would double their money, and the other one would see their money gone. Let's stay with Stan.

Stan bought 100,000 units @ $1.00 per unit and deposited the $5,000 standard margin:

Standard margin	**$5,000**
Variation margin	**0**
Balance	**$5,000**

The units rise to $1.05 each. Stan's account is marked to the market and is credited (given) $5,000 variation margin.

Standard margin	**$5,000**
Variation margin	**+$5,000**
Balance	**$10,000**

The variation margin in Stan's account is enough for him to buy a second contract. His choice is to do nothing and let the variation margin serve to protect the $1.00 per contract price, or use it to buy a second contract, which would give him two contracts at $1.05. In the first case Stan has a nice cushion in case the price should fall, but he is earning or losing $1,000 per point. In the latter case, if the price falls more than 3 points, he would be on call for margin on two contracts but he is making or losing $2,000 per point.

Stan's account is long two contracts at $1.05:

Standard margin	**$10,000**
Variation margin	**0**
	$10,000

Let's assume the price rises to $1.10 per contract. Stan now has $10,000 variation margin ($5,000 per contract) that he can leave alone or reinvest or buy two more contracts, which would give Stan four contracts at $1.10.

Stan's account is long two contracts at $1.10:

Standard margin	**$10,000**
Variation margin	**$10,000**
	$20,000

Stan uses the variation margin to acquire two additional contracts and is now long four contracts at $1.10:

Standard margin	**$20,000**
Variation margin	**0**
	$20,000

As long as the price continues to rise, Stan can keep acquiring more contracts. He is now earning or losing $4,000 per point. If the price fell 3 points the account would be as follows:

Standard margin	**$20,000**
Variation margin	**–$12,000**
	$8,000

$8,000/4 = $2,000 per contract, which would put Stan on call for $3,000 per contract to bring each contract back to $5,000. $3,000 × 4 = $12,000. Therefore, on the $5,000 investment Stan deposited, he has lost $12,000 up to this point. Had he stayed with his original investment, he would still have had a profit of $7,000.

$1.00 original value + $0.05 = $1.05, $1.05 + $0.05 = $1.10, $1.10 – $0.03 = $1.07 current value

Greed

If we follow the above example, where the price of the product continues to move in the position holder's favor, it will continue to generate variation margin. As the position holder uses the variation margin to increase his position, he is changing the contract price to reflect a new level. When Stan Tahl used his variation margin to acquire a second contract, he owned two contracts at $1.05. The use of the variation margin negates the commission merchant's or financial institution's ability to honor the contract at the old price.

While the position is increasing through the use of the variation margin, the maintenance spread between current value and maintenance level (in the above example = 3 points) remains the same. If and when the market turns and gets to the point where a maintenance call is issued, it will be on the entire position. Using the previous example, had Stan run the one-contract position into twenty contracts through the conversion of variation margin into contract positions, while Stan was dreaming of earning $20,000 per point ($1,000 per contract), if the price for the underlying contracts fell by 3 points, Stan would be awakened from his dream to a maintenance call of $60,000 (3 points x twenty 100,000 widget contracts). Remember, this starts off as a $5,000 investment.

• STANDARDIZED PORTFOLIO ANALYSIS OF RISK, OR SPAN MARGIN •

SPAN margin is a holistic view of the risk contained in a portfolio of futures and options on futures. In the case of an FCM that is carrying client accounts, the clearing corporation would want adequate collateral (margin) to protect the clearing corporation and its members. The relationship of options positions to futures changes as the future price changes. Options that were in the money become out of the money; options that were out of the money are now in the money. The clearing corporation is interested in what the risk of these positions is to it, and couldn't care less about the individual accounts' positions. That is the problem between the FCM and its traders or between the FCM and its clients. The clearing corporation must protect itself from the exposure of its member firms.

SPAN takes into account the price and the volatility of each instrument and its related options. By re-sorting the future contract positions and their overlying option positions into an arrangement that will isolate the maximum risk at different price points, the worst exposure or risk can be identified. Based on that configuration, the margin requirement will be determined. The following is a simple example of its purpose. Remember, in the real world we are working with future products and all the positioned option series using that future as an underlying product for all the clients or proprietary accounts of that entity.

For example:

Long 1 Call widgets six months strike price $1.05

Short 1 Put widgets six months strike price $1.03

Short 1 future six months future contract original cost $1.00

Short 1 Call widgets six months strike price $0.98

Long 1 Put widgets six months strike price $0.95

If the current market price of Widgets was:

$0.97 = The long call at $1.05, the short call at 98, and the long put at $.95 are all out of the money. There would be a $0.03 gain on the future contract position and the short $1.03 strike price put is in the money by $0.06. If the $1.03 short put was exercised for a loss of $0.06 ($6,000) and with the exercise against the short put, the account would now be flat the future contract with a net loss of $3,000 and three out-of-the-money options.

$1.00 = The long call at $1.05 and the long put at 95 are out of the money. The future contract is even. The short $1.03 put is in the money by $0.03 and the short $0.98 call is in the money by $0.02. If both options were exercised, the short put at $1.03 and the short call at $0.98 would cancel each other out, contract-wise, with a trading loss total of $0.05, and the account would be left with a short position of one future and two out-of-the-money option contracts. Margin

would be required for the future contract and account short $5,000 ($0.05 × 100,000 widgets) loss as a result of the two exercises.

$1.04 = Both puts are out of the money, as is the 105 call. The short future contract has a .04 point loss, the $0.98 short call is in the money by 6 points. If the in-the-money call was exercised, the account would have a 6-point loss and be short two futures contracts and three out-of-the-money options.

Future member firms use SPAN margin on their professional clients' accounts for the same reason. They too want to ensure that there is sufficient collateral in their clients' accounts. The individual strategies of the clients, such as hedge funds or pension funds, are ignored and in their place is the worst outcome, reflecting their current position at different price points. Besides highlighting the worst-case scenario, the clearing corporation, the future member, regulators, and auditors can all run "what if" tests to see the vulnerability of the test subject at different price points. As you will see in the option section, the application of a long position can easily be synthetically made to resemble a short position and vice versa.

• EXCHANGE FOR PHYSICAL (EFP) •

Some of the products that are traded have what could look like an escape valve; it's called an "exchange for physical" (EFP). The owner of the physical property or product goes into a contract to exchange the delivery of that product to another party for a different future contract.

For example, supposing an oil importer owns a shipment of oil that is coming into port, but for whatever reason, a client of his cancels a contract. The importer does not have any place to store or hold the oil, but while it is the importer's oil, the importer has not paid for it yet because it hasn't been received.

The importer looks to the market to find another importer who could use that supply of oil. They negotiate a price for the exchange. The oil will be delivered to the new owner/importer. In exchange, the importer has sold to the old importer a future contract that will be delivered in the near future. The oil exporter or shipping company whose tankers are shipping this oil doesn't really care who owns the oil as long as it gets paid.

There are some advantages that can be gained from an EFP. Suppose that in the preceding example, the individual who had the oil contract being delivered to him was also short a future contract for delivery at a different time. In other words, he had hedged his oil contract. Suppose the individual or company that had the future contract was short the physical oil. So we have two parties operating in the same market; one owned oil that was coming in at a set price and was short a future, which allowed it to know what price it could get if it delivered the oil out against the future, and another party that was short physical oil but longed contracts in the same products as a hedge against rising prices. If these two parties were to trade with each other, they would close out the position at an agreeable price to both. The owner of the oil, who does not have any place to store it, would have it delivered to the party that was short the oil. That short contract would be voided against the other party's long contract, and both parties would walk away from the trades with a price for the oil and without any further exposure.

This is just one benefit of EFP. A second benefit is that through the direct negotiation between the parties, they know who they are dealing with. They actually know about and are choosing the counterparty, so they are not trading in the blind. While these negotiations are done in private, they are sent to the clearing corporation of exchanges, such as the CME Group, for processing and recording purposes. The CME Group offers a suite of these types of products under the heading "Exchange for Related Positions," or EFRPs. The group includes the aforementioned exchange for physical, and also the exchange for risk and the exchange for option. All of these transactions go through the same process of a private negotiation where the trades are being reported to a clearing corporation. These products are applicable for use on foreign exchange contracts, interest rate contracts, stock index contracts, agricultural contracts, commodity index contracts, energy contracts, and metal contracts.

CHAPTER 16

FORWARD CONTRACTS AND FORWARD RATE AGREEMENTS

A business, at times, faces the dilemma of knowing it must borrow money if an event, such as an opportunity to acquire a wanted asset, occurs in the near future. The business knows the approximate amount needed for the acquisition, but the borrowing cost of the money needed to pay for the asset may dampen its appeal or even negate it. If the business had some way of knowing what its borrowing cost (interest rate cost primarily) would be, it could more accurately assess the cost of the opportunity. The derivatives market offers two products that give some control of borrowing cost to business management. One product is similar to a future product; the other is similar to a call option. The one that is similar to a future product is known as a forward contract. Unlike a future, all terms of the forward contract are negotiated, and there isn't a secondary market for trading in or out of position. The other product is a forward rate agreement, which locks in a negotiated interest rate for a period of time. By that predetermined time, the owner of the FRA activates the contract or lets it expire.

• FORWARD CONTRACTS •

As future products trade on exchanges, forwards trade over-the-counter. The terms of a future product are set by the exchange on which it trades. The quantity, quality, and delivery requirements are stated in the specifications. The specification for the contract is the same for all contracts in that product with a deliverable in that month. In other words, the contracts are standardized. In the case of forwards, each contract is negotiated. With both products, there are advantages and disadvantages to this method of trading. In the case of the future, the contract is predescribed by the exchange on which it trades. Therefore an April contract on a particular oil product is the same as any other April contract on that same oil product. In the case of a forward contract, all terms are negotiated; therefore you have different quantity quality and different delivery periods. Because of the standardization of contracts on the future exchanges, there is liquidity and a secondary market.

As stated above, the contracts are the same no matter what differences there are in the products on delivery. These differences are addressed when the products are actually delivered. The future contract on coffee, for example, has seven different grades. What is traded while the coffee is in the future state is grade 4. The adjustments are then made later through the clearing corporation at the time of delivery. If a forward agreement was enacted to trade coffee, the participants would identify the exact grade and type of coffee that is going to be delivered; thus forward contracts lend themselves to one-off negotiated agreements. Forwards do not clear and settle through a clearing corporation, so each transaction must be settled one by one without the benefit of netting. Unless provided for in the agreement, mark to markets are not usually performed. Pricing of a forward is the same process as used for a future contract: the current commodity price, plus the cost of carry, insurance, storage, etc. As there isn't a clearing corporation involved, there may be an additional charge for credit risk.

The British pound future contract traded in the United States is 62,500 British pounds denominated in dollars. What would happen to a client who only needed 25,000 British pounds? She could not go into the future market to secure this sum, so she would have to turn to the forward currency market, where there are dealers willing to trade 25,000 British pound contracts. The terms of the contract would be negotiated as far as the conversion rate, the delivery date, and the delivery location.

The major products that trade in the forward market are currencies, interest rates, and precious metals. The currency forward is especially important, as many of the nonmajor currencies that trade on the future market are needed for business dealings around the world. Let's take a look at forward trade: the U.S. dollar versus the British pound. It would be written GBP/USD, meaning we are using U.S. dollars to buy the British pound. Assume the British pound would cost $1.50 per. The converse of that would be that you would need 66.7 pence to buy one U.S. dollar.

Now let's set up a hypothetical case: The company Crumpets Importers is a U.S. business. It is going to buy 100,000 British pounds' worth of crumpets for sale in America. At the current exchange rate this would cost $150,000. The company is hoping to sell the crumpets and make a 10 percent markup on the transactions. Therefore, to accomplish this feat, it must sell its crumpets for $165,000. The crumpets will be delivered six months from the day of the transaction. Crumpets Importers has a choice: it can buy the British pounds now, it could hold off and buy the British pounds six months from now, or it could buy a forward contract on the British pound at $1.50 a pound. Each of these alternatives has its positives and negatives. If it buys the British pounds it needs now, it is without the use of $150,000 for the next six months; therefore the company may have to borrow money should it run into some processing problem or some other need.

The $150,000 that the company surrogated is very dear funds. If it waits until the crumpets are delivered, it's exposed to market risk because no one knows exactly what the conversion rate will be six months from now. The safest and surest approach to this problem would be if Crumpets Importers went into the forward market and bought a contract that would lock in a price of $1.50 per pound to be delivered six months from now. This contract would cost a fee of course, but that fee is factored into the overall cost of the project. Let's assume a forward cost of 2 percent a year or 1 percent for the six months. So on the 100,000 British pound contract, it's going to cost Crumpets Importers 1,000 British pounds or $1,500. For that fee of $1,500 it has locked in the rate of $1.50 per British pound.

Let's assume that over the six-month period of time, the dollar weakened against the British pound, so that six months from today, it will cost $1.60 to buy one British pound (or in this case $160,000 to buy 100,000 British pounds). Assuming that Crumpets Importers has no latitude as far as the selling price goes, its profit of $15,000 has now been reduced to $5,000 since it would have to go into the market if it did not have the contract and pay $1.60 a pound or $160,000 for 100,000 pounds.

Of course the dollar could have strengthened over the six months, so now let's assume it was $1.40 to buy the 100,000 pounds; it would cost the company $140,000 to convert to 100,000 British pounds to pay the company in England. If it could still retail the product at the assumed $165,000 it would have increased its profit margin from 10 percent to almost 18 percent. However, if it had purchased the forward contract and assumed that it could still sell the product for $165,000, it would only make the 10 percent less the cost of the contract.

• FORWARD RATE AGREEMENTS (FRAs) •

A forward rate agreement (FRA) is an agreement that sets either an interest rate or an exchange rate to be effective sometime in the future. It is an integral part of money markets and is basically a kind of delayed loan. An interest rate FRA is a delayed interest payment on a notional amount set by the two parties. Let's suppose that a business wants to lock in a rate commencing two months from the time the contract is signed and terminating eight months after the contract is signed. In other words, the duration of the contract would be six months. That would be designated "2x8," which translates to a contract that becomes effective two months from the signing of the agreement and terminates eight months from the signing of the agreement, the difference being the six months that the business is looking to protect. This product is basically a short-term derivative with a single payment at the end, depending on the interest rates that are involved or the difference between the reference rate, which is decided, and the actual rate that is in place when the period of time involved occurs.

The FRA has two parties involved in the contract: the buyer, who is protecting against interest rates rising, and the seller, who is protecting against interest rates falling. What is involved, as mentioned above, is the notional amount and the time period during which the FRA will exist. The interest rate that is applied is based on the notional amount. What is settled between the buyer and the seller is the difference between the reference rate and the effective rate that is in force at that time.

If interest rates should rise, then the seller will pay the buyer the difference between the reference rate and the contract rate because it is costing the buyer more money to borrow money. If, on the other hand, interest rates should fall, the buyer would pay the seller the difference to make up for that shortfall in interest income. Let's suppose a reference rate of 5 percent is set at the time of the contract signing. On the date the FRA takes effect, the borrower/buyer has to borrow money at 5.5 percent. After the agreed-upon period of time has elapsed, the seller would pay the buyer the difference between the 5.5 percent rate the borrower paid and what the reference rate called for. Therefore, the effect of this compensation would be to adjust the borrow rate to the contracted rate. If on the other hand the interest rates were to fall to 4.75 percent, which is below the reference rate of 5 percent, the buyer would pay the seller the difference so that the effective rate is the contract rate. Therefore the seller would receive the same benefit as if the rate itself had remained at 5 percent.

Since the reference rate and the actual rate are both known at the beginning of the FRA, the difference between the two is settled at the effective date. The formula for computing the amount of money owed to the individual who is benefiting from the FRA is as follows:

> notional amount × (reference interest rate − FRA rate) ×
> number of days / base number of annual days [360 or 365]
> divided by 1 + (reference rate × number of days / base number
> of annual days)

Here's how that concept would look as a numerical example:

Loster Motors negotiated $10 million of a 2x8 FRA (180 days) at 5% rate. Referenced rate is 5.50%. Using a 360 basis the formula would be:

1. $$\frac{\$10,000,000 \times (5.50\% - 5.00\% = .005) \times 180/360}{1 + (5.50\% \times 180/360)}$$

2. $$\frac{\$10,000,000 \times 0.5/100 \times \frac{1}{2}}{1 + (5.5/100 \times \frac{1}{2})}$$

3. $5,000,000/200 = 25,000$

In the next chapter, we will be taking a look at swaps.

CHAPTER 17

SWAPS AND THEIR PARTICIPANTS

O ne of the concepts that apparently people understand when they are very young but seem to misunderstand as they grow older is the word "swap." Ask any child between the ages of five and ten years old if they "want to swap" and they understand they have the option to give up something in exchange for something else. Yet some articles in newspapers and periodicals seem to ignore this simple factual explanation—either that, or they've replaced the simple explanation with fantasy language. The swap product is real, though, and used in many parts of the industry for a multitude of purposes. We will introduce the swap and its participants in this chapter.

• SWAP OVERVIEW •

A swap is an agreement between two or more parties to exchange value on some prearranged schedule. The form that this value takes is usually that of cash flows. As such, one of its benefits is allowing a company to rebalance its debt cost to better accommodate current needs. A simple example of this concept would be two companies that are active in the debt market. One is engaged in making medium- to short-term loans, whereas the other company's business model requires the continuous ability to offer long-term loans. The object of both of these companies is to profit from the spread between what the money being borrowed cost and the interest being received from the loans they make. Both companies know with a good degree of certainty what their cost of money is versus their expected revenue receivable. Both companies have to continually come to the debt market to borrow the funds that they need to make the loans.

As the debt market is multifaceted, different events or forces will change some rates of one time period while having little or no effect on rates from other time periods. The interest rate spread between short-term interest rates and long-term interest rates is constantly changing to the point where it is possible that the interest rate curve could be convex, with short-term rates being more expensive than long-term rates.

There are many different kinds of swaps. On one layer, there are interest rate swaps, domestic currency swaps, foreign currency swaps, exchange for physical (EFP) swaps, equity swaps, credit swaps, and swaptions. Then in the next layer down the instruments are fine tuned to meet the users' need. There are fixed-for-floating rate swaps, which involve the swapping of fixed continuous periodic payments for floating rate payments that are continuous, though variable. In this market there is also fixed rate for fixed rate, with the difference being the payment dates. There is a floating-for-floating rate swap with different reset dates as well as forward swaps, where payments start in a later time period, and so on. As each swap is a negotiation in and of itself, each one is different and stands alone.

Here's an example:

Let's suppose that the company making long-term loans finds itself in a very tight market where the interest rate for funds borrowed is almost the same as or higher than the rates being received on long-term loans, and therefore the company looks for alternative funding sources and finds them in the short-term funds market. The company may have to borrow the short-term money to maintain its business. At a different time, the lenders of short-term loans find their source of funds dried up, or the interest rates of long-term loans are now more attractive than the short-term rates, so they borrow long-term funds and continue to make their short-term loans. Both companies now have market risk because cash inflow of funds is not directly tied to their cash outflow. In other words, both companies cannot "pair off" their payables against their receivables as the spread between the two is constantly changing. This exposure can be minimized or greatly reduced by a swap broker or swap dealer who will "find the other side."

The long-term borrower will swap the borrowed contracts with a short-term borrower, thereby allowing both companies to "parallel their loans versus borrows" or "match receivables versus payables," which in turn gives them better control of the profitability. The swap has freed both companies from the risk of a market segment they do not belong in or want to be in. The long-term lender now has borrowed long-term funds; the short-term lender has borrowed short-term funds.

• PARTICIPANTS •

In the above example we saw how the swap product was used to efficiently "better" an existing situation for two companies. Only three entities know the swap took place, namely the two companies and the swap broker or dealer. The terms "swap broker" and "swap dealer" are often used interchangeably, even though there is a major difference between the two functions.

Swap Broker

A swap broker does not take positions. It acts as a conduit between parties for which it collects a fee. The swap broker maintains a cadre of financial institutions that have exposed their needs to the swap broker in the past and because of the nature of their business may be willing to be the contra party to a swap if offered interesting terms. Think of the swap broker as a clearinghouse for swap information. When a broker is contacted, the caller explains what he or she is trying to accomplish along with the size, duration, quality, and other pertinent information. Armed with this information, the broker determines if there are any known parties that may be interested in participating in this swap. If there aren't any, the broker will so inform the inquirer, who will, in turn, have to go elsewhere. If the broker believes there could be interest, the broker will call that party or those parties that may have an interest, and find a contra party to the swap. Depending on the size and/or the asset being swapped, the broker may have to assemble the contra side from several sources. The time used by the broker in assembling the deal frees the participant up to perform other functions.

Another benefit offered by a swap broker is participants' anonymity. While the broker is working to put the swap together, the broker doesn't have to divulge who is being represented until the deal is just about agreed to. The nondisclosure could be important to the initiating party for financial or security reasons. Brokers obtain knowledge from conversations containing facts or rumors, and some participating firms have the power or ability to stir the market by just the mention of their name. Also the initiating party may be operating for a client who wants anonymity and fears that, if the initiating party was known, others would put the pieces together as to who was behind this transaction and make its completion more difficult.

Let's assume the Starfire Corporation realizes that based on current market and economic conditions, it would be better if it could extend its debt borrowings for a longer period of time. Some of the short-term debt the firm is facing was originally issued as long-term debt, which was issued a long time ago but now makes up part of its short-term debt. Starfire Corporation is concerned that if this strategic realignment of its debt—converting short-term debt into longer-term debt— was known, it might have a negative impact on its ability to continue day-to-day financing. The company would seek out a broker who would shield its name until the broker and Starfire were sure that the deal could be done. If it couldn't be accomplished, then the effort remains a secret.

Swap Dealer

A swap dealer will position, when necessary, the whole or part of a swap transaction that will be traded out of its position at a later time. Like a broker, the dealer will choose those opportunities that are

| SWAP PLAYERS |

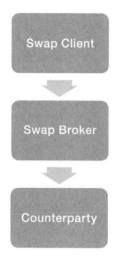

attractive to him or her. Unlike a broker, the dealer can participate in a transaction—either to make up the deficient side so that a trade can be completed, or closing out an existing position to establish a new position. Swap dealers are profit-oriented businesspeople who earn their livelihood trading. Swap dealers rely on swap brokers for the merchandise or inventory that the brokers bring to the market. The brokers are, in effect, the dealer's customers. Occasionally a dealer will even be asked to do a facilitation trade to satisfy a client of a good broker customer of the dealer's. The facilitation trade is one that the dealer wouldn't usually take the other side of, but because of the relationship with the broker, the trader takes it on. The dealer includes this transaction when assessing his market risk.

While the swap broker has to be concerned about the creditworthiness of those they transact business with, the dealer must also be concerned with market risk. The dealer will hedge his swap positions using futures, options, or other derivative products. A broker renders an execution and information service while a dealer trades against his positions. The misuse of the terms "broker" and "dealer" generally comes from the party to a swap transaction; it is insignificant to the party whether it is dealing with a swap dealer or a swap broker, as long as it accomplishes the desired results.

| STRUCTURE OF SWAP DEAL |

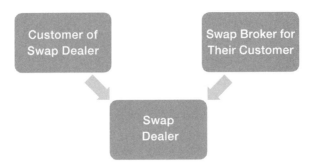

Interdealer Broker

The last participant in the swap marketplace that we will look at is the interdealer broker. One of the attractions of any market is its liquidity, or to put it another way, the ease of getting into and out of a position. Some markets are order driven, such as the listed equity markets where the volume of trades propels the market. Other markets require an intermediary to step in and trade against buyers and sellers, when the two cannot agree on price. That party is referred to as a market maker. They exist in many over-the-counter markets. This brings us to a unique member of the community, which operates as a broker between dealers.

In thin markets or ones where there are voluminous variations of a product and a need for anonymity, the dealer's broker function thrives. Such is the case with some products in the swap markets. Dealers will look for interdealer brokers when they are trying to unwind a position, or hedge a position, or disguise the brokerage firm they are representing. Dealers will also seek out interdealer brokers when they do a facilitation trade. The contacts and current market knowledge that the interdealer broker has can be most helpful in the dealer's closing out or hedging the facilitation trade.

| SWAP PLAYERS' INTERACTION |

CHAPTER 18

RANGE OF SWAPS

D ue to the true simplicity of the basic swap (i.e., an exchange of assets), the application of the concept is applied to many needs. Some are very straightforward, some are more complex, but the basic theme remains. Actually, the swap concept is applied to three major categories: currency, cash flows, and commodities.

• ACCRETING SWAP •

The opposite version of an amortizing swap discussed later is called an accreting swap. In this type of swap the notional amount that the swap is based on is increasing over the life of the swap and therefore the swap payments going back and forth in the case of the fixed payment leg and the floating payment leg increase accordingly. An accreting swap's notional value increases over time. The users are those whose assets are increasing over time also, such as building or development companies. In a swap that could span years, the creditworthiness of the counterparty becomes even more important than in a conventional swap because the exposure and risk is increasing as the notional value is increasing. Other names for this type of swap are accumulation swap, appreciating swap, and step-up swap.

• AMORTIZING •

An amortizing swap is one that has a fixed rate of interest on one leg and a floating rate of interest on the other. Both of the legs are based on a notional amount of principal that is amortized over time, therefore as the amount of outstanding principal decreases, so does the amount of the interest payments. A mortgage is this type of product; rather than maturing, it is just amortized to zero. Each interest payment in an amortized swap is less than the one preceding it because the notional value is decreasing, and therefore the swap payments decrease accordingly. The payments are based on the amount of principal or notional value that is enforced at that particular period of time. There are several asset-backed securities that use this type of swap. The amortizing schedule can be a set dollar amount each period, a delayed amortizing swap (kicking in after X years), or modeled after mortgage payments. Mortgaged-backed securities and collateralized mortgage obligations (CMOs) are examples of this type of product.

• ASSET •

An asset swap is the "swapping" of two cash flows emanating from two assets. The major difference between an asset swap and a credit is that in an asset swap a tangible asset is the referenced object. Credit swaps use interest rates or the rates of credit interest. The payments are based on a notional value of a fixed dollar amount. As with other derivatives, the notional value is never exchanged. The payments are prescheduled and do not have to occur at the same time. For example: one leg could be a quarterly payer, the other could be a semiannual payer. In a similar manner one leg could be fixed, and the other could be floating. The rate and payment schedule are completely negotiable. This type of swap has many uses. An institution with a large long-term bond portfolio can hedge its short-term needs by entering into a swap. An investor who has seen a bond investment deteriorate can swap out into a more flexible position.

Here's an example:

The owner of a bond wanting to convert the bond's fixed interest pay-ments for a floating rate enters into a fixed-for-floating swap. As the bond is tangible, having a real issuer, interest rate, maturity date, and price, the asset swap spread. This is the amount over floating rate (LIBOR) that the bond owner receives. To find the asset swap spread, first determine the yield to maturity. This yield is used as the bond or income-paying debt asset will not be sold during the swap on period. Next determine the appropriate floating rate from the yield curve of the floating rate source. After that, subtract the appropriate floating rate from the asset's yield. The larger the number in the answer, the riskier the bond is, and the lower the number the safer the instrument.

Many of the types of swaps mentioned in this section are applicable by substituting the cash flow from an income-paying asset instead of the cash flows based on LIBOR or U.S. Treasury rates.

• BASIS •

The next type of swap is a basis swap. Here's how it works: 100 basis points equals 1 percentage point. Therefore a basis swap would be based on two floating-rate instruments, with each leg of the swap backed by, or affected by, one of these floating interest rates, such as the Treasury bill rate and the LIBOR rate. These could also be of the same underlying rate but cover a different period of time, such as the three-month versus six-month bill rates.

The concept of a basis swap can also be applied to a cross-currency situation. Payments would be based on the two streams of money mar-ket floating rates represented by these two different currencies. What is exchanged is not the rates themselves, but the basis/difference be-tween the two rates. While the U.S. Treasury bill rate and the LIBOR rate are most often recited, other domestic rates used include the fed-eral funds rate, prime rate, cost of funds index (COFI) rate, and the certificate of deposit (CD) rate.

• CALLABLE/PUTABLE •

A swap may have a call or put feature built into the terms of the agreement. In the case of a callable swap, the party who holds the fixed leg, the payer of the fixed amount, has the right at their "option" to terminate the swap on or before the scheduled maturity date. The party of the other leg, the floating-rate payer, is compensated for this option either by a premium paid at the start of the swap or an increase in the fixed rate received. As this is a fixed-income instrument and also an interest-rate instrument, the person paying the fixed rate would "call" the swap and terminate it only if he or she believed interest rates were going to fall. The person paying the fixed rate might also terminate it if the interest rates have fallen and might now enter into a similar agreement for far less cost.

Since there's a callable swap, there must be a putable swap. The putable swap allows the party paying the floating rate to terminate the swap. For this privilege the floating-rate payer would reduce the fixed rate received by making an up-front fee payment to the fixed-rate payer. One use of a putable swap would be for an issuer of fixed-rate callable bonds. Should interest rates drop, the bonds could be called in and it will simultaneously exercise the right to terminate the swap. By doing so, the fixed-rate bond payer has converted it into a floating-rate instrument, and as interest rates fall they can get out of the situation by calling the bonds in and then terminating the floating-rate leg of the swap. If agreed to in the initial contract, or later in the swap's life, a swap can be extended if the parties agree to the extension and the new terms that will follow when the original swap expires.

• CAPPED •

In this type of swap, one or both of the legs is a floating-rate swap. If one of the legs is a fixed rate, that rate is determined at the beginning of the swap and consistent throughout the duration. The floating rate is unknown from period to period, therefore, should interest rates rise, the floating rate will also increase. The side that is paying the floating rate has to be concerned as to how high interest rates could go; remember that the other side of that swap is either a fixed rate with a steady income stream or a floating-rate that may not be affected as much as the rate that the floating rate payer is paying. To protect themselves, the fixed-rate side will cap that rate, putting a maximum amount that the floating-rate side or sides will pay during the duration of the swap. Once that cap is reached, that's the maximum rate that will be paid for the duration of the swap unless interest rates fall again, at which time the floating rates will be adjusted downward. In return for the cap, the floating-rate payer either pays an up-front fee for compensation purposes or lowers the rate of the fixed-income side they are receiving.

Since there is a cap that sets the maximum that the floating-rate payer would have to pay in interest, there must also be a floor. The floor sets the minimum amount that the floating-rate payer would have to pay. Should interest rates drop so that the floating rate goes below the floor, the payer of the floating rate is responsible for that floor amount. It is also possible to have a cap and a floor, which set the maximum that the floating-rate payer will pay and the minimum that the floating-rate payer will pay. For each of these features the participants of the swap will negotiate a lower fixed-income payment base.

• Circus •

A circus swap is one that has one currency and a fixed rate on one side and a different currency and floating rate on the other side. It may also have two different currencies that can also have fixed-for-fixed or floating-for-floating. The term "circus" stands for "combined interest rate and currency swap."

For example, a Canadian firm has swapped a 5¾ percent fixed-rate U.S. dollar obligation for a U.S. Treasury three-month rate plus 1½ percent. The company then turns around and swaps a U.S. Treasury three-month rate plus 1½ percent for a fixed-rate 5⅛ percent Canadian dollar obligation.

| RATES AND SWAPS—U.S. AND CANADIAN DOLLARS |

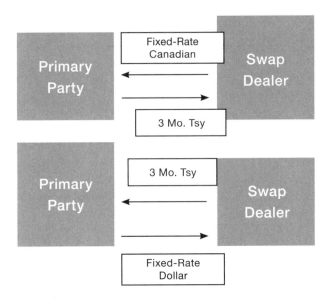

• COMMODITY •

Mainly used in the oil sector, the commodity swap is based on one leg having a fixed price and the other leg floating. In the following example both the farmer and the processor have floating rates, versus the swap broker that has the fixed rate.

> *A contract of 100,000 widgets has been trading between $0.95 and $1.05 per widget for several months. The widget farmer and the widget processor want to level monthly variance in pricing. A swap is set up by which the widget farmer will receive $0.99 per widget, and the processor will pay $1.01. The $0.02 difference is paid to the swap broker for setting up the agreement.*

MONTH 1

Widget contracts settle at $1.05.

| WIDGETS SWAP EXAMPLE ($1.05 PRICE) |

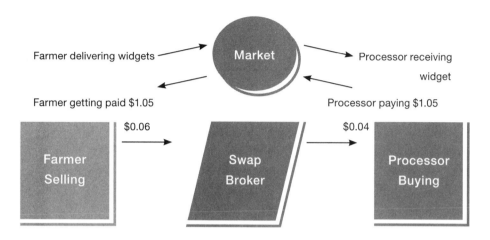

Farmer delivers widget contracts into the market and receives $1.05 per widget. From the proceeds the farmer pays the swap broker $0.06 = net $0.99.

Processor receives the widgets from the market and pays $1.05. The swap broker pays the processor $0.04 = Net $1.01.

MONTH 2

Widget contracts settle at $0.95.

| WIDGETS SWAP EXAMPLE ($0.95 PRICE) |

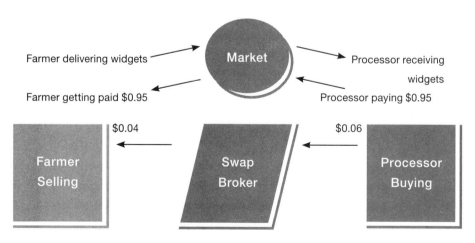

Farmer delivers widget contracts into the market and receives $0.95 per widget. The swap broker pays the farmer $0.04 for a net of $0.99.

Processor buys the widget from the market, paying $0.95 per widget, and then pays $0.06 to the swap broker for a net cost of $1.01.

• CONSTANT MATURITY •

A constant maturity swap (CMS) is one where the interest rate on one leg can be periodically reset by referencing a market swap rate other than LIBOR. The other leg is tied to LIBOR, however. It is a variation on the regular interest rate swap. Both legs are floating rate, with one being the referenced rate. Due to the use of two floating rates, the constant maturity swap can be single- or multicurrency. Usually the reset rate is shorter-term than the referenced rate. The referenced rate is a fixed maturity market rate. By being able to reset the rate, the investor can adjust the spread between the two rates to his or her advantage.

• INFLATION •

Inflation swaps are long-term swaps consisting of one leg tied to the rate of inflation and the other tied to a periodic interest payment or a zero-coupon bond discounted at a predetermined rate. That rate determines the value of the bond at the beginning of the swap. At the end of the swap's tenor the two legs are compared and the greater side keeps the difference. Inflation swaps are also called real rate swaps or inflation-indexed swaps. Those swaps that involve a zero coupon usually settle the monetary difference at the end of the swap. Those that have one leg tied to an interest-bearing instrument settle periodically and can reset rates at that time.

• INTEREST RATE •

In order to delve deeper into interest rate swaps, we first must understand their purpose. While we refer to the interest rate, it is the resulting cash flow it produces that is important. The two critical aspects here are principal versus rate. Interest rates in the market are constantly changing. Not only are the rates rising and falling, the spread between long-term and short-term rates is also changing. Products that are interest rate sensitive react to these changes. The more sensitive to interest rate changes an issue is, the more it will react to them. Those instruments that are expected to pay the same rate of interest from initiation until maturity (a fixed rate) will see their market price change so as to adjust their yield to reflect the new benchmark rate. Those instruments that have a floating rate will see their price remain stagnant but their interest rate change to reflect the current condition.

Fixed for Floating

We will start with a basic fixed-for-floating rate swap, which has a life span of five years. The referenced instrument has a notional value (in this case the principal amount) of $10 million. The LIBOR rate is 4 percent.

> *Let's assume the debt is a promissory note with a fixed 5 percent annual interest payment. The owner of the note, Mr. Michael Rafone, would prefer a floating-rate note to better offset other investments in his portfolio. Mike is more interested in preservation of capital than he is in income. He contacts his broker at Stone, Forrest and Rivers (SF&R), which is also a swap dealer, and arranges a swap of 5% fixed vs. LIBOR + 1%, with a contra side of LIBOR + 1% vs. 4.90% fixed for five years on $10,000,000. Mike is a swap payer. Therefore every year Mike will:*

| STONE, FORREST & RIVERS EXAMPLE |

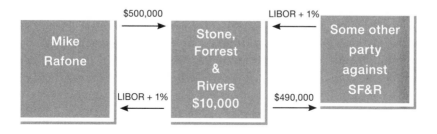

Pay $500,000, the fixed interest payment, and receive LIBOR + 1%, while the contra party will pay LIBOR + 1% and receive $490,000.

To Stone, Forrest and Rivers, the LIBOR payments cancel each other out and Stone, Forrest and Rivers is left with an annual profit of $10,000 ($500,000 received − $490,000 paid out = $10,000). Stone, Forrest and Rivers would stand to make $50,000 for the five years if all parties held their positions for the full tenor of the contract. Let's take a look at the situation from a different angle now.

What would happen if SF&R could only offset the position for four years? Unless a favorable offsetting position materializes, SF&R would receive $500,000 from Mike Rafone and have to pay LIBOR + 1%, which could result in a greater profit (if LIBOR is lower than it was at LIBOR + 1% setting) or a loss (if LIBOR is higher than it was at LIBOR + 1% setting), all other things being equal. If the LIBOR "leg" was to rise to 5%, SFR would receive $500,000 from Mike but would have to pay $590,000 (LIBOR at 5% = $490,000 + 1% = $100,000 for a total of $590,000). Therefore, unless SF&R wanted the risk, it would hedge the open side with some other derivative product such as an index derivative that tracks the LIBOR.

Fixed for Fixed

Fixed rate for fixed rate is primarily used when the payment dates need to be better aligned or in currency transactions. In the United States, corporate bonds pay interest every six months. As explained in the bond section of this book, the payment dates are January–July, February–August, March–September, April–October, May–November, and June–December. In other countries, bonds may pay interest only annually. This schedule only exacerbates the misalignment problem.

While those who rely on interest income try to acquire bonds whose interest payments meet their needs, there is the ongoing value rating dilemma known as the bond market. When acquiring new bond assets, either as an addition to a portfolio or as a replacement for called or matured bonds, the desired payment period may not be available. What's more likely, though, is that it might not be the best investment choice. Therefore the portfolio manager will make the correct bond choice, and in doing so, unbalance the interest payments. Depending on when the payments are needed and the amount involved, this disconnect could cause an obligatory payment shortfall. To mitigate the risk, the portfolio manager may enter into a fixed-for-fixed swap on terms that are beneficial to the counterparty, who may need to realign its payment schedule or who is just willing, for a fee or some other compensation, to accommodate the portfolio manager.

Fixed for Fixed, with Currency Exchange

Another, and perhaps the more dominant type of fixed-for-fixed swap, involves currency and interest rates.

Stone, Forrest and Rivers has an American client trying to fund the building of a German residential complex. The client must transact business in euros. The current funding rate in the United States for that type of dollar loan would cost the client 4 percent. In Germany that same type of loan would cost 6 percent. Stone, Forrest and Rivers also has a German client who is trying to expand business in the United States. It would cost 7 percent for the German company to borrow U.S. dollars for the expansion project. In Germany, the same type of loan in euros would cost the company 5 percent. SF&R enters into a swap agreement with both parties, by which the German client borrows euros at 5 percent and the U.S. client borrows dollars at 4 percent and SF&R sees that the swap is executed. The effect is that the German client has borrowed dollars at 4 percent and the U.S. client has borrowed euros at 5 percent.

	U.S. DOLLARS	EUROS
U.S. Client	4%	6%
German Client	7%	5%

The swap occurs:

	U.S. DOLLARS	EUROS
U.S. Client		5%
German Client	4%	

The German company will pay the interest in U.S. dollars and repay the loan in U.S. dollars. The U.S. client pays both interest and principal in euros.

The German client has saved 3 percent per million, while the U.S. client has saved 1 percent per million.

As with most of the examples presented, these are simple because their purpose is explanatory. In the above example, the terms of the swap, the duration, payment periods, and amortization, etc., would all have been negotiated and listed in the swap agreement.

Floating for Floating

Another name for a floating-for-floating rate swap is a "basis swap." Unlike the swaps where one leg or both legs are set to some fixed rate (the current twenty-year Treasury bond rate, for instance), here the legs are tied to two different money rates (for instance, one might be tied to the three-month U.S. Treasury bill and the other might be tied to the three-month LIBOR rate). The object of the basis swap is to try to take advantage of aberrations in the basis spreads between the two rates. The spread could widen if the more expensive one increased and/or the less expensive one lost value. The spread could decrease if the reverse happened.

Let's assume the three-month LIBOR rate is 0.46685 and the six-month LIBOR rate is 0.73640. The current spread between the two is 0.26955. If two parties took loans, with Cindy Ash paying six-month LIBOR to the other party, and Carol Ling paying three-month LIBOR plus 27 basis points, which party would be in a better position if the three-month LIBOR remained the same but the spread decreased to 25 basis points? In order for this to happen, the six-month LIBOR would have to have fallen to 0.71685. Cindy Ash is better off in this scenario because the three-month is costing more: 0.46685 + 0.27 = 0.73685.

A floating-for-floating rate swap may be based on different reset dates. Some events occur periodically, but on a regular basis—such as annually, semiannually, quarterly, or monthly. The first three occurrences create a potential liability to a company. Mismatching of any of the payment schedules could cause a firm embarrassment and/or penalties if payment cannot be made on time. The annual receivable versus annual payable situation is, perhaps, the schedule with the greatest risk, as it could include an accumulation of what would be shorter-term payments, and/or incur the greatest credit risk. In the case of a long payment period, it can even be worse if the receivable is paid well in advance of when it is needed. In that scenario, when the offsetting payable is due, the firm might find itself short of funds. In today's world, effective cash management increases the ability and possibility of profit. In the global business environment, it is imperative that the correct sum of money, in the correct currency, arrive at the correct location exactly when it is needed.

Scheduling Payment

As mentioned above, the semiannual payment schemes are J & J (January and July), F & A, M & S, A & O, M & N, and J & D. The quarterly cycle is J,A,J,O (January, April, July, and October); F,M,A,N (February, May, August, November); and M,J,S,D (March, June, September, December). Many of the payments, expiration dates, and maturity dates in most business transactions follow one or more of these conventions. In America, most bonds pay interest *twice a year*, some debt pays *quarterly*, GNMA pass-through instruments pay down *interest and principal monthly*, and U.S. Treasury bills are issued on a three-month, six-month, and one-year tenor. They are discounted instruments that pay interest at maturity. In swaps agreements where payments are to be made during the tenor of the swap, these conventions are employed.

• ROLLER-COASTER •

In the standard multipayment swap, the dates of payment are preset and the amount of money due at each payment is fixed. This type of swap, which is the dominant form, is not always in the best interest of the users. As the terms of the swap are negotiable, the parties may be better off using a variable payment schedule. Companies whose businesses are of a cyclical nature would be much better served by a swap where the payments follow the company's cash flow. During periods when the business is at the height of its annual or seasonal period, the payments should be at the highest point. During periods when there is a lull in the business, the payments should be at a much lower point. The type of swap where payments change from period to period is called a roller-coaster swap. A business such as a sporting goods company specializing in outdoor sporting equipment would be better served if the payments were larger in the summer than in the winter when business is in a lull. Of course the structure of this type of swap would be dependent on the business itself and the geographic area it serves. Businesses involved with seasonal decorations would also benefit from this type of swap.

· TOTAL RATE OF RETURN (TROR) ·

The total rate of return (TROR) swap is a contract between two parties in which one party transfers market risk and credit risk to another for a flow of income and a guarantee of principal for a predetermined period of time.

This type of swap obtains its name from the fact that the swap seller is buying insurance that will protect the principal of the investment at a point in time, as well as receiving a cash flow based on a predetermined floating rate. In return for this, the swap seller will forfeit any appreciation in the reference asset's value and any interest payments made by the referenced asset. The swap buyer is going to receive any appreciation in value of the referenced asset plus all interest payments made to the asset, but pay out any depreciation in the referenced asset's value as well as paying out a floating rate of interest. In other words, the swap seller owns the referenced asset without market risk. The swap buyer synthetically owns the referenced asset, as he or she will benefit from any appreciation in value and incur loss from any depreciation.

Here's an example:

Loster Financial owns 5,000 Regal Corporation bonds (nominal value $5,000,000) that pay 5 percent interest annually. The bonds are currently trading at "96" ($0.96 on the dollar). The present value is $4,800,000 and the semiannual interest payment is $125,000 ($5,000,000 × 5%/2). Loster Financial enters into a TROR with Mercury Bank. In return for

Regal Bonds' interest payments, Mercury Bank will pay Loster Financial LIBOR plus x basis points. Should the bonds increase in value, Loster Financial will pay Mercury Bank the amount over the referenced value. If, on the other hand, the bonds lose market value, Mercury Bank will pay Loster Financial the amount under the referenced value.

In this total return swap the paying party of the TROR swap will be paying periodic interest payments that the bond pays in return for a negotiated steady income based on some other rate, such as LIBOR plus basis points. At the end of the swap's tenor, with each interest payment having been received, the value of underlying referenced issue at the time of the swap transaction is still intact. The swap does not have to expire at the same time that the bond matures. Therefore, in the above example, if the TROR was for three full years, the TROR payee would pay the TROR receiver the interest payments received from the bonds plus any appreciation in the value of the bond. In return, the receiver pays the payer a floating rate based on LIBOR plus basis points, as well as any depreciation in the value of the underlying bond.

Let's compare the two parties:

TROR Seller	TROR Buyer
Owns the referenced asset	Synthetically owns referenced asset
Buys the insurance	Sells the insurance
Has lower cost of finance	Does not tie up capital
Pays out referenced asset's interest payments	Receives referenced asset's interest payments
Receives floating-rate interest	Pays floating-rate interest
Receives any depreciation in referenced value	Pays any depreciation in referenced value
Pays any appreciation in referenced value	Receives any depreciation in referenced value
Transfers market risk	Accepts market risk
Has interest-rate risk	Has interest-rate risk

The duration of the TROR is negotiated and not preset in the marketplace. The typical transaction contains the following: details of the referenced asset, its interest rate, its nominal value, its agreed-to price or value, a start date, an end date, the duration, the interest payment dates, the floating rate (with basis points), floating-rate payment dates, settlement date, and method of payment.

Referring back to the example above, let's start with Loster Financial. It owns the bonds, having acquired $5 million worth of bonds. Whether it paid for the acquisition in full or on margin is not for discussion at this time as it brings in tangential topics. However, as owner of the bonds, Loster Financial is expecting to receive periodic interest payments. These payments, from Regal's paying agent, should be in Loster's control on the payment due date. What if they aren't? Depending on the cause, Loster Financial may be held in default of the contract. Mercury Bank would begin legal remedies up to and including claiming the bonds themselves. In other words, payment from Loster Financial to Mercury Bank is not contingent on Regal Corporation's paying Loster Financial. There are exceptions, such as a force majeure, which may negate the ability of Loster Financial to make payment.

• YIELD CURVE •

Since there is a need for swaps based on short-term rates, we don't have to look too far to find a need for swaps on long-term rates also. The yield curve swap is one that involves a bond or other long-term instrument, and a very similar instrument with a different duration. The swap involves the difference between two interest rates that these bonds or debt instruments are carrying. So in the case of a corporation issuing a fifteen-year bond and a twenty-year bond, all other things being equal except for the duration of the two bonds, the twenty-year bond should carry a higher interest rate than the fifteen-year bond. However, the prices for those bonds in the market are determined by the Treasury benchmark yield curve and the relationship of this company's bonds to it. As the yield curve changes due to the supply and demand for funding at various periods of longevity, the difference between the prices of the two bonds will change also, which creates a basis price difference. The swaps could be based on those differences.

• Zero-Coupon •

One form of swap that is much different from all the rest we've looked at is one with a floating rate against a zero-coupon bond or a fixed rate against a zero-coupon bond. In both cases, the fixed-rate and the floating-rate sides, the swap will receive periodic payments; the zero-coupon bond will not. At the end of the instrument's life or at the end of the swap, the zero-coupon bond will pay off. For those not familiar with the zero-coupon bond, it is a deep-discounted instrument that pays its principal at the end of its life; therefore, while the zero-bond owner is paying annual income tax on the interest it is theoretically earning, but not paying out, the owner will receive full payment at the end of the bond's life. If the zero-coupon bond has a longer tenor than the swap, the bond will be valued at the present value of its cash flow based on the negotiated interest rate up to the end of the swap.

• The Principal Amount and the Notional Amount •

Throughout this book, we are using two terms that seem to be the same, but they are not. The "principal amount" is one term and the "notional amount" is the other term. While in some cases they are the same, in many cases they do not refer to the same product. The principal amount is the amount that is going to be changed or the amount that something is computed from, such as on a standard bond. The accruing of interest is a percentage of the face amount known as the principal amount. If you were to buy or sell that bond, the amount of money that would be exchanged would be based on the price multiplied by the principal amount. A $1,000 bond selling at 60 would cost $600. The interest on that bond would be computed based on the $1,000 amount. The notional value is one that has value but is not pertinent to the computations.

CHAPTER 19

CREDIT DEFAULT SWAPS

As commercial loans, certain collateral debt obligations, and intercompany loans grew in size, the need for lenders to hedge or offset their risk grew also. Some of these huge multimillion-dollar loans were fragmented; other loans, which required periodic payment of principal, had the payment periods sold; still others sold some or all of the interest payments. Several investment firms saw an opportunity, and for a fee guaranteed payment should the borrower of a loan or part of loan fail to do so. Enter the credit default swap.

A credit default swap (CDS) is similar to an insurance policy, where the buyer pays a fee to the seller to cover a certain obligation in case a third party defaults on a particular event. As with an insurance policy, the buyer pays a premium and the seller has to react only if certain events occur. These events are referred to as "credit events." Here's a basic example: Party A and Party C enter into an agreement by which Party A acquires an asset from Party C. The asset is to pay Party A a periodic return over time. At the end of the contract, the asset pays Party A the predetermined amount outlined in the contract. (Think of a bond that pays semiannual interest and at its maturity date pays the required principal amount.) To protect the investment, Party A enters into an agreement with Party B that should Party C default on any of the payments, Party B will pay the amount owed. For this protection, Party A pays Party B a fee known as a premium.

There is some unique terminology associated with this product. The terms "buyer" and "seller" could refer to the protection under consideration. The seller or writer is offering to sell protection to the referenced asset owner in return for a fee or premium. The referenced asset owner is buying the protection. However, the term "buyer" is also applied to the acquirer of the asset who sells the risk to another and pays the risk buyer a fee to take the responsibility. To confuse the issue even more, both parties to the transaction are called counterparties.

· ASSESSING RISK IN CREDIT DEFAULT SWAPS ·

The negotiation of the fee is based on the level or amount of presumed risk and the duration of time the credit default swap will be in existence. As the CDS exists in a dynamic environment and as time erodes the risk period, the value of the CDS changes. It is therefore a tradable instrument. As the perceived possibility of default diminishes, the premium on the default diminishes; as the possibility of risk increases, the premium increases.

Here's an example: Party A enters into an investment project with Party C. The project is to last five years. Party A is to pay Party C a lump sum payment on day one. The one-time payment will be used by Party C to fund the project. Party C is to make five consecutive annual payments that are scaled upward, so that the last payment is the largest payment. This is because all the parts or units should be operational and generating revenue. With that last payment Party C should have fulfilled the obligation as required by the original contract. Each annual payment is obtained from parts of the project that begin to generate revenue as they become operative.

Party A knows that there are events that could occur during the contract's life that would cause late payments, partial payments, or no payments at all. While the risk is slim, Party A doesn't want to have to face that risk should any of the events occur. Party A enters into a contract with Party B, which stipulates that for a fee (premium), Party B will make Party A whole for any shortfall. The amount of the fee is negotiated between the two parties based on their assessment of the risk.

Purpose

What outcomes face Party B? There are four probable outcomes. From best to worst they are:

1. Party C pays Party A in full and on time, and Party B retains the fee.

2. Party C makes full payment but it is late, causing Party B to make payment on C's behalf. Thereby Party B would be incurring an expense from when the payment was originally due by Party C until it was finally paid by Party C. Even though Party C paid, Party B is entitled to the compensation for the use of its funds during the period. The terms and rate are spelled out in the agreement. The profit or loss to Party B on the entire transaction would depend on the size of the premium (fee) received from Party A and on whether any penalties could be assessed based on the contract between Party A and Party C.

3. In the next scenario, Party C makes only a partial payment and defaults on the remainder. Party B must make up for the shortfall and follow up with Party C for the remainder of the payment. This would involve legal proceedings between Party C and Party B, as Party B went after Party C to collect the balance due.

4. The last scenario is where Party C doesn't pay at all, and Party B must make the full payment on the due dates with anticipation of recovering part or all at a later date. In this last situation, depending on the terms of the contract and the marketability of the investment project, Party A may have to surrender the asset to Party B, who would be able to sell it to recover part or all of the expense.

• MARKETABILITY •

There is indeed a market for these credit default swaps. Initially, Party A would "shop" the risk around to various contra-side financial institutions to obtain the lowest premium cost for the assumed risk. The proposed parties on the opposing side are performing their own risk analysis on Party C, and/or the asset itself, to determine the degree of risk they are looking at. Once the risk analysis is performed, a fee or premium is set.

For long-term contracts, the risk may diminish or increase during the CDS's existence. If it diminishes, the premium initially demanded by the risk inherent in the CDS will decrease, and in the above case, Party B could try to trade out of the obligation for a lower premium than they received when they accepted the risk. The difference between the premium they received when they originally accepted the risk and what they paid to get out of the contract would be a profit to them. Conversely, should the risk increase, Party B may not want that exposure to risk and may close the position to another party for a higher premium, thereby incurring the loss, rather than maintaining the position and being exposed to an even larger loss.

On the other side of the CDS, Party A, who sold the risk to Party B (or who bought the CDS), paid a premium based on the observed risk and agreed to credit risk assessment at that time. Should the risk increase over time, the value of the CDS would increase too. As this is all occurring in a dynamic marketplace, where events are affecting even Party A itself, should Party A decide, for whatever reason, to close the position by selling it out, it would have a profit. For example, should Party A decide to sell the referenced investment itself, it wouldn't have need of the CDS any longer. Conversely, if the perceived risk should dissipate, the premium would dissipate also. Then Party A would perceive the level of risk as manageable and could sell off the CDS and recoup some of the original cost.

Remember, the party receiving the premium is obligated to perform the activity being covered. Therefore should there be a default, the owner of the CDS must make good on the defaulted amount. We will discuss recourse later in this chapter.

• NEGOTIATING A CREDIT DEFAULT SWAP •

So far, the process seems very straightforward. However, the negotiations are rather detailed. Many questions must be answered before the agreements become active. For example: What constitutes default?

What constitutes late payment? Each party is trying to clarify the terms so that there cannot be any misunderstanding at a later time. The main component parts of a credit default swap are:

1. The counterparties to the CDS
2. The referenced obligation
3. The notional amount under contract
4. The longevity or term of the CDS
5. Premium or fee involved
6. Clear definition of what constitutes default
7. Method of settlement
8. Recourse in case of default

Counterparties to the Contract

The question "Whom am I dealing with?" becomes ever more important, as the value under consideration is millions of dollars. First and foremost, what do you know about the counterparty firm's finances and faculty? What is known about the firm?

Clear Definition of What Constitutes Default

Culled from *The Washington Post,* February 29, 2012:

Referencing Greece restructuring its debt could cause a credit event:

"It will be the first time that the obscure but influential International Swaps and Derivatives Association has made such an inquiry into a sovereign government's actions, and the possibility that Greece could be found to have wronged its creditors is something European officials have worked for two years to avoid.

"Such an outcome could leave the entire euro zone with the unwanted stigma of being a region where governments stiff the people who lend it money, and could trigger payouts under thousands of bond insurance contracts known as credit default swaps."

· The ISDA Master Agreement ·

The swap agreement has been through several iterations over the years. Now, under the auspices of the International Swaps and Derivatives Association (ISDA), the contract comprises five parts that collectively form one agreement. The five parts are:

- The master agreement, which, except for the participants' names, is never altered and contains the standard terms that apply to all transactions.
- A schedule, a negotiated arrangement that establishes the basic trading terms between the parties.
- A credit support annex, including establishing and governing the collateral between parties.
- The confirmation, which contains the specific terms of the deal.
- A definition booklet.

The intent of the master agreements is to avoid conflicts or misunderstandings at a later date. There are two forms of the ISDA master agreement. The first is the single jurisdiction/currency, and the second is the multiple jurisdiction/currency version. Some of the more pressing issues are highlighted below:

1. Who are the parties to the swap?
   a. Authority
      i. What authority gives this entity the right to enter into the swap?
      ii. By whose authority does this (these) individual(s) enter into this agreement?
      iii. What is the counterparty's reputation?
      iv. Is this contract legal under state or other law?

(continued on next page)

(continued from previous page)

   b. Financial

      i. What source was verified concerning the counterparty's financial condition?

      ii. What is their financial history?

      iii. Were their year-end financial statements signed off on by:

         1) The proper officer of the counterparty

         2) An approved or acceptable certified public accounting firm?

      iv. How active are they in the swap market?

2. Notional Amount

   a. What is the notional amount?

   b. What is the actual amount that interest and other such computations will be based on?

   c. Does the amount stay the same over time or is depreciation or accretion applied?

3. Interest

   a. What interest rate or rates are in effect?

   b. Under what terms do they change?

   c. What basis is used to accrue interest?

   d. Do holidays or other nonworkdays affect the interest calculation?

   e. What is the payment frequency?

   f. What is/are the payment date(s)?

   g. Is it a level payment or day count payment?

   h. If the payment date falls on a nonworkday,

      i. When is the payment due?

      ii. Is there an adjustment to the payment for the nonworkdays?

4. Fixed vs. Floating Rate

   a. Under what conditions, if any, may the fixed rate be changed?

   b. What is the floating rate based on?

      i. What is the spread between the referenced rate and applicable rate?

    ii. Under what conditions does the spread change?

    iii. When are the reset dates?

5. Currency

    a. What currency is to be used?

    b. What form is the currency to take?

    c. Where are the payments to be made?

6. Early Termination

    a. What are valid causes for early termination?

    b. What penalties, if any, are applied?

    c. Parties to the agreement

7. Force Majeure

    a. What constitutes force majeure?

    b. Responsibilities of the parties under force majeure.

    c. Failure of parties to honor responsibilities.

8. Default

    a. What constitutes default?

    b. What recourse is available?

    c. How is restitution determined?

9. Maturity

    a. What are the parties' obligations?

    b. When are they to be performed?

    c. What constitutes final settlement?

CHAPTER 20

SWAPTIONS

The chapter on option products earlier in this book stated that an option gave its owner the privilege of taking a market action at a later time, if she so desired. If the owner didn't want to, she didn't have to—it was her option. The chapter on swaps stated that a swap involved an exchange of assets or cash flow. The terms of the swap have been agreed to and the swap is alive. However, what if a participant wanted to delay the start of the swap, but use current rates only if they were better than the then-going rates? In other words, the party to the swap can decide at a later date which rate to use. The party would have an option to choose which rate best served him. He would have an option on the swap, which is called a "swaption."

Let's take this one step further: suppose the party to the swap wasn't sure the swap would be needed at a later time, but was concerned that by the time the swap was needed, the swap rates might not be as beneficial as they are at present. The parties to the swap would negotiate the terms so that, if desired, the swap could be executed at a later time. The parties would have a swaption.

• Swaptions in Action •

Let's look at a hypothetical situation where a swaption may be used. Say there is a company unsure whether a swap will be needed at a later date, but the company likes the current swap rates. It faces three choices: do nothing and risk having to enter into a swap on less favorable terms at a later time; get involved in a potentially adverse, hard-to-get-out-of transaction if the swap turns out not to be needed; or find a product that has an activation delay mechanism built into it. The last choice is called a swaption. This option permits its owner to enter into a swap agreement under prearranged terms and conditions only if it wants to. If it does not want to enter into it at this time, it does not have to do so and the swaption will expire.

• Components of a Swaption •

The typical swaption contains three parts, the option itself and two "legs." One leg is a fixed-interest-rate leg pegged to longer-term interest rates, and the other leg is a floating-interest-rate leg pegged to a floating rate such as LIBOR. The option portion of the swaption may be one of three types: Bermudan, American, or European. The Bermudan option permits the swaption owner to enter the swap on several predetermined dates. The American form can be exercised any time during its life. The European form is only exercisable at the end of the option's life. The negotiated terms of the option include the notional amount of the swap that the option is based on; the strike price, which is obtained from the fixed rate of the underlying swap; the tenor of the option, which usually is set to expire approximately when the swap would be expected to be needed; and the premium at which the transaction will take place.

Receiver Swaption and Payer Swaption

The terms of exercise are set in the negotiation stage of the swaption. However, a swaption is unlike a standard equity option, where the buyer can acquire a call option, giving its owner the ability to purchase a trading unit of the underlying issue, or a put option, giving its owner the ability to sell a trading unit of the underlying issue or product. The owner of the swap is neither buying nor selling anything. Instead, as one leg of the swaption is paying a fixed interest rate and the other leg paying a floating rate, the buyer of the swaption is either receiving or paying a fixed rate of interest. Therefore, by definition, the seller of the swaption is either paying or receiving a floating rate of interest. The term used keys off the fixed-payment side, with the buyer receiving fixed payments known as the "receiver swaption," or paying fixed payments known as the "payer swaption." The floating-rate side is understood or assumed.

Call and Put Swaptions

The concept of when a call or a put option would have intrinsic value (be in the money) still applies. In the case of a call, it would be an advantageous exercise when the market price of the reference issue's value is greater than the strike or exercise price of the option. A put would have intrinsic value when the referenced issue's value is lower than the strike or exercise price of the put option. When working with swaptions, the buyer of the swaption who is paying fixed payments has an "in the money" option when the going fixed rate for a similar product with the same tenor and credit risk has a higher rate than the swaption rate.

An example of this would be a swaption with a fixed rate of 6 percent in a market of equivalent products paying a fixed rate of 7 percent. Likewise, a swaption owner who is a fixed-income receiver has an in-the-money option when the going fixed-income rate is lower than the swaption rate. For example, a swaption receiver has a fixed rate of 6 percent when the going rate for a similar product is 5 percent. Another way of saying the same thing involves the difference between the swap rate that was set at the time the swaption was negotiated and the actual swap rate that is applicable at the end of the swaption on the same referenced asset for the same tenor, quality, etc.

• OTHER SWAPTION SCENARIOS •

Upon expiration of a European swaption, the buying counterparty has the choice of letting the option expire or exercising it. The decision is based on whether the option portion of the swaption is in the money or not. If expiration is the decision, the opportunity ceases to exist and the seller retains the premium. On the other hand, if the option is in the money and the holder counterparty decides to exercise, the holder will enter into the swap.

Here is a simplified explanation of these concepts:

Negotiated Swap Rate at the beginning of the swaption = NSR
Actual Applicable Rate for swap at end of swaption tenor
   = AAR
In the money when (Payer) = AAR > NSR
In the money when (Receiver) = NSR > AAR

Swaptions trade in an over-the-counter environment. The participants are primarily financial institutions such as banks, corporations, and hedge funds. The product is used as a tool for managing the interest rate risk brought about by these companies' primary business activities. It is not a main product but is necessary in managing interest rate risk. While swaptions involve only two parties to the trade, there are major swap dealers who make markets in swaptions and maintain large swap positions. Among these are Bank of America and Merrill Lynch.

Market price of the swaption is discussed in basis points. As covered earlier, a basis point is one one-hundredth of 1 percent (that is, 25 basis points is a quarter of a percent). The basis point price amount that the swap trades at follows the usual sources that option premiums are based on. These include the relationship between current interest rates and the strike rate of the swap, the tenor of the option, and the volatility of the interest rates at present. The value of the swaption when it is at the money is the forward swap rate of the option.

CHAPTER 21

COLLATERALIZED DEBT OBLIGATIONS

Investors in long-term debt sometimes prefer to have their risk spread over several different long-term instruments rather than dedicated to one. For example: A bank will lend a client $100,000 to buy a home. The home is used to collateralize the loan, which becomes a mortgage. The bank then sells the mortgage to an investor. The investor is one on one with the homeowner. Whatever actions the homeowner takes that affect the home could affect the mortgage, which in turn affects the investor. In other words, all of the risk the investor has is tied up in this one mortgage. To diversify the risk, the investor would have been better off investing the $100,000 in a pool containing ten or twenty mortgages. This risk sharing is what is behind all of the following collateral debt obligation products. Investors are more willing to spread their risk than they are willing to put all their eggs in one basket.

"Collateralized debt obligation" (CDO) is a term that applies to several different securitized products, including a derivative, that spread the risk. First let us look at the variety of securitized products.

• THE DIFFERENT TYPES OF CDOs •

Under the umbrella of collateralized debt obligations are the following products: collateralized mortgage obligations (CMOs), collateralized bond obligations (CBOs), and collateralized loan obligations (CLOs). The purpose of the securitization of these loans is to spread the risk of default among several debt contracts of the same type. There can be one hundred debt contracts in an individual CDO. Once securitized, the CDO is disbursed to investors, thereby permitting investors to spread the risk of default over a multitude of debts of a certain variety. In addition, there are synthetic CDOs in which the underlying asset is not actually owned. Instead, the issuing firm has amassed credit exposure by selling credit default swaps and using the proceeds to buy low-risk debt.

Collateralized Mortgage Obligations (CMOs)

Let's go back to the beginning of this segment of the industry. Government National Mortgage Association (GNMA, or Ginnie Mae), a division of the Department of Housing and Urban Development (HUD), issued the first collateralized mortgage debt in 1970. GNMA contained a pool of government-insured or -guaranteed home mortgages. These mortgages were backed by the Department of Veterans Affairs (VA), the Federal Housing Administration (FHA), the Office of Public and Indian Housing (PIH), and the Department of Agriculture's Rural Housing Service (RHS). GNMA guarantees the timely payment of principal and interest due on the pools to the GNMA holders. It was structured as a "pass-through" instrument that tracked the mortgage payments made by those homeowners whose mortgages were part of the pool. As the homeowners made their monthly payments (comprising principal pay-downs and interest payments on the mortgages' outstanding principal), the payments were passed through to the GNMA pool owners in proportion to the amount of the pool they owned. Generally speaking, GNMA receives 6 basis points and the mortgage servicer retains 44 basis points, which means that GNMA mortgages of 5 percent will pay the GNMA pool holder 4½ percent. The owners received monthly payments of principal and interest. As mortgages do not mature, their principal depletes to zero.

Owners

These monthly payments were affected by mortgages that either refinanced homes, sold homes, or took some other action that negated the

| POOL / OWNERS |

Initial Pass-Through
Principal Outstanding

After Time Has Passed
Principal Outstanding

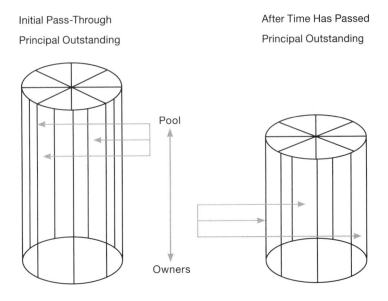

original mortgages. Mortgages could be paid off and ceased to exist and the proceeds passed through to the GNMA pool owner. New qualified mortgages are added to new pools, not existing ones. As a result, the GNMA owner will receive scheduled principal pay-downs and prepayments when they occur.

Issuance

GNMA's modified pass-throughs are issued through the efforts of a mortgage banker. While not a true banker, a mortgage banker has as its primary function arranging financing for buyers of new homes. The mortgage banker must also sell the approved mortgages and enforce them to buyers. Some of these mortgages will qualify for coverage under GNMA as stated previously. Those that qualify will be sold as GNMA pooled mortgages. Those that do not qualify will be sold as conventional mortgages, either as whole loans or pooled as collateralized mortgage obligations (CMO) as part of the asset-backed securities (ABS) universe.

There is a period of time between when homeowners get their mortgages approved and when they move into their new homes and the mortgages go live or are enforced. During that period of time the mortgage banker, or the financing agent, is at risk for changes that may occur in mortgage market interest rates. As it is not a primary function of mortgage bankers to take on any interest rate risk that they do not have to in the course of their business, they will go into the GNMA market and offer the approved but not enforced pool of mortgages to GNMA dealers. The span of time until the pool is alive could be several months. At this point the amount of mortgage principal, the rate of interest the pool will carry, the "maturity" date of the mortgages, and the delivery day of the actual pool are known. What is not known is the unique number that GNMA will assign to this pool. That unassigned unnumbered pool is known as a TBA (to be announced).

TBA

The GNMA dealer will offer the TBAs for trading in the over-the-counter market. They are sold into the market and during this period of time will not pay any interest or principal, as the mortgages representing the pool are not enforced and the homeowners are not yet paying them down. So the TBAs are traded as purely as an interest rate value.

In the marketplace there are many TBAs being offered and traded. All those that have in their nomenclature the same product, interest rate, delivery date, and debt maturity date will trade as one instrument. Members of the Mortgage-Backed Security Division (MBSD) of the Fixed Income Clearing Corporation (FICC) of Depository Trust & Clearing Corporation (DTCC) will assign an ID number to each TBA being traded. Therefore, as with many derivatives, it is possible for there to be more TBAs of one class being traded than are actually going to be delivered.

Participants in the market sell and buy or buy and sell TBAs. Depending on the financial strength or nature of the firm's client, some clients must post margin against their positions while others may not. As the TBA period nears its end, participants "unwind" their positions, leaving only those who want to be recipients or deliverers of the actual pool. As mortgage rates fluctuate from day to day the participants' maintaining positions will see the value of holdings increase or decrease. It is important to note that as the actual pool has not been issued, there isn't any real product outstanding. Therefore, the buyers of the product cannot really buy anything and the sellers cannot deliver anything. This permits them to go in and out of TBA positions at almost no cost. The resulting profit or loss from this trading activity is real and will be settled at the appropriate time.

Mortgage Backed Security Clearing Corporation (MBSD) keeps a daily tally of the trading and activity of its members from the time the TBA starts to trade until settlement. At the end of the TBA period, it will issue receive and deliver instructions to its participating members. The obligation to receive or deliver will be based on the unilateral net balance of their activity. All clearing members of the corporation will be processed through the same unilateral netting process. As a result, the contra side to the settlement instruction may be a clearing member that the member did not trade with, but ended up on the other side for the settlement. It's worth noting that MBSD will act as a central counterparty (CCP) to all trades. Therefore, in this process, all TBA buy trades will be submitted against MBSD and all TBA sell trades will be submitted against MBSD. At the end of the trading period MBSD will issue settlement balance orders to the netted members. Market participants that are not members of MBSD will settle their transactions directly with their contra parties on a trade-for-trade basis or may choose to use a bilateral netting service against contra firms.

Clients who conduct TBA transactions through these member firms will net out at the end of the TBA period. Those clients that have positions will make arrangements for settlement. Most of these arrangements will enlist the services of a clearing bank.

The GNMA Market

An industry suddenly grew out of this product. At issuance, all mortgages in the pools are assumed to mature within a few months of one another. Once they are issued, however, the demographics of the mortgage owners set the tone. For example, mortgages issued to homeowners in a geographic area appealing to retired homeowners would have a much longer life expectancy than mortgages given to homeowners who reside in a transient area, such as a high-tech region where homeowners change jobs frequently. Therefore, GNMA pooled mortgages were priced at their weighted average maturity (WAM), which was developed from experiences gained from previous pools and observations.

Even though the mortgages were all issued with the same or similar "maturity," the passage of time and the actions of the homeowners and the changes in interest rates would cause the average life of the pool to change—and through that change, the market price of individual pools would also change. In addition, the mortgages are debt instruments and interest rate sensitive. Therefore, as mortgage interest rates fell, homeowners would refinance their homes, retiring their higher-rate mortgages with the proceeds from their new lower-rate mortgages. To the GNMA pool owner, it was as if there were an unwritten, hidden call feature. Their pool of twenty-five-year mortgages was suddenly partially retired in X years as Y number of homeowners refinanced.

Other factors would also affect the life of a mortgage. Relocation of the homeowner and the need to capture the built-up equity for expenses such as children's education are just two reasons for early termination. In recent years, we witnessed a new situation: homeowners' walking away from their responsibilities as the value of the property fell below the mortgage balance, or because of economic hardship. During the life of the mortgages, the payments of interest or principal were overseen by a mortgage servicer.

The GNMA market continues to grow and GNMA-IIs were introduced, which allowed for single-rate mortgages as in GNMA-I, or mortgages with different interest rates in the same pool. With these multirate pools, the division of the rates affected the pricing. This change gave way to WAC (weighted average coupon) pricing.

REMIC

Investors were looking for a way to better control their cash flow. Some wanted a shorter loan period; many wanted more flexibility than was afforded them with the pass-through format. In 1983, Freddie Mac (Federal Home Loan Mortgage Corporation) issued its first collateralized mortgage obligation (CMO). Since then Freddie Mac and Fannie Mae (Federal National Mortgage Association) have been issuing CMOs.

In order to clarify possible confusion, a change in the tax law in 1986 introduced real estate mortgage investment conduits (REMICs), which are legal entities that issue CMOs. REMICs allow CMOs to be issued with a minimum of tax complications.

Freddie Mac and Fannie Mae were created by Congress and established as government-sponsored enterprises (GSEs). The CMOs are backed by the agency. While Fannie Mae and Freddie Mac do not make direct loans, they assist lenders by providing funds. They acquire mortgages from lenders, package them, and sell the securitized products into the market.

Tranches

Let's take a look at how a CMO works with the tranches below, and how they "mature" sequentially.

Each tranche pays a stipulated rate of interest based on the time to maturity. Principal received from the mortgagees is applied against the first tranche. When it is paid down, the principal flows to the second tranche and so on. As with pass-throughs, the prepayment of mortgages hastens the retirement of the pool. Using the above example, let's

| TRANCHES |

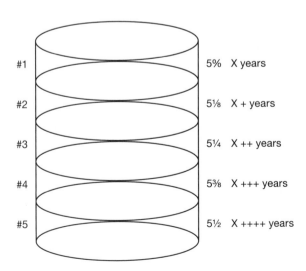

#1	5%	X years
#2	5⅛	X + years
#3	5¼	X ++ years
#4	5⅜	X +++ years
#5	5½	X ++++ years

assume tranche #5 is supposed to be receiving principal payments from years 21 to 25. The owner of the tranche would be receiving that rate of interest on the outstanding principal from day one. Now let's suppose that the tranches were paying down faster so that by year 16 the first four tranches were paid down. Then from year 16 on, the owner of tranche #5 is receiving interest on a 16+ year instrument at a rate of a 21+ year instrument.

The CMO trades of Freddie Mac and Fannie Mae are cleared through MBSCC.

Non-Government–Backed Collateralized Mortgage Obligations

Private mortgage companies, like banks, issue CMOs also, but these do not have any government guarantees. Therefore, the structure of their CMOs is different from those that are government issued. As is the case with those of Freddie Mac and Fannie Mae, the CMOs are divided into tranches. These tranches cover different parts of the CMO. They could be divided into classes, such as A class, B class, C class, etc. All the tranches of the particular CMO collectively make up the CMO's capital structure. A rating agency such as Moody's rates the tranches.

The CMO prospectus details the hierarchy of the tranches. They are listed from AAA, the most senior, down to unrated, the most junior. The tranches below the senior tranches but above the equity tranche are known as "mezzanine tranches." The most junior tranche is known as the "equity tranche" because, if all goes right, it stands to earn the most as it has the highest coupon. Naturally, the AAA rated are the safest but have the lowest "coupon rate" of the tranches. Cash flowing in from the underlying debt is directed to the AAA tranche first and then down to the riskiest of all, the equity tranche. The equity tranche is also referred to as the "toxic waste" tranche because if anything goes wrong, this tranche gets hit with it first, including any defaults, short payments, drops in market value, etc. In the case of losses, the equity tranche absorbs them first, then the tranches up the line absorb them in order of seniority, with the senior tranche absorbing them last.

Z Tranche

Some CMOs have a "Z" tranche, which acts like a zero-coupon bond not receiving any interest or principal until all other tranches have been paid down. It is an interest tranche because, being the lowest on the totem pole, it absorbs any defaults first. However, the interest that it is supposed to receive accrues in its principal, so that in a perfect world, at the end of the CMO or CDO, the Z-tranche owner receives the principal plus the accrued interest, which can now start to earn interest itself.

Collateralized Bond Obligations (CBOs)

Collateralized bond obligations are pools of corporate bonds of varying degrees of risk, including junk bonds that are securitized and sold to the public. Due to the diversity of risk that these bonds represent, they offer an opportunity to receive a higher rate of interest without concern that the entire issue may fail at one time. That fear is evident in the acquisition of a single junk bond. In other words, the risk of default is spread over many bonds. The CBO is issued in tranche format. The idea is to take the possibility of default from one product, with the bond owner(s) absorbing the whole loss, to many diversified junk bond products and many shareholders, where the loss of a bond due to default is shared among many.

Collateralized bond obligations are rated as investment grade based on the possibility that all the bonds won't default at the same time. Therefore there is safety in numbers. As the primary content of the CBO is junk bonds, the bonds must be yielding a high rate of return, which is passed on to the investor. If, when the bonds were originally issued, they were considered non-investment-grade or junk, then they issued with a high "coupon" rate compared with other less risky bonds. If, on the other hand, the bonds were investment grade when issued, but the issuer's finances have weakened and are now at a point where they are considered below investment grade or junk, then the bonds' market price would have fallen in value to the point that they were yielding a high rate—one that is equivalent to the coupon rate of a junk bond. An investor obtaining a position in CBOs who can close it out before a default occurs would have done exceptionally well with the investment. If there were defaults during the holding period, the size of the default compared with the whole would determine the outcome of the investment.

It may still be a better option than one bond, one investment, one default. The tranches are rated by a rating service, with senior, mezzanine, and equity tranches.

Collateralized Loan Obligations (CLOs)

Major corporations in good financial condition usually find it easy to borrow money. Even those whose financial condition isn't stellar can generally negotiate good terms. Midsize and larger businesses may find good borrowing rates harder to come by because of the nature of their business, their location, competition from bigger or foreign companies, or just the economic climate in general. Financial institutions will take these loans and pool them together and sell them as a unit, in a manner following the tranche format with senior, mezzanine, and equity tranches.

The concept of a collateralized loan obligation is to spread the default over many participants, thereby lowering the risk per individual. As with other tranche-issued debt, the tranches descend from senior to equity tranches as the risk of default grows. As the risk of default rises, so does the interest rate paid on the respective tranche.

CLOs are made up of car loans, credit card loans, boat loans, and other commercial loans. One of the major users of this market is Sallie Mae (SLM Corporation, originally the Student Loan Marketing Association). The product is developed by banks and other lending institutions as a way of recouping funds so that they can continue their business of making loans. The loans are not guaranteed by the developers. Therefore, a bank would gather loans of a certain type that it has made and package them. The package is sold to a third party, who securitizes them and sells them into the market. That third party is known as a special purpose vehicle (SPV) or special purpose entity (SPE). The buyer of the securitized product may be a special investment vehicle (SIV) that sells shares of the CLO to its clients or may sell the shares in the over-the-counter marketplace.

| FINANCIAL INSTITUTION TO BROKER |

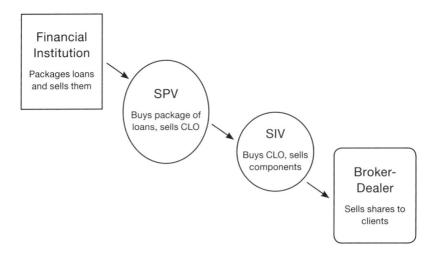

• COVERED BONDS •

Covered bonds originated in Europe centuries ago. Only recently did they begin to appear in the United States. They were brought to the forefront by former secretary of the treasury Henry Paulson. These instruments offered a more secure method for investors and distributors to enter a liquid debt market. The introduction of the product occurred during the credit crises and has the structure to avoid many of the pitfalls of collateralized debt obligations.

What separates covered bonds from other debt derivatives is the recourse that investors have in case of default. Unlike the typical collateral debt obligation, where the investor can lose his or her entire investment should the pool of debt instruments go into default, the investor has recourse against the issuer or the organization the issuer is affiliated with, as well as the covered pool itself.

The assets that make up the pool are segregated from the issuer's other assets. The issuer cannot use these assets for any purpose other than to support the covered bonds. Because the assets are locked in, investors can examine the quality of the assets to determine value and risk.

Another difference between covered bonds and CDOs is that covered bonds remain on the issuer's or distributor's books and are not sold off to another entity, as is the case with CDOs. The lender issuer of

CDOs sells the pools to a special purpose vehicle, which in turn issues shares against the pool. Therefore any malady that befalls the pools also affects the issuing party.

In addition to Europe and the United States, New Zealand and Australia are in the midst of offering these instruments. The product trades in an over-the-counter environment with several institutions creating it. Transactions are settled between parties through correspondent banks.

CHAPTER 22

STRUCTURED "PACKAGED" PRODUCTS

The U.S. Securities and Exchange Commission has a rule regarding certain prospectus deliveries. Rule 434 of the Securities Act of 1933 defines structured securities as "securities whose cash flow characteristics depend upon one or more indices or that have embedded forwards or options or securities where an investor's investment return and the issuer's payment obligations are contingent on, or highly sensitive to, changes in the value of underlying assets, indices, interest rates or cash flows."

Structured products are a group of "packaged" issues that are designed to accomplish certain objectives unavailable through conventional product offerings. As they comprise products from different markets, they are also known as "market-linked investments" or "market-linked products." Structured products are custom made to suit a particular purpose and therefore do not have a fixed format, but instead are made up of a combination of two or more products, one or more of which is a derivative. This specialization using unique features is one of the reasons that technology used in other products cannot be employed here. These products are "packaged" by the issuer, which is usually a financial institution such as a bank. They are then sold to institutions, such as hedge funds, and, depending on the price a trading unit, to the general public.

• OBJECTIVE •

The objective will determine which products will be used in an attempt to achieve success. It may be performance-oriented products that are structured to look at longer-term investments in markets that reflect growth and volatility. The events happening in the BRIC countries (Brazil, Russia, India, and China) have been an example of such goals. The product may be structured to participate in a high-risk/return scenario using a basket of equities and option derivatives, representing the more volatile segment of the market, or simply a principal protection product that focuses on preservation of capital and earning a higher rate of return than can be obtained through the acquisition of AAA-rated debt through the use of bonds and options.

As with any investment, the objective is always at risk. If one was to consider these financial products as musical instruments, then the selection and placement of the correct instruments will go a long way to making beautiful music. Therefore the financial instruments involved are: debt products, equities, commodities, credit instruments, currencies, futures, forwards, forward rate agreements, indexes, options, other securities, and swaps. Some of these tools are applied individually while others are placed into baskets. As such, each structured product must be examined as if it is a "one and only" because it probably is.

• STRUCTURED PRODUCTS AT WORK •

Structured products may be called different names by different users, such as a buy/write, income writing, income enhancement, etc. A buy/write consists of a dividend-paying common stock and a call option. Let's take a look at some examples.

Client Pete Koll is interested in investing in income-producing securities. He buys 1,000 shares of RAM common stock at 37. RAM is paying $1.00 per share per year or $0.25 per share per quarter. At its current price RAM is yielding 2.7 percent. Pete sees that there is a *six-month call on RAM with a strike price of $40 trading at 1½. This is an out-of-the-money option as no one will call a stock and pay $40 per share when the stock is trading at $37. Pete decides to sell (write) ten calls (10 contracts × 100 shares per contract × 1½ = $1,500) and take in $1,500. With that one move, Pete has collected one and a half years' worth of dividends by the next day. If all stays status quo, at the end of the six months the option will expire worthless. Pete has earned two dividend payments (2 × $0.25 = $0.50 × 1,000 shares = $500). And because the options are out of the money, Pete can do it again.*

What is the downside of this strategy? First: The stock rises above $40 and gets called away. Since Pete paid $37 for the stock and had it called away at $40 he earned $3 per share times 1,000 shares = $3,000 (three years' worth of dividends). However, in doing so, he lost his income stream and now must find a new one. Second: What if the stock rose from $37 to $100 per share or higher? Pete gave up the opportunity to profit from the capital appreciation because of the calls. The most he can earn from the capital appreciation is 3 points, from $37 to $40.

What if the stock starts to fall in value? As Pete paid $37 per share, and received 1½ points from the sale of the calls, he has a breakeven of $35½. If the stock falls below that price, Pete has a loss. What should he do? If he sells the stock, he has ten uncovered calls that expose him to market risk and further loss, hinging upon whether the stock turns and starts a run-up in value. Since the short calls are no longer covered by the stock, Pete must post margin.

As a structured product is an actual product plus one or more derivatives, in this case common stock and one derivative with a call option were used to enhance Pete's income.

Here's a more complicated example. Again it uses common stock, but with two option products.

If a brokerage firm, Stone, Forrest and Rivers, was to acquire 1,000 shares of Zappo Corp (ZAP) common stock at $37 per share and write (sell) ten six-month European calls on ZAP with a strike price of $40 @ 4 and at the same time buy ten six-month European put options on ZAP with a strike price of $35 @ 2, the firm could sell this package or *structured product, guaranteeing the package buyer its principal investment returned as well as the possibility of earning better than 15 percent on its investment.*

Here's the formula:

Owns 1,000 shares of ZAP @ 37 =	**$37,000**
Owns 10 puts (10 puts representing	
100 shares each = 1,000 shares)	
strike price 35 @ 2 =	**$ 2,000**
Short 10 calls (10 calls representing	
100 shares each = 1,000 shares)	
strike price 40 @ 4 =	**($ 4,000)**
Total Cost	**$35,000**

Reviewing the position:

The purpose of the position is to preserve capital while attempting to earn a profit. Stone, Forrest and Rivers owns 1,000 shares of ZAP common stock at $37 per share. At this point in the analysis, the risk of loss is $37,000. The company owns ten of the European puts at a cost of 2 points per option, which permits it to sell (put out) 1,000 shares of ZAP at $35 at the expiration of the options. Stone, Forrest and Rivers would only do this if ZAP was selling at $35 per share or below. The firm has now invested $39,000 ($37,000 cost of ZAP stock + $2,000 cost of ZAP put options), and then sells ten calls with a strike price $40 at 4 points each times 100 underlying shares times ten contracts = $4,000 received. The $4,000 they received for the calls subtracted from the $39,000 position acquisition cost nets to a cost of $35,000. Should ZAP fall in price and be below $35 per share at the time of put option expiration, the puts would be exercised and the account would be credited $35,000 in proceeds from the exercise (10 puts × 100 shares each × $35 = $35,000).

In the case where the puts would be exercised, the account paid $35,000 net for the position, minus $35,000 received from the exercise of the puts. If that outcome occurred, the investment would be intact. But what if the stock rose and was trading above $40 when the call was about to expire? SF&R sold ten out-of-the-money European *call options with a strike price of $40 @ 4, which grants the call option owner the ability to buy (call in) the ZAP stock at $40 per share. (Note: the term "out-of-the-money option" refers to the relationship between the current market value of the underlying security and the strike price of the option.) With the stock being called away at $40 per share (× 1,000 shares = $40,000) there would be a $5 per share profit ($40,000 received from the exercise of the calls minus $35,000 total cost) for an annualized maximum return of 14.28 percent in six months.*

If it turns out that ZAP stock was trading between $35 per share and $40 at the expiration date of the options, the options would be allowed to expire and the ZAP security liquidated. No one would call the stock in at $40 per share if it was trading for less. Had the package been sold to one of SF&R's clients, the company would not put the stock out at $35 if it was trading above it. Therefore, the only part of the package that remains is the stock, which now has an adjusted purchase price of $35. If it was sold the proceeds from the sale would be applied to the cost and any residual would be a profit. (This example excludes expenses.)

Had the structured product been sold to a client of Stone, Forrest and Rivers, then should the stock pay a dividend during the holding period, its distribution would depend on the terms set at the time the package was originated. As Stone, Forrest and Rivers took the necessary market action to develop the structured product, the respective clearing and settlement companies, namely the Depository Trust & Clearing Corporation (DTCC) and Options Clearing Corporation, could be maintaining the positions on behalf of Stone, Forrest and Rivers so that any dividend paid on the stock would go to the broker-dealer's account. The dividend would be paid to the broker-dealer, which would either retain it or pass it on to the client. (This example ignores all fees, commissions, etc.) However, if such a product was packaged by a bank or a broker-dealer, the issuer's fee would be less than it would cost the client for the package if the client was to transact all parts individually.

In the above example, the European form of option was selected to remove the possibility of premature exercise by the call option owner.

The American form of option could be exercised at any time during its life. Therefore, should the call owner exercise options before expiration, the owner of the package would not be in control of the position and might have to take unwanted action to protect it.

While the above example appears to be a win or breakeven situation, there are many factors, variables, and dynamics that have been frozen in time for explanatory reasons. For example, what if the stock is trading way above $40 at the end of the package's existence, and the profit opportunity to cash in on this bonanza is lost? What value would be assigned to the three parts if the company merged or was acquired?

• STRUCTURED NOTES •

One of the major products sold in the structured product market is structured notes. These notes consist of a bond and a derivative product, which may be an option, a future, a swap, etc. It is the intent of the product to protect the investor's investment and to outperform the bond itself. The note is issued for anywhere from six months to ten years. At the end of the note the issuer is supposed to pay the investor the principal amount originally paid by the investor, plus all or part of the profit made from the derivative.

Let's look at a couple of examples and then compare them.

Example A uses an outright purchase of a bond:

A client of Stone, Forrest and Rivers, a broker-dealer, acquires a $10,000 bond that is currently trading at $9,000 for a client. The reason for the discounted price is that since the time the bond was issued, interest rates, in general, have risen. New instruments with the same or similar qualities are commanding higher interest rates, therefore this bond's value has to be adjusted downward to compete in the market. The bond in this example is a fixed-income instrument. As interest rates rise, bond prices fall, and yields rise so that the bond remains competitive with the newer issued bonds.

The bond carries a 5 percent interest rate, which means the bond will pay $500 ($10,000 × .05 = $500 per year or $250 semiannually). If the bond position is maintained by the client until maturity and the *issuer is still financially sound, the client would receive the face value of the bond ($10,000) regardless of the current interest rates. The bond is a loan obligation and must be paid in full at maturity. The owner would have received semiannual interest payments over the time the bond was owned and was maintained, less whatever interest had accrued but had not been paid to the previous owner when the buyer initially acquired the position. If during the period the bond is owned the bondholder wants to sell it, he or she is free to do so as there is a ready market for the product. Of course, during this period, the client is facing credit risk (changes to the financial worthiness of the issuer) and market risk (changes to the current or near-term interest rates). When the bond matures, the bonds are surrendered and the client receives $10,000. The client has earned $1,000 plus accrued interest.*

Here's Example B:

Broker-dealer Stone, Forrest and Rivers is assembling a structured note. The firm acquires a $10,000 bond with a current value of $9,000. The bond is paying 5 percent interest. The bond is packaged with a long (owned) call option on an index as a structured note. The note is structured so that the maturity of the bond coincides with the maturity of the structured note. The package is sold to a client for $10,000. The client has purchased a "guarantee" that the investment is safe and that there is a possibility of a greater return than by just owning the bond. Of the client's $10,000 investment, $9,000 is used to pay for the bond, and the remaining $1,000 is applied to the purchase of the option (or other derivative). In this example, the documentation covering the structured note states that during the duration of the structured note, the client would not receive the bond's semiannual interest payments.

Comparing Examples A and B

In Example A, the client owns a $10,000 bond and paid $9,000 for it. At maturity the bond owner will receive par or face value of $10,000, assuming the bond issuer is in the financial position to retire the bonds. During the period of ownership, the bond owner has received the accrued periodic interest payments. While the bond owner is exposed to market and credit risk, the owner has the ability to sell the bond into a liquid market whenever it is desirable. The price he or she receives should represent the fair market value at that time. Should the bond-issuing company experience financial hardship or even bankruptcy, the bondholder would suffer a financial loss.

In Example B the investor has paid $10,000 for an instrument that is only worth $9,000 plus whatever the potentially illiquid customized derivative is valued at. He or she has also given up receiving the 5 percent periodic interest payment. The structured note would have to earn at least the 5 percent for the owner to break even, had he or she just purchased the bond by itself. However, the expectation is that the $1,000 remaining from the bond purchase ($10,000 paid versus a $9,000 bond) will be invested in a derivative that will have to outperform the bond's return. Had the investor actually paid $10,000 for the bond, he or she would have $10,500 at the maturity of the bond, comprising the bond's face value and two interest payments. Therefore, as the bonds issuer will pay $10,000 at its maturity, the derivative portion must have a value of better than $500 to make the effort worthwhile.

The profits that may be obtained from the derivative leg may be paid under different arrangements. Some notes pay 100 percent of the profits to the note holder, some share only under certain circumstances, and still others cap the amount to be paid, or any combination of these. The "guarantee" of principal is only applicable at the expiration of the structured note and the maturity of the bond. Therefore the return at maturity may total less than what the bondholder in Example A above would have received.

Should the note holder want to or need to close out the position, he or she may be selling into an illiquid market, or if there isn't any market for the product, the investor may have to sell it back to the issuer, which may or may not be interested in participating. The note holder may be offered a price far below what was anticipated.

The same outcome discussed above would occur if a zero-coupon bond was employed instead of the interest-bearing instrument. As explained in the debt section, a zero-coupon bond is a bond priced to the present value of its cash flows. Over time the interest owed accrues in the value of the bond and is not paid out periodically. At maturity, the bond is worth face value. The difference between what was paid for the bond originally and its face value at maturity is the interest earned.

The fact that the principal is "guaranteed" could be a misnomer. The questions are: who is giving the guarantee, and what exactly is guaranteed? Some guarantees have caveats as to when they apply or what events would trigger the guarantee. The caveat may be that the guarantee becomes effective only if the firm files for bankruptcy, but if it merges or goes through some capital restructuring it is not applicable. The guarantee may only cover the value of the bond at purchase, which would mean that, initially, the investor would be losing $1,000. Other guarantees "kick out" if the level of the bond falls below a certain value. In addition, structured notes may be callable or able to be terminated by the issuer. The latter is especially true if the second component has an index as an underlying product. The index portion may be permitted to increase to a point or percentage. Once that point is reached, the holder of the structured note ceases to participate. The terms and conditions for termination of the agreement may include cases of bankruptcy, inability or failure to meet the obligations, or a force majeure or other unexpected event that was disclosed in the offering document, or if the value of the benchmark or referenced security falls below the requirements of the contract.

• INVERSE FLOATER STRUCTURED PRODUCT •

Another form of structured note is one that employs the use of an instrument that reacts contrary to interest rates. The structured note may contain an inverse floating instrument. As interest rises in the market, the interest rate paid on this instrument falls, and vice versa.

For example, a structured product contains a debt instrument yielding 5 percent and a reverse floater yielding 3 percent, for a total yield of 8 percent. Interest rates are not static; rather, they fluctuate over time. As interest rates in the market rise, debt prices are falling, and the debt instrument is now yielding 6 percent in this situation. The reverse floater would have to be yielding 2 percent for a total of 8 percent. If interest falls, and bond prices are rising, the debt instrument is now yielding 4 percent. The reverse floater would have to be yielding 4 percent in this instance.

Reverse floaters emanate from two primary sources: security issuers and financial institutions. During volatile interest periods, issues composed of a floating-rate or fixed-rate debt instrument and a reverse floating rate will trade at a higher value than a similar instrument without the reverse floating part, because the sum of the parts is greater than the whole. With a floating-rate instrument, the interest rate changes and the value (price) remains about the same; with a fixed-rate instrument the rate remains the same but the value (price) changes. Both have the same effect on the instrument's yield. A financial institution will marry a debt instrument to a floating rate and sell the package to a client. The financial institution has sold a debt instrument that it has issued or bought for resale and enters into a swap trade, reversing the reverse floating position so that the position is neutral.

In the above example where the debt instrument was yielding 5 percent and the reverse floater was yielding 3 percent, what would happen if interest rose to where the bond had to yield 10 percent? The reverse floater is at -2 percent yield. Obviously the owner of the reverse floater is not going to turn around and begin paying the issuer interest. The structured product nomenclature would state that once interest rates rose so that the yield would have to be greater than 8 percent, the floater would cease paying and the debt instrument would remain as an 8 percent instrument.

• Equity-Linked Notes and Index-Linked Notes •

Equity-linked notes and index-linked notes are actually debt instruments and not equities. They represent a promise from the issuer to pay the investor an amount based on a predetermined formula. They are totally unsecured as they do not have any real asset behind them. What they are is a note combined with a derivative, such as an option, issued on a referenced asset. This asset may be a stock (an equity-linked note) or an index (an index-linked note). They are acquired at a discounted price from par; therefore, the safety of the note is directly connected to the safety of the issuer. At maturity the investor is to get back par plus any gains made by the derivative.

Due to the recent financial crisis, equity-linked notes and index-linked notes are now being issued with collateral backing. Therefore, the notes could be offered as secured, partially secured, or nonsecured. As always, the value and quality of the assets supporting the note then become of concern.

Regulatory authorities are concerned that the broker-dealers selling these products make sure that their sales personnel are well aware of their complexities and have informed their prospective clients of the risk.

• REVERSE CONVERTIBLE •

A reverse convertible security consists of a long (owned) zero-coupon bond and a short (sold) European-type put on an index or common stock. The option expires at the same time the zero-coupon bond matures. The rate of interest paid by the zero-coupon bond is factored into the bond's price, and at maturity, it will be part of the maturity payment made. The premium received from the put sale is added to the final sum received, thereby offering the investor a higher rate of return.

Here's an example:

Assume a $10,000 investment in a zero-coupon bond that is priced to yield 5 percent, and a sale of put options on $10,000 worth of Regal Corp common stock with a strike price of $50 which netted $400. At maturity of the note, the investor would get a return of 9 percent (5% interest on the bond + 4% premium on the option). If the stock drops in price and at maturity is selling below $50 per share, the investor would absorb the loss between the market value of the stock or index and the strike price of the put option.

The investor stands to make a profit of 9 percent, which is capped at that point. The price of the zero-coupon bond cannot go higher than par (face value, which is $10,000) and should Regal trade above $50 per share the option is worthless as it is out of the money (no one *would put [sell] stock at $50 if it was selling at a price above $50 in the market). On the downside, the underlying stock could fall 9 percent before the investor would have a loss. The investor's maximum loss on the put is the difference between $50 and 0 (Regal Corp is bankrupt) less the $400 premium = $4,600 per 100 shares. The owner of the European put would exercise the option and receive $50 per share for the worthless stock. In addition, the issuer of the zero-coupon bond could be in financial trouble and thus unable to retire the bond. Because of that, the investor would also lose all or most of the investment in the bond.*

(The reason a European-type put was chosen was to prevent early exercise. The European form of option is only exercisable at the end of its life, whereas the American form is exercisable any time during its life.)

We have looked at the investor; now let's look at the issuer. The issuer has structured a product consisting of a zero-coupon bond and bought a European $50 strike price put for $400 per contract. Assuming the issuer, First Continental Bank, issued a zero-coupon bond, it would have the use of the funds for free up until the bonds matured and the structured product ceased to exist, or until the client prematurely terminated the agreement. At that time, it would have to pay the interest owed. As to the put with a strike price of $50, the result ranges from a loss of $400 per contract because the option expired worthless, as Regal Corp was trading at $50 or above, to a profit of $4,600 ($5,000 [100 shares @ $50] − $400 [the price of the put] = $4,600).

CHAPTER 23

REGULATORS AND INDUSTRY ASSOCIATIONS

T he securities industry as well as the commodities industry are regulated by federal and state governments and industry organizations. Those financial entities operating in the global space have other regulators, with other rules and regulations to contend with. Collectively, these institutions have provided us with the framework that we must operate under. The regulations include: Who can operate and what their limitations are, how the markets are to operate, what clients may or may not do, the regimen for processing transactions, the requirements for the lending of money and securities, and the maintenance of records. All are mandated via these directives.

• SECURITIES AND EXCHANGE COMMISSION •

The Securities and Exchange Commission was created by Congress to develop and enforce rules and regulations regarding securities exchanges, securities trading markets, and the members and firms operating through these facilities. The SEC's purview includes all firms and individuals that conduct securities business with the public. The exceptions are those entities covered by other federal agencies, such as the Office of the Comptroller of the Currency (OCC), which regulates federal banks and federal savings associations. State banks are regulated by the individual states.

The scope of the commission's regulations is vast, covering:

- Firm and individual registration requirements
- Financial requirements including threshold minimums and reporting obligations
- Enforcement of the Federal Reserve Board's regulations
- Regulation T (lending of funds to clients by broker-dealers)
- The 1933 Truth in Securities Act covering the issuance of new securities
- The 1934 Securities Exchange Act, which created the Securities and Exchange Commission and covers the requirements of operating as a broker-dealer, secondary trading, record keeping, auditing, and proper processes for conducting business with the public
- The Trust Indenture Act of 1939
- The Investment Company Act of 1940
- The Investment Advisers Act of 1940
- The Sarbanes-Oxley Act of 2002

Divisions of the Securities and Exchange Commission

The Securities and Exchange Commission is divided into five main divisions:

CORPORATE FINANCE oversees disclosures made by public companies and operates EDGAR (Electronic Data Gathering, Analysis, and Retrieval), which is a system for public notification of financial events affecting those companies. The division is also responsible for the registration of securities for sale to the public and for overseeing the processes that accompany offerings.

TRADING AND MARKETS oversees the self-regulating organizations such as FINRA, broker-dealer firms, and investment firms. This is the division that promulgates rules as to the levels of qualification examinations industry personnel are required to pass.

INVESTMENT MANAGEMENT OVERSEES mutual funds and investment advisers and oversees compliance with the Investment Company Act and the Investment Advisers Act.

ENFORCEMENTS WORKS WITH the aforementioned divisions, investigating alleged rule and/or regulation violations and bringing charges against parties when such conditions are found.

RISK, STRATEGY, AND FINANCIAL INNOVATION applies academic disciplines and quantitative and nonquantitative concepts to complex matters, provides economic and statistical analysis to the commission, and also develops economic and risk models for the commission and market participants.

• COMMODITY FUTURES TRADING COMMISSION •

The Commodity Futures Trading Commission (CFTC) is an independent agency of the federal government that regulates the futures, options on futures and credit derivative markets. It is the successor to the Commodity Exchange Act of 1936, which prohibited fraudulent trading acts. In 1974, Congress amended the act and replaced the Commodity Exchange Authority with the Commodity Futures Trading Commission. The commission's mission was expanded and is now stated thus: "to protect market users and the public from fraud, manipulation, and abusive practices related to the sale of commodity and financial futures and options, and to foster open, competitive, and financially sound futures and option markets." Originally, the commission was focused on agricultural products; over the years, however, its area of jurisdiction has widened, partly because of the multitude of new products that we now trade and because of some of these products' unique structure.

Divisions of the Commodity Futures Trading Commission

The Commodity Exchange Act (CEA) was a successor to earlier legislation aimed at stopping fraud and the manipulation of commodity prices. It required all regulated commodities to trade on licensed contract markets. In addition, it mandated that all broker-dealers who had customers that traded commodity orders be registered with the federal government. These firms became known as futures commission merchants (FCMs).

The CFTC is composed of five commissioners appointed by the president with the consent of the Senate, and operating in five-year terms. Its major operating units are:

DIVISION OF CLEARING AND INTERMEDIARY OVERSIGHT is responsible for the oversight of derivative clearing organizations (such as CME Group clearing entities), registrants' financial integrity, customer fund protection, stock-index margin requirements, registration and financial/operational condition of intermediaries, futures commission merchants, commodity pool operators (CPOs) and commodity trading advisors (CTAs), sales practice reviews, and National Futures Association activities as they relate to intermediaries and foreign market access by intermediaries.

DIVISION OF MARKET OVERSIGHT is responsible for the oversight of trade execution facilities, with a primary focus on market surveillance, trade practice reviews in accordance with best practices, and the investigation of possible violations, verifying that rules and procedures are being enforced.

DIVISION OF ENFORCEMENT investigates alleged violations of the CFTC and CEA rules and regulations and, when parties are found guilty, it proceeds with prosecution. Violations range from unauthorized transactions, to improper marketing of commodity and/or option products, to criminal violations of the Commodity Exchange Act or of other federal rules, and may be referred to the Justice Department for prosecution.

OFFICE OF CHIEF ECONOMIST is an independent office whose purpose is to render policy analysis and economic research. Its members may be called upon to give expert testimony and to provide education and training.

OFFICE OF GENERAL COUNSEL (OGC) is the commission's legal adviser. The staff represents the OGC in appellate litigation and certain trial-required cases. The OGC reviews all regulatory, legislative, and administrative matters. It also advises the commission on the application and interpretation of the Commodity Exchange Act.

OFFICE OF THE EXECUTIVE DIRECTOR (OED) develops the management and administrative policies the commission will follow. The OED performs management accounting functions such as the formulation of the budget and the allocation and use of resources, oversees management controls, assures financial integrity, and updates and maintains its automated systems. Located within the OED is the Office of Proceedings, which provides an inexpensive and expedient forum for processing customer complaints against the National Futures Association's registered personnel and entities. The office has the responsibility for recording and monitoring futures contracts traded on United States futures exchanges.

• FINANCIAL INDUSTRY REGULATORY AUTHORITY (FINRA) •

The Financial Industry Regulatory Authority is the largest independent regulator of broker-dealers and affiliated firms in the United States. It is dedicated to protecting investor and market integrity through regulation of the securities industry.

FINRA is the industry's own police force. It is empowered to enforce the rules of the Securities and Exchange Commission, other federal agencies, and its own rules and regulations. For example, it is responsible for enforcing the Securities and Exchange Commission's rules covering the Federal Reserve Board's Regulation T, which covers the lending of funds to clients to perform transactions in securities. FINRA eventually appended to it rules covering account maintenance.

Divisions of Financial Industry Regulatory Authority

There are four main sections of FINRA:

REGULATIONS: works on maintaining FINRA rules, develops new and updates current rules, distributes information notices, and solicits comments for members and other interested parties.

COMPLIANCE: maintains broker-dealers' and individuals' registrations, operates continuing education programs, and performs compliance examinations of member firms.

EDUCATION: conducts conferences and events, provides online learning and university programs.

ENFORCEMENT: enforces the sanction guidelines, adjudicates disputes and infractions, and assigns disciplinary actions.

FINRA also provides tools to assist investors and industry personnel to perform various tasks, such as its Fund Analyzer and Retirement Calculator.

• INTERNATIONAL SWAPS AND DERIVATIVES ASSOCIATION (ISDA) •

The International Swaps and Derivatives Association is an international organization dedicated to representing derivative and structured product participants and products through communication, education, and cooperative cohesive efforts. It works to foster a safe and efficient derivatives market that will in turn facilitate effective risk management for all users of derivative products.

The organization has eight functional areas. They are:

- Legal and Documentation
- Public Policy
- Risk Management
- Infrastructure Management
- Research
- Accounting and Tax
- Protocol Management
- Technology Infrastructure

These areas are the focus of the association's attention as its members work with global regulatory and industry groups in setting policy, regulations, and processes. The products involved are credit default swaps, credit, equity, interest, and foreign exchange derivatives, and select commodity and structured products.

The main ISDA document, the master agreement, and its accompanying documents have gone a long way in reducing misunderstanding and confusion in transactions of these products as well as codifying the core components into a standard form.

Securities Industry and Financial Markets Association (SIFMA)

The Securities Industry and Financial Markets Association is a non-regulatory industry organization that develops policies and practices that augment the rules and regulations enforced by the Securities and Exchange Commission and FINRA. It comprises broker-dealers, banks, asset managers, and industry professionals who devote their time and efforts for the mutual good. It develops policies that strengthen financial markets and encourage capital availability, job creation, and economic growth, while building trust and confidence in the financial industry.

SIFMA organizes committees to address issues facing the industry. As of the writing of this book, committees are addressing the Dodd-Frank Act and systemic risk, just to name two. There are also committees whose role is to represent the industry to federal and state government bodies.

· National Futures Association (NFA) ·

The National Futures Association (NFA) is an industry-run self-regulatory organization made up of its members. To trade on a U.S. futures market, the person or entity must be registered with the NFA. Currently the NFA has 4,200 firms and 55,000 associates. Its purpose is to provide rules and regulations that protect clients and maintain the industry's integrity.

The NFA establishes and administers qualification examinations. It performs a thorough background check on all applicants, including fingerprint scanning. The entity reserves the right to deny any applicant and revoke, suspend, or fine any registered firm or individual.

The CFTC develops rules and regulations and the NFA enforces them. A complete suite of rules and regulations are being updated on a regular basis to keep the National Futures Association in step with current trends and trading techniques. These rules and regulations, which focus on the dealings between clients and firms, are being expanded to cover the new products continually being added to the futures exchanges.

CHAPTER 24

DERIVATIVE TRANSACTION PROCESSING AND THE DODD-FRANK ACT

Passed in 2010, the Dodd-Frank Wall Street Reform and Consumer Protection Act addressed three main serious problems. First, the amount of capital required to support derivative positions maintained by financial institutions was deemed to be insufficient. Second, the amount of trading risk being taken by institutions whose primary purpose was clients' financial services was growing. Third, there was a lack of transparency (disintermediation of a third party) in the market because there wasn't any reporting of price and other transaction information through a central facility.

Thus one of the major parts of the Dodd-Frank Act focused on product processing and transparency, via an entity called a swap execution facility (SEF). The European Market Infrastructure Regulation (EMIR) and Markets in Financial Instruments Directive (MiFID) are both addressing the same issues. The main concern is both the number of trades and the billions of dollars' (and other currencies) worth of derivatives and structured products that are not in a "controlled harbor" but floating around somewhere in the "clouds" (either systemically or archaically). Section VII of the Dodd-Frank Act requires that certain over-the-counter derivatives (the Act's term is "swaps") be cleared through exchanges or clearinghouses. Currently some exchanges offer systems that operate from product trading through to settlement, as in some futures markets. In other markets, the exchanges and clearing facilities are separate entities.

For example, the Chicago Board Option Exchange (CBOE), where option products are traded, and the Options Clearing Corporation (OCC), where all CBOE-traded options settle (as do the option trades from exchanges), are two separate entities. Dodd-Frank further clarifies the responsibilities of the Securities and Exchange Commission (SEC) and Commodity Futures Trading Commission (CFTC), with the SEC having the authority over "security swaps" and the CFTC having authority over all other swaps. As of the writing of this book, the trading, clearance, and settlement of some derivative products are highly automated, while others are at the opposite end of the spectrum.

• CUSTOMIZED VS. NONCUSTOMIZED PRODUCTS •

The term "customized" takes on a completely different meaning when it comes to processing. Transaction processing involves the structure of the product and not what it is composed of. Listed issues, those that trade on exchanges, follow a regimented format. A trading lot of ZAP common stock, structure-wise, is the same as a trading lot of RAM common stock, and so on. Certain over-the-counter products, by their very nature, also follow the same format as other similar products. GNMA pass-through securities are an example of this. While the number of pools that make up the trading unit, as well as the coupon rate and mortgage expiration date, may all be different, the product conforms to a set of processing requirements. This structure requirement makes processing of transactions more efficient through the use of electronic processing and through the employment of clearing corporations. In the case of GNMA pass-through securities, the clearing corporation Mortgage-Backed Securities (MBSCC) is one of the divisions of the Depository Trust & Clearing Corporation (DTCC). Some over-the-counter products are not automated because the volume of transactions is so low it's not warranted.

Noncustomized Transactions

Not all derivatives are customized. Many are standardized in structure. For instance, futures, listed options, options on futures, and mortgage-backed securities issued by GNMA, Freddie Mac, or Fannie Mae are all customized products but standardized in structure. Credit-linked notes are an example of where the structure is missing, as the component parts, individually, require their own processing and are not the same from one note to another.

Customized Transactions

In terms of operations, a customized product is synonymous with a one-off transaction: a trade so different from the rest that it must be manually processed or one that, as a group, has such little volume that the cost of developing, running, and servicing a system is not cost effective. The customization of a transaction can involve a product or a transaction. A product would be a call option on 150 shares of ZAP preferred stock with a strike price of $53.35 expiring at 12:00 noon on May 24. The structure is that of an option, its nomenclature is a one of a kind. A customized transaction would be a structured product where an ETF on TAN index of the top fifty European stocks is acquired and two of the stocks that are in the ETF are shorted and five other stocks, not in the ETF, are acquired in quantities other than their trading lots. This type of trade requires special handling and processing and its purpose is known only to the principal.

• EVOLUTION OF DERIVATIVE PROCESSING •

The first item that must be addressed is the misconception that the processing of nonderivative products is all "straight-through processing" and that derivative products are processed by chisel and stone. To understand the concepts and steps along the way, we will follow the listed option market from before the Chicago Board Option Exchange (CBOE), the first "listed" option exchange, was launched, and the effects it had on the option world. In many ways some of our derivatives products of today run the same way the option market did back then.

Prior to 1973, almost all put and call options were on common stock and were traded in an over-the-counter environment. The marketplace was small. SEC-registered broker-dealers known as put and call dealers made markets, published prices on a half dozen of their "offerings" in the newspaper to attract interest, and investors would call their broker-dealers, who in turn would call the put and call dealers and negotiate the terms of the new contract. Once this was agreed upon between client, broker-dealer, and put and call dealer, the broker-dealer would trade against whichever dealer gave the best terms and price. The broker-dealer then wrote up the terms and price on an order ticket. The ticket was used as a source to print out the customer's trade confirmation, which was mailed to the client with a copy going to the broker-dealer's operation department to be matched to the actual put or call option contract when it arrived from the put and call dealer.

At the same time the put and call dealers would type the terms of the option contract and physically deliver the option paper contract to the client's broker-dealer, who in turn would match the terms against the customer's confirmation and hold the contract pending later instruction. This is the genesis of the current terms "holder," the one who can exercise the option, and "writer," the one who can be assigned to perform the terms of the contract. There wasn't any record maintained by the put and call dealer as to who actually retained the paper contracts; rather, the put and call dealers knew their positions but didn't know who actually held them. If a "holder" should lose the paper contract, there wasn't any replacement to be had because the document was in bearer form, so whoever should surrender the option paper to the put and call dealer was assumed to be the owner. Therefore, anyone turning in the paper contract to the put and call dealer could exercise it.

Trading between the investors did not exist, as there wasn't a secondary market. All trades were against the put and call dealers. Broker-dealers would exercise options on behalf of a client or for their own proprietary account, surrendering the option paper to the put and call dealer. Both firms would then submit trade report tickets to their operation departments and the trades would be manually processed by the two firms. This should sound familiar, because some of the derivative trades we process today look very similar.

The Opening of the Chicago Board Options Exchange

On April 26, 1973, the CBOE opened its doors and the options world changed forever. The listed options market accomplished the following:

- Standardization of the product was accomplished when option format structure was established. The core or structure of all listed options is the same; details of the individual trades are different. The option must be a put or call, it must be a buy or sell, and it must be for a trading lot, etc.

- New options products that are to be listed for trading must be approved for trading by the Securities and Exchange Commission and by the Options Clearing Corporation (OCC). Additional option series that may be required due to price movement of the underlying product are added by OCC as provided for by rules for put and call options, with the same series designation added at the same time.

As a result of the standardization and the orderly way options are issued, a secondary market developed with participation from brokerage firms (and their customers) trading against other member brokerage firms and against member floor traders (market makers who added liquidity to the market). Therefore brokerage firms executed their customer orders against other brokers and market makers on the trading floor of the CBOE. Brokerage firms executed "upstairs" proprietary orders against other brokers and traders as well. Traders, operating on the exchange floor and from "upstairs" trading rooms in their respective firms, added liquidity to the market.

Execution price transparency was accomplished when trade prices were captured by an independent third party known as the Options Price Reporting Authority (OPRA). These prices were made readily available to the public. Historical pricing records were available to auditors, regulatory personnel, and the public. It is this pricing element that is missing from some derivative products and addressed in the Dodd-Frank Act.

Option products and members were assigned to areas of the floor to balance trading volume and product servicing. Today, physical floor locations are no longer needed, as technology has improved and the use of electronic markets has been replacing the need of a physical trading floor.

Another area addressed by the Dodd-Frank Act was the lack of any execution detail for certain derivative transactions being captured by an independent third party. In the case of listed options, execution details are reported to the source of the order and to the OCC. It is the OCC that is responsible for reporting trade comparison and verification between submitting brokerage firms. The matching and comparison are now performed systemically, with trades where the buying and selling firm do not agree as to details (known as "uncompared trades") identified and highlighted, leaving no doubt as to the validity of each trade. Firms' management, internal and external auditors, as well as regulators can review current position risk, problem transactions, and exposure to potential loss.

As options involve a "second life"—the period between the opening or establishing of a position and option expiration or closing of the position—a record is maintained of outstanding option positions by the OCC, and the respective broker-dealers maintain the positions in customer, firm (proprietary), and market maker control accounts. In addition, firms must adhere to SEC rules forbidding commingling of aforementioned positions. This record keeping by an independent third party, in this case OCC, is another requirement of the Dodd-Frank Act.

Margin requirements were established based on the perceived risk of the overall positions maintained by the firm. The amount of margin required was deposited with OCC, which operates as a central clearing party (CCP) to all compared trades. Trade settlement involves unilateral netting—all compared transactions will net out to zero! For each buy transaction there must be a sell transaction. The two parties must agree as to trade and settlement date, type, class, series, and price. Therefore this allowed unilateral netting for both product and cash, and cash netting is financial entity bound, not product bound.

In summation, this is what the Dodd-Frank Act requires for actively traded derivatives. The concerns that led to the act's passage are especially urgent, as many of these trades are global in nature and not under one regulatory authority.

• A NONSYSTEMATIZED EXAMPLE •

Party A (an investment bank) receives a phone call from a client who discusses a transaction he would want to do if the terms are amenable. The client has an established account at Party A so that part of the process is in place. Party A contacts Party B (another financial institution and possible contra party to the transaction) and discusses the requested transaction. Party A is representing the client. Assuming it is a swap, Party A is a swap broker, and Party B is a swap dealer. If Party A does not have a master agreement with Party B, the terms and conditions contained in the master agreement must be agreed to, approved, and signed by the appropriate personnel of both firms.

Next, the two parties, A and B, negotiate and review the terms of the transaction. Once those terms are agreed on and approved by Party A's client, written confirmation is sent to the client giving the

| ORDER, NEGOTIATION, REPORT OF EXECUTION |

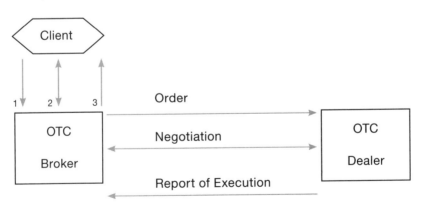

KEY: 1 = Order
2 = Negotiation
3 = Report of Execution

details of the agreed terms. The transaction is consummated. Confirmations are also exchanged between Party A and Party B. At this point, a third independent party is not involved in recognizing and/or recording the transaction between Party A and Party B. The client is in the care of Party A. Should a problem arise between them, the client and financial institution that accepted the client will have to work it out; Party B is not involved in their problem. The terms agreed to are known by only three parties: the client, Party A, and Party B.

• Clearing Facilities and Trade Transparencies in the Derivative World •

The Dodd-Frank Act discusses the need for clearing facilities and trade transparencies. The derivative product world is a perfect place to discuss it, as its products cover the entire spectrum.

There are products whose trades involve the transmission of confirmations that form part of a master agreement package or stand alone and after transmission require the confirmation sender to await affirmation from the contra party. These transactions are at the bottom of the list and are the least automated. (Note: These exclude the many daily transaction notifications known as "negative confirms" that *do not* require a response unless something is incorrect.) This process is expensive, labor intensive, and error prone. As only two people will see the confirmation details, the sender and the recipient, the chances of catching errors or detecting other problems early are minimal. It is only the buyer and seller, or the receiver and deliverer, or the payer and receiver, who know about the transaction's existence. Therefore, confidence in the risk assessment and/or exposure analysis is low.

If the contra party to the trade doesn't respond, the sender has an open transaction that may or may not be a valid transaction. This has a kind of "heads or tails" scenario. The parties do not know if the transaction is valid until the contra party is supposed to take some sort of action. The confirmation sender can call or send the contra party another confirmation in trying to get acknowledgement. Contracts could run for long periods of time, although the contra party may not exist by the tenor's end. That is a long time to find out if the transaction is null and void.

Without the aforementioned transparency, transaction price versus actual market price verification is impossible. There isn't a central independent pricing data source available for verification.

With each transaction standing alone, unilateral netting is not available. If the same security was traded by Dealer A twenty times, where Dealer A was buying from ten different broker-dealers and Dealer A was selling the same security to ten other broker-dealers, Dealer A would have to settle each trade individually with each contra party.

Each transaction must be monitored during its tenor to assure that periodic payments and other requirements are completed. This monitoring function could be performed by a central facility system instead of each participant performing its own.

Mark to markets, to assess risk and balance collateral deposits, during the life of the derivative product, is not universal. Where it exists or when it is called for, it is a manual process, and manual, one-at-a-time processes are error prone, inaccurate, and unreliable. In addition both parties must agree as to whether mark to markets is permitted on this particular transaction, the amount to be called for, the collateral being used, and the delivery date of same.

Payments that are to be made during the tenor of the derivative transaction must be collected. This includes prenegotiated amounts and method of payment, and could include acceptable currency and location payment is to be made to, as well as time and date. Periodic interest rate changes must be confirmed as to rate and applicable date. Accruals of interest must be verified and any differences reconciled.

Settlement at end of tenor creates a new set of problems. Settlement monies need to be agreed to, or if not, rebalancing using contract terms and applications must be performed to determine the settlement amount involved. This is time consuming and expensive as reconciling the difference often costs more than the difference is worth. With a central facility, there is ongoing interparty communication, and parties are notified by the central facility whenever there is any change to any part of the transaction.

Currency exchange transactions have their own life, as they could have a new set of potential problems separate and apart from the initial transaction. These include the source that determines the conversion rate to be used, the effective date for the conversion rate to be applied, the payment currency to be used, or the instruction of where and when the exchange of assets is to be delivered.

These details are supposed to be agreed to at inception. The central facility would be notified of terms and controls entries for both parties. Any discrepancies that may occur are highlighted and rectified by the parties quickly.

Customer Side

Once upon a time there were retail accounts and institutional accounts. Because it was inadvisable for a prudent person to leave assets that belong to other people in anything other than the safest location, custodial banks were permitted to settle transactions between the custodian and the trading financial institution on a delivery-versus-payment basis. Whereas retail had to settle trades in accordance with normal convention, which was T + 5 (trade date plus five days), T + 3 is now standard for most SEC-regulated products. CFTC, which is concerned with the public and their futures trades, is concerned with standard or initial margin that must be deposited immediately.

| FCM REPORTING |

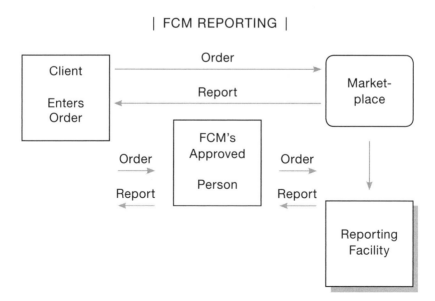

System Supported

A client calls her broker (Party A) and discusses a transaction she wants to perform. Assuming that the client has an account in good standing, Party A transmits the order to the marketplace. Once there, by either electronic trading venue or open outcry on a trading floor, the order is exposed to dealers and or other brokers. The order is executed and the price of the transaction is reported to Party A, the contra party or parties (the other side to the trade), and the reporting authority of that marketplace, which in turn broadcasts it to the public across many networks. The terms of the trade are known to anyone who cares to check on it. The client's order could also be transmitted directly to the marketplace, with copies going to Party A, or to a client representative, who, after verifying the terms of the order to ensure they are in line with the client's profile, forwards it to the marketplace for execution.

| FLOW OF A "LISTED" TRADE TO CLEARING |

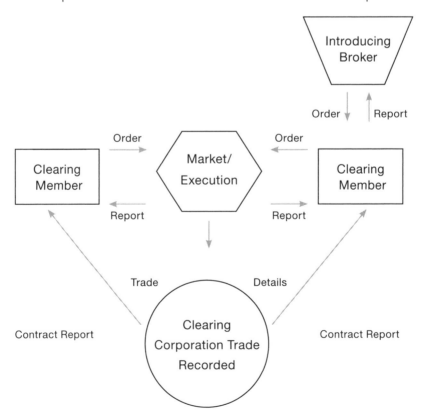

• THE MATCHING FACILITY •

From here on the product determines process.

Those products traded on an exchange, such as the Chicago Board of Trade or the International Securities Exchange, have the terms of the trade captured at the point of execution and recorded as matched between clearing members. The trades executed by nonclearing members "give up" the names of their clearing member firms as only clearing firms have recognition at the clearing corporation.

At this point in the processing, the member clearing firms have "compared" the details of the trade and the clearing corporation has a record of the agreed-to transactions. Both firms now enter into the netting phase. This can entail bilateral netting for cash or bilateral netting for cash and securities.

• NETTING VS. NONNETTING •

Each trade stands alone and must be settled independently of the others.

| FLOW WITH NO NETTING |

Party A Buys 100,000 Widgets	← B owes A 100,000 widgets	Party B Sells 100,000 Widgets
	A owes B $100,000 →	

Party A Sells 200,000 Widgets	A owes B 200,000 widgets →	Party B Buys 200,000 Widgets
	B owes A $202,000 →	

• BILATERAL AND UNILATERAL NETTING •

| FLOW WITH BILATERAL NETTING |

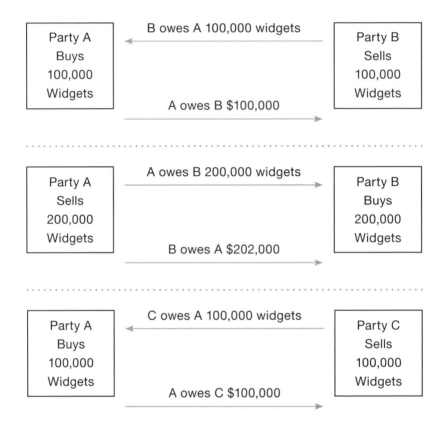

After Bilateral Netting

FIRST SCENARIO

Party A owes Party B 100,000 widgets

Party B owes Party A $102,000

| FLOW WITH UNILATERAL NETTING |

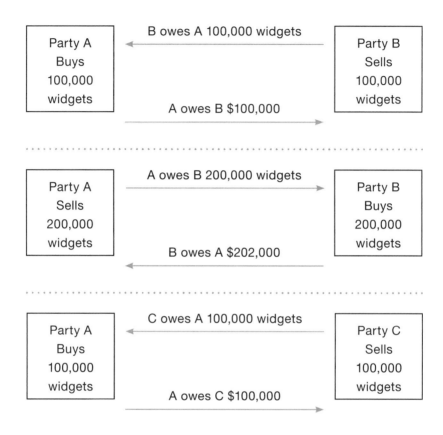

SECOND SCENARIO, APPENDED
TO PREVIOUS EXAMPLE

Party C owes Party A 100,000 widgets

Party A owes Party C $100,000

After Unilateral Netting

Widgets

Party A bought 100,000 widgets from Party B and 100,000 widgets from Party C. Party A sold 200,000 widgets to Party B. Party A's widget balance is zero.

Party B bought 100,000 widgets more than it sold. Party C sold 100,000 widgets more than it bought. Party C owes Party B 100,000 widgets.

Cash

Party A bought $100,000 worth of widgets from Party B and $100,000 worth of widgets from Party C. Party A sold $202,000 worth of widgets to Party B. Party A is owed $2,000.

Party C is owed $100,000 from its sale of widgets to Party A. It will settle with Party B.

Party B owes $202,000 from its purchase of 200,000 widgets from Party A and is owed $100,000 from its sale of 100,000 widgets for a net $102,000 that it owes. Party B will pay Party A $2,000 and Party C $100,000.

All of the above calculations are processed electronically by the clearing facility.

| CASH / UNILATERAL NETTING |

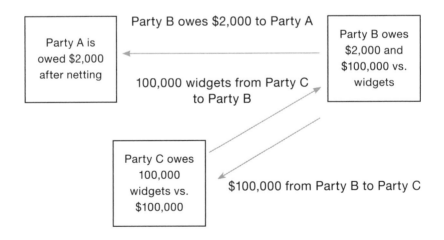

| Party A is owed $2,000 after netting |

Party B owes $2,000 to Party A

100,000 widgets from Party C to Party B

| Party B owes $2,000 and $100,000 vs. widgets |

| Party C owes 100,000 widgets vs. $100,000 |

$100,000 from Party B to Party C

• A Repository •

A repository records the details of transactions, which include who the parties were to a transaction, the terms and requirements, trade date and settlement dates, and whether the details of the transaction are the same for the contra parties.

SUMMARY OF BENEFITS OF A CENTRAL REPOSITORY

1. Independent third party is a witness to the transaction. The details of the negotiated contract reside on the records of the repository.

| REPOSITORY FLOW |

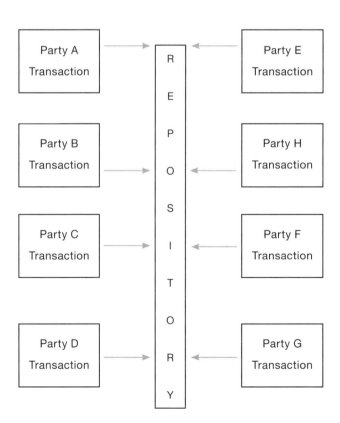

2. The transaction input from the contra parties is captured in one location. Differences can be addressed immediately.
3. Transactions in which both sides agree are recorded.
4. Unmatched trades are carried that way until resolved or deleted.
5. The third-party repository reports status of transactions to contra parties.
6. Problem items are dated and aged.
7. Price verification against actual market prices or similar derivatives can be accomplished.
8. Confidence in prices and market is improved.
9. Entitlements as required by the contract are easier to track with the repository tracking required entries.
10. Cash movement entries are netted, simplifying the process by removing redundancy (where permitted).
11. A financially or operationally troubled contra party is easier to detect.
12. Auditing—internal and external—is easier to perform, more accurately, with less chance of "surprises."

SUMMARY OF USE
OF A CLEARING CORPORATION

1. Transaction matching and comparison. Transaction locked in.
2. Transactions that do not compare are dropped off system if not resolved in set time. Cannot have one side of transaction believing it is good and the other side believing it is not.
3. Unilateral netting reduces entries to a minimum.
4. Money and contract balances roll forward.
5. Clearing corporation becomes central contra party to all compared trades.
6. Clearing corporation forwards delivery/receive instruction to participants.
7. Price transparency for regulators and interested parties.
8. Auditing: Firm positions checked against clearing corporation.
9. Differences detected on a timely basis.

10. Transactions unwound in case of default and rebalanced without defaulting party and its contra firms.

SUMMARY OF USE
OF CLEARING CORPORATION WITH
TRANSACTION GUARANTEE

1. Same as clearing corp without guarantee except for #10.
2. Member firms maintain deposits.
3. All compared transactions guaranteed by clearing corporation.

SUMMARY OF SETTLEMENT

1. Trade for trade through custodian or clearing bank.
2. Clearing corporation balances orders.
3. Physical receiver vs. deliverer (commodities).
4. Electronic entry through clearing banks (mortgage backed).
5. Clearing corporation electronic transmission to depositories.
6. Products such as options expire but their cash balances carry on with remaining products.

CHAPTER 25

USING INDEXES

The use of indexes is a method of expressing the value of a group of like products. However, to appreciate the index value, the observer must know exactly what the index's purpose is. A stock index made up of the common stock of the one thousand largest corporations by capitalization would have some different components and a different value from an index of the one thousand largest corporations by common shares price weighting. Similarly, an index of growth stocks would have different components from an index of high dividend payers, even though they may have the same index manager and the same primary names.

• STRUCTURE •

Some indexes that we use, such as the Dow Jones Industrial Average, are price weighted, which means that each component corporation's contribution to the index is the same set share quantity for all component shares multiplied by its price, divided by a preset denominator known as the base. Some other stock indexes are capitalization-weighted indexes or are market value weighted, which involves a formula of the shares outstanding times price divided by some preset denominator. The NASDAQ Composite index is this type of index. In the second method, the larger capitalized companies have sway.

A variation of the capitalization-weighted index is the floating adjusted weighting index. The purpose of the adjustment is to account for the shares that are closely held and not readily available for trading. Shares that were issued and outstanding, but are reacquired by a company for use in some corporate strategy and are temporarily held as treasury stock, are examples of this concept. If the amount held totals 10 percent, the weighting would be multiplied by 90 percent.

• TYPE •

The most well-known stock indexes are the general market indexes. The index is composed of selected common shares traded on a country's financial markets. Listed below are some of the more popular ones:

NORTH AMERICA

CANADA

S&P TSX Composite = Based on the common shares of the largest companies traded on the Toronto Stock Exchange. It also includes income trust units.

MEXICO

IPC = Índice de Precios y Cotizaciones (Index of Prices and Quotations), a market-weighted selection of shares trading on the Mexican Bolsa representing all sectors of Mexico's economy.

UNITED STATES

Dow Jones Industrial Average = Comprises thirty major industrial companies and is price weighted.

Standard & Poor's 500 index = A free-floating index capitalization weighted index.

Standard & Poor's 100 index = Known as the OEX, this is a capitalization-weighted index best known for the options that trade on it.

NASDAQ Index = A capitalization weighted index of approximately five thousand companies.

EUROPE

UNITED KINGDOM

FTSE 100 (aka "Footsie") = *Financial Times* London Stock Exchange, a capitalization float weighted index comprising the one hundred largest market-capitalized stocks traded on the London Stock Exchange.

FRANCE

CAC 40 = Cotation Assistée en Continu (Continuous Assisted Quotation) = A free-floating market-capitalized index. The common shares selected from forty of the top one hundred companies traded on the Euronext exchange.

GERMANY

DAX = Deutscher Aktienindex (German Shares Index) = Thirty blue-chip stocks traded on the Frankfurt Stock Exchange and market capitalization weighted.

SPAIN

IBEX 35 = A capitalization-weighted index containing the thirty-five most liquid stocks traded on the Madrid Stock Exchange's continuous market.

ASIA AND PACIFIC

AUSTRALIA

All Ordinaries = The equities of more than three hundred companies traded on the Australian Stock Exchange make up this market-weighted index.

CHINA

SSE = Shanghai Stock Exchange Composite Index = Contains shares of all the stocks, both A and B shares, traded on the Shanghai Stock Exchange. It is a market capitalization index.

HONG KONG

Hang Seng = Capitalization-weighted forty-stock index of companies traded on the Hong Kong Stock Exchange.

INDIA

Nifty = Known as the Nifty Fifty, this is a free-floating capitalization index of stocks traded on the National Exchange of India.

JAPAN

Topix = A capitalization-weighted index of all the stocks traded on the First Section of the Tokyo Stock Exchange.

Nikkei 225 = A price-weighted index of shares of the 225 largest companies traded on the Tokyo Stock Exchange.

KOREA

KOSPI Composite Index = A market capitalization index based on all the stocks traded on the South Korean Stock Exchange (Korea Stock Exchange).

SINGAPORE

Straits Times = Capitalization-weighted index of thirty companies traded on the Singapore Stock Exchange.

TURKEY

ISE = Istanbul Stock Exchange = 100 = stock index is a price-weighted index.

SOUTH AMERICA

ARGENTINA

MerVal = Mercado de Valores is a price-weighted index. The weighting is based on the stocks' share of the overall trading done on the Argentina Stock Exchange.

BRAZIL

Bovespa (Bolsa de Valores do Estado de São Paulo) = A total return price-weighted index of fifty stocks. Its value represents the current worth of an investment made in the then fifty stocks on January 2, 1968, and includes all distributions, such as dividends (a total return index).

CHILE

IPSA = Índice de Precios Selectivo de Acciones comprises the forty most heavily traded stocks, revised quarterly.

GLOBAL

BBC Global 30 = Comprises the thirty largest companies by stock market value in the Americas, Asia, and Europe.

S&P Global 1200 = Covering thirty countries and about 70 percent of the global capitalization.

Subindexes

Many of the indexes above are accompanied by subindexes. The DAX index, for example, has a DAX subsector All Airlines index, and a DAX subsector Auto Parts and Equipment index to name just two. There are many indexes that are not listed here, such as the Russell and the Wilshire indexes, which are umbrella names for many subindexes. Russell indexes cover eighty-three markets worldwide and capture 98 percent of investible global equity.

• FORMULAS •

One of the primary formulas used to calculate indexes are:

Laspeyres Index

The Laspeyres index is calculated from the value of a basket of fixed assets, which is set as the base. The base is assigned the number 1. A calculation is then made on the value of the same basket of assets at a later time. The index value is equal to the ratio of the value of the basket at the end of the second period divided by the value of the first period.

Here's an example:

On day 1 = Market value of 100 stocks set as Base 1.

On day X = Market value of same 100 stocks on day X divided by value determined in Base 1. The difference is the index.

• ECONOMIC INDEXES •

While not directly involved with common stocks, many economic indexes are studied as they have an impact on the stock market. Among these are the Consumer Confidence Index (CCI) and the Consumer Price Index (CPI).

The Consumer Confidence Index measures the attitude of a sample of the public toward their current financial condition and what they see coming in the near term. Their collective attitude is thought to affect their spending habits, which in turn affects what and how much they will purchase.

The Consumer Price Index is the primary index that measures inflation. A variation of the CPI is the chain-weighted CPI, which not only tracks prices but tracks changes in the choices people are making. If product A and product B are in both indexes and the public begins to buy more of product B and less of product A, the chain-weighted CPI will reflect this; the CPI will not.

Here's an example:

Last year the cost of an apple pie was $7.00 and a chocolate cake was $5.00. Your bakery sold twice as many chocolate cakes as apple pies. This year, apple pie was $6.00 and the chocolate cake was $9.00. Your bakery sold twice as many apple pies as it did chocolate cakes.

Your base year is (1 pie × $7.00 + 2 cakes × $5.00)

The CPI calculation would be:

(1 pie × $6.00 + 2 cakes × $9.00) / (1 pie × $7.00 + 2 cakes × $5.00)

$6.00 + $18.00 = $24.00 / $7.00 + $10.00 = $17.00

$24.00 / $17.00 = 1.411764 or an inflation level of 41.17%

The chained CPI calculation would be:

(2 pies × $6.00 + 1 cake × $9.00) / (1 pie × $7.00 + 2 cakes × $5.00)

$12.00 + $9.00 = $21.00 / $7.00 + $10.00 = $17.00

$21.00 / $17.00 = 1.235294 or an inflation level of
23.53% (rounded upward)

There are many other aspects related to working with stock indexes. Among the more important is the application of corporate actions such as stock splits, dividends, and mergers. Another key element is the criteria required to make changes to the indexes' components. Let's take a look at how they relate to derivative products.

• USE OF INDEXES IN DERIVATIVE PRODUCTS •

Throughout this book, the mention of indexes has been as prevalent as the underlying product for derivative issues. The OEX options, which are listed for trading on the Chicago Board Options Exchange, have the Standard & Poor's (S&P) 100 index as their underlying issue. There is an exchange-traded fund that uses the NASDAQ 100 index for a base. Companies such as Vanguard offer many products that are index based. Portfolio managers will "index" a portfolio—meaning they will structure a portfolio to replicate the performance of a particular index.

With the success of ETFs, the proliferation of indexes has grown geometrically. Indexes can be designed to cover debt instruments as well as equities. There are indexes that measure the volatility of financial products, or the activity of sectors, or the relationships between different industries. There is a volatility index (VIX) that measures the volatility in the prices and volume relation of put and call options on the S&P 500 index. The world of commodities has its own indexes, such as the Commodity Price Index and the Commodity Research Board (CRB) indexes.

The CRB Index, known as the CRB Futures Price Index, calculated by Thomson Reuters/Jefferies, measures the price movements of commodity sectors. The CRB BLS (Bureau of Labor Statistics) produces spot market indexes. Included in the group are the CRB BLS Spot Index, CRB BLS Metals Sub-Index, CRB BLS Textiles Sub-Index, CRB BLS Raw Industrials Sub-Index, CRB BLS Food Stuff Sub-Index,

CRB BLS Fats and Oils Sub-Index, and CRB BLS Livestock Sub-Index.

Goldman Sachs has developed its own commodity index, now known as the S&P GSCI.

• INDEXING PORTFOLIOS •

During different periods certain indexes have outperformed those of managed portfolios. In other words we have a tortoise and hare situation, with the index being the tortoise and the managers' researched information and recommended strategies being the hare. Investors may request that the money manager "index" their portfolio to replicate a particular index. The money manager will then focus on altering the portfolio so that the securities contained therein will have a high correlation to the index.

The wide world of indexes and their uses can fill a book by itself. This section was merely intended to show their relevance to the derivatives market.

• CONCLUSION •

New derivative products will be introduced as the need arises, and those that become redundant or unnecessary will cease to exist. The industry is and always has been in transition. It has always been interesting to see how nonfinancial events affect different segments of the financial markets. For example, a drought or a flood in a particular region can affect prices of certain futures contracts, or a change in the tax law, such as the creation of individual retirement accounts, can have effects on the mutual fund industry segment. The increase in asset gathering by financial institutions, when combined with advancements in technology, allowed for the introduction of exchange-traded fund products.

The evolution of products, processes, and regulations will continue to move forward and events will raise new problems; resolution of those problems will be accomplished via new solutions. The Dodd-Frank Act, in its blending with other markets' efforts, such as EMIR, will lead to global standards that we will all adhere to. In short order, the "mysterious" products discussed in this book will become commonplace and the next batch of "exotic" products will come along. It is all part of this dynamic and exciting industry. Those who look at their employment in the financial industry as just a "job" are missing out on participating in this interesting and ever-changing market. I trust this book answered some of your questions and that your time spent with it was worthwhile.

ACKNOWLEDGMENTS

I have been fortunate to be part of an industry that is forever changing. It is constantly growing; growing productwise as well as growing products within existing product. Some of these new products must be supported by new markets, other are housed in older markets that suddenly sprout new trading venues. The expansion of the industry's financial infrastructure migrated into new geographical locations and within these newly developed financial centers comes their own domestic growth, which feeds back into the new markets. This is all caused, in part, by advancements in technology that have permitted questions to be answered faster, complicated computations to be performed in seconds, and countries' borders to disappear. The question is: Does this growth fuel the advancement in technology or does the advancement in technology fuel this growth? This is and will continue to be debated for years to come.

As the industry advances to new horizons, current rules and regulations must be altered and new rules and regulations promulgated when and where needed. Globalization of the markets has introduced a new need—standardization of these rules and regulations so that barriers are removed and transactions flow in a borderless environment.

Even before there was an information highway, the industry has always provided those curious with educational material. The phrase "seek and ye shall find" had been part of my work ethic from day one. As the years pass, obtaining information became easier due to my employment status and the industries' technical advancements. My daily e-mails contain notification alerts, newsletters, and bulletins from various industry organizations and general informational documents. And of course there is the Web, where richly pertinent information abounds for those truly interested and make the effort to seek it.

During my varied career I have met and worked with many colleagues who took the time to explain the many different aspects of the industry. I thank them for their time and more than that: their patience. I owe a debt of gratitude to the individuals and institutions that extended employment opportunities to me over the years. I trust they view their investment in me as well worth the exercise.

As I have done in my previous books, as well as in seminars and lectures that I have conducted, I would like to take this time to share this information. I hope this book accomplishes that task.

Thank you.

GLOSSARY

AAR

See Actual applicable rate.

Accretion

The amount that the principal of an asset increases over time.

Accretion swap

A swap in which the amount of principal increases over time.

Accrual

The accumulation of cash or other value from the same origin over time. Interest owed on a debt instrument accrues day by day until it is paid or the debt matures.

Accrual swap

A swap in which interest accrues to one party when a certain event occurs.

Accrued interest

The interest owed on a debt instrument covering a period of time.

Activity date

The day that the action or event is recorded or formally "booked."

Actual applicable rate

Refers to the rate realized on a swap at end of tenor.

Actual value

The quantity or sum that is used in interest and other computations, as apart from notional value. A stock option trading at the notional value of $6 has an actual value of $600 because the option is on a trading unit of 100 shares.

Agent

A broker-dealer or other party who acts as a conduit assisting customers in buying and selling financial instruments. An agent does not have any financial interest in the transaction. Usually charges a fee known as a commission.

American form of option
A put or call option that can be exercised at any time during its life.

Amortization
1. The process whereby the principal amount of the debt decreases over time. 2. How the cost or payment of a product is apportioned over its life.

Amortization swap
A swap that pays down its initial value during its tenor.

AP
See Associated person.

Arbitrage
See Risk arbitrage, Risk-free arbitrage.

Asian option
By some preestablished methodology, an average strike price is determined between the underlying's market price the day the contact position was acquired and the price at expiration.

Asset-backed security
A group of similar loans, mortgages, and other debt that are pooled into a single collateralized security. See Collateralized debt obligation.

Asset swaps
A transaction where the referenced asset is being swapped for another (e.g., a fixed-income bond being swapped for a floating-rate note).

Assignment
When used in listed options, the process used by Options Clearing Corporation to elect an option writer (or seller) who must perform the terms of the contract due an exercise by an option owner.

Associated person
Registered employee who is permitted to conduct business with the public. Term is used in the futures market.

Audit
Verification of the account balances and positions in the "books and records" of a company by a third party or its internal staff.

Authorized participant
An entity empowered to "create or redeem" ETF shares.

Backwardation
Term used in the futures market when the price of a futures contract is below that of the spot (cash or current) deliverable.

Bankruptcy

Legal process that occurs when a creditor does not meet its financial obligations and the remaining assets are placed in the care of a trustee.

Barrier option

A knock-in or knock-out option. A price is set (the barrier) by the negotiating parties and when the price is reached the option will come alive (knock in) or the option is terminated (knock out).

Basis point

One one-hundredth of a percent. Therefore, 50 basis points equals ½ of a percent. Used as a pricing guide in the evaluation of certain debt products. Example: debt product X trades at 50 basis points over debt product Y.

Basis swap

A floating-for-floating swap where the swap legs are tied to different referenced indexes or money rates. Example: one leg is tied to the three-month LIBOR rate, the other leg is tied to the three-month U.S. Treasury bill rate.

Basket default swap

Basket containing several entities from which the credit default swap (CDS) negotiation will determine which credit event will be the trigger enacting the terms of the CDS contract.

Bear option spread

Long and short put or call options on the same underlying product but different series constructed so that the spread owner profits if the underlying product loses value.

Bellwether

A bond or other instrument from which other products' values are set.

Benchmark

The referenced object that sets prices or values of other products.

Beneficial owner

The principal or actual owner of an instrument, regardless of how it is registered.

Bermuda option

Option that can only be exercised on certain predetermined dates.

Beta

Relationship of two products to each other. One of the two is generally an index. The closer the beta is to the number one (1), the more closely the issue replicates the referenced issue's movements.

Binary default swap

This swap contract states that should a certain credit event occur, the credit default swap (CDS) seller pays a predetermined amount. Example: a scheduled payment is missed.

Binary option

An option with a predetermined underlying asset price, which if and when reached will pay a preset amount. If the target price is not reached, the option expires worthless.

Borrowers

The users of other parties' funds on a temporary basis.

BOT

Industry abbreviation meaning "bought."

Brady bonds

Treasury zero-coupon bonds issued as backing for sovereign debt of troubled Latin American countries of the 1980s.

Broker

Individual or entity that acts on behalf of others transacting futures, securities, or other types of contracts for a fee or commission. The broker does not have any financial interest in the transaction.

Brokerage firm

An entity registered with the Securities and Exchange Commission that offers financial products and services including the trading of securities in the marketplace.

Broker-dealer

1. A license obtained from the Securities and Exchange Commission that permits a firm to carry on security business with the public. 2. A firm that acts as an agent (broker) and/or principal (dealer) in transactions with the public.

Bull option spread

Long and short put or call options on the same underlying product but having different series, designed to profit from a rise in the underlying value.

Buy/write

The simultaneous purchase of stock and the writing of a call, on the same security, against it.

C-a-R

Capital at risk. The amount of an investment's current value being exposed to possible loss.

Callable bond

A bond that can be retired in part or whole, by the issuer, in accordance with the terms of the bond's indenture, before the bond's maturity date.

Call option

Product that permits its owner to buy the underlying product at a predetermined price during a predetermined time period.

Cancellable swap

A swap that includes a stipulation that if a particular event was to occur, the swap would be terminated. Example: the issuance of additional debt by the referenced asset's issuer thereby diluting the collateral or security backing the reference asset.

Capped option

An "out of the money" option that is automatically exercised if the strike price of the option is reached or passed by the underlying issue's price, which places the option in the "in the money" state.

Capped swap

A floating-rate swap that sets a limit to which the floating rate can increase.

Cash settlement

The use of currency to settle a transaction in lieu of a physical delivery settlement. Example: Several derivative products are based on the value of indexes. The indexes themselves are undeliverable, so cash is used instead for settlement purposes.

Cash trade

A trade that settles on its trade date.

CBO

See Collateralized bond obligation.

CCP

See Central clearing party.

CDO

See Collateralized debt obligation.

CDX index

A family of credit default swap indexes covering different sectors.

CEA

See Commodity Exchange Act.

Central clearing party

The process by which a clearing corporation inserts itself and becomes the contra party to both sides of each compared trade.

CFTC

See Commodity Futures Trading Commission.

Circus swap

Two swaps where each has one identical but offsetting leg with the same party that can be netted out against each other, leaving the remaining leg in each swap active.

Class

1. A type of option (i.e., put or call). 2. A product comprising components that have distinct characteristics (e.g., Class A common stock has voting rights, Class B does not). 3. A grouping of products having the same or similar characteristics (e.g., asset class).

Clean price

A debt's price that is free from any interest calculations which may have accrued, and from commission or other fees. The present value of all of the debt instrument's cash flows.

Clearing broker-dealer

See Clearing member.

Clearing corporation

An industry organization that acts as a third party to a transaction while expediting the settlement process.

Clearing firm

See Clearing member.

Clearing member

A member of a clearing corporation, which uses the corporation's facilities to expedite and settle transactions with and/or against other clearing members.

CLO

See Collateralized loan obligation.

Closed-end fund

A type of mutual fund where buyers and sellers of the fund shares trade with each other in a marketplace and not against the mutual fund itself as they do with open-end funds.

Closed-end investment company

See Closed-end fund.

CMO

See Collateralized mortgage obligation.

Collateral

1. An asset that is pooled with similar assets to form a new product. Example: as used in support of a collateralized debt obligation (CDO). 2. An asset whose value is used to support or back another issue's risk. 3. An asset that is pledged against a loan.

Collateralized bond obligation (CBO)

An instrument comprising a pool of corporate bonds; most, if not all, are rated "junk" but due to the wide range of issuers and issues, they are considered investment grade. The instruments are issued in tranche format.

Collateralized debt obligation

Umbrella term covering collateralized bond obligations (CBOs), collateralized loan obligations (CLOs), collateralized mortgage obligations (CMOs).

Collateralized loan obligation (CLO)

Pools of different types of bank-issued commercial loans that are securitized. Among the loans included are car loans and credit card loans. They are issued in tranche format.

Collateralized mortgage obligation (CMO)

An instrument set in a tranche format where each tranche has its own credit risk profile. It comprises mortgages from different issuers. The mortgages of the Federal Home Loan Mortgage Corporation (Freddie Mac) and Federal National Mortgage Association (FNMA, Fannie Mae) are classified as mortgage-backed securities (MBS). Mortgages issued by conventional issuers, such as banks and savings and loan institutions, are referred to as asset-backed securities (ABS).

Combined interest rate and currency swap

See Circus swap.

Committee for Uniform Security Identification Procedures (CUSIP)

A nine-digit number assigned to identify a particular security. Only one issue can have that particular number.

Commodity Exchange Act

Passed in 1936; ultimately led to creation of the Commodity Futures Trading Commission (CFTC).

Commodity Futures Trading Commission

Established in 1974 as an independent federal regulator of the commodity and futures markets.

Commodity pool operator

Funds are gathered and pooled by the operator for the purpose of trading in the futures market.

Commodity Research Bureau (CRB)

One of the oldest commodity data gathering companies in the world. Publishes many commodity data books that include prices, production, and analysis.

Commodity trading advisor

An individual or entity that offers trading strategies for a fee.

Common stock

Voting (usually) shares representing ownership of a corporation.

Compared transaction

Official (written) agreement between contra firms to the terms of a trade.

Confirmation

Document detailing the components of a transaction that is given by one party involved in a transaction to another. It may be in electronic or paper form and is usually delivered by a brokerage firm to its client.

Constant maturity swap

Two floating rates, one pegged to the swap rate, the other pegged to LIBOR. Spread can constantly be adjusted as the rates change.

Consumer Price Index

Measures changes in the cost of a select list of goods that consumers purchase.

Contingent swap

A swap that becomes enforceable when some other event occurs.

Contra party

See Counterparty.

Conversion

An option strategy involving the buying of stock, the buying of puts, and the selling of calls, all with the same expiration date on the same security. No matter which way the security price moves, the position will be closed out upon the exercise of the option.

Convertible security

Security that contains a feature permitting its owner to exchange it for another security of the same issuer. A one-time event.

Convexity

The sensitivity of a bond price to a change in interest rate.

Cost of carry

The charges associated with storage or holding on to an asset pending settlement.

Counterparty

The other party to a transaction as it goes through processes leading up to final transaction settlement.

Coupon rate

Percentage of a debt instrument's face value that interest payments are based on.

Covenant

A clause in a contract that mandates an obligation on either or both parties to do or refrain from doing certain actions or deeds.

Covered bonds

Pooled mortgages that are securitized and sold, *but* remain on the issuer's books and give investors access to the assets in case of issuer's default.

CPI

See Consumer Price Index.

CPO

See Commodity pool operator.

CRB

See Commodity Research Bureau.

Creation units

The assembling of ETP shares by an authorized participant.

Credit balance

The sum in a client's account that is owed to the client.

Credit default swap

A contract between two parties that obligates one of the parties to step up should a third party fail to perform its obligations.

Credit Default Swap Index

See CDX index.

Credit derivative

A generic term for a group of products designed to transfer credit risk from the issuer to another entity.

Credit event

Occurrence that triggers the CDS seller (risk buyer) to act as required by contract.

Credit-linked notes

A note with a credit default swap embedded in it.

Credit market

The trading of debt instruments among practitioners.

Credit risk
Exposure to a counterparty's defaulting risk.

Credit spread option
An option on the spread between two debt instruments.

Credit support annex
Provides credit protection between parties by establishing mutual rules concerning the posting of collateral.

CTA
See Commodity trading advisor.

Currency
Umbrella name for cash or nomenclature of a type of cash.

Currency swap
The contract that oversees the exchanging of one currency for another at predetermined rates and conditions.

Current yield
Annual compensation divided by price. Annual interest rate times principal divided by market price.

CUSIP
See Committee for Uniform Security Identification Procedures.

Customer side
That part of a transaction or entry affecting customer accounts.

Day order
An order entered into a marketplace that is canceled at the end of the day if not executed.

Dealer
A firm that trades for its own account and risk. Makes a market (quote) for others to trade against.

Debit balance
The sum in a client's account owed to the financial institution.

Debt market
General term where all loan or borrow types of securities can be traded.

Default swap
An agreement that states that if Party A doesn't honor its obligation to Party C, Party B will.

Delivery risk
The exposure to a failure of delivery occurring.

Delivery versus payment (DVP)

Where assets are exchanged simultaneously. For example: a seller is paid at the same time that it delivers the sold item.

Delta

The amount of change in an option's or other derivative's price relative to the price change in the underlying or referenced product.

Depository Trust & Clearing Corporation

See DTCC.

Depository Trust Company

Industry custodian for the immobilization of securities.

DerivSERV

A product of DTCC used as a repository for OTC derivative transactions.

Dirty price

The instrument's price including the present value of all cash flows plus accrued interest less commission and other fees.

Discount instrument

A debt instrument, issued below par, whose interest accrues in its price and at maturity pays par or its face value. The value at maturity is composed of the initial principal amount plus interest that has accrued over the life of the instrument.

Dividend

A per-share payment or earnings which is sometimes made to the equity share owners of an entity.

Dodd-Frank Act

Set in motion regulations codifying financial requirements, trading restrictions, and development of clearing and settlement facilities (see SEF) for certain derivatives.

Dow DIAMONDS

An ETF that tracks the Dow Jones Industrial Average and is managed by State Street Global Advisors.

DTCC

The domestic clearing corporation and depository for stocks, bonds, and unit investment trusts, expediting transactions; a major participant as a repository in global derivative transactions.

Duration

1. The time remaining in an event. 2. The conversion of the present value of a debt's cash flow into years. 3. Measures the change in a bond's price due to a change in interest rates.

DVP

See Delivery versus payment.

Equity

1. Ownership portion of a corporation's balance sheet. 2. The balance in a margin or cash account minus any money or value owed the institution carrying said account. 3. The value of any asset minus any encumbrance.

Equity-linked note

A note in which the return is based on the performance of a specified security, basket of securities, or index.

Equity tranche

Lowest-level tranche in a collateralized debt obligation issue.

ETF

See Exchange-traded fund.

ETN

See Exchange-traded note.

ETP

See Exchange-traded products.

Euribor

Interest rate charged between European banks.

European form of option

A put or call option that can only be exercised at the end of its life.

Event

An occurrence that triggers a derivative product to respond.

Exchange

A federally regulated organized marketplace that has membership standards and product listing requirements on which trading and price dissemination are carried out.

Exchange-traded fund (ETF)

An equity index that trades its shares on exchanges as if they were shares of stock.

Exchange-traded note (ETN)

Senior debt offered by a bank or provider backed by the creditworthiness of the issuer.

Exchange-traded product (ETP)

A basket of similar products that have been put into a fund or trust and qualified for listing to trade on an exchange. It's an umbrella name which includes ETFs and ETNs.

Executing broker or party
The initial broker-dealer or other financial intermediary involved in the contracted execution of an order or contract.

Exercise price
The contracted price, as stated in an option description, to be paid upon exercise of the option. Also known as strike price.

Expiration date
The last day of a derivative's life. After this date the contract that existed between parties is no longer enforceable.

External audit
A verification of a firm's books and record by an independent "outside" auditing firm.

Facilitation trade
A trade executed by a dealer to clear the way for other transactions to occur. These are sometimes executed for $1 for the entire lot as a way of recording an execution for audit trail purposes.

Fact sheet
See Term sheet.

FCM
See Futures commission merchant.

Federal funds rate
Rate charged on overnight loans between U.S. banks.

Federal Home Loan Mortgage Corporation (FHLMC)
A government-sponsored entity (GSE) that issues mortgage-backed CMO-type securities. Also known as Freddie Mac.

Federal National Mortgage Association (FNMA)
A government-sponsored entity (GSE) that issues mortgage-backed CMO-type securities. Also known as Fannie Mae.

Financial Industry Regulatory Association
See FINRA.

FINRA
A self-policing and rule-enforcing organization of the securities industry. Enforces SEC rules as well as promulgates its own rules. It can fine, suspend, or take other action against offenders.

Fitch
One of three major rating services. The other two are Moody's and Standard & Poor's.

Fixed-for-fixed swap
An agreement between two or more counterparties in which fixed rates of cash flows are exchanged. This usually involves debt instruments with different payment cycles. For example: One party's cash flow occurs every January 15 and July 15; the other party's cash flow occurs every April 15 and October 15.

Fixed-for-floating swap
An agreement between two or more counterparties during which one party exchanges a fixed-rate cash flow for another party's floating rate which is pegged to some standard, such as LIBOR or the federal funds rate.

Fixed rate
A debt instrument whose interest rate is set for the entire duration of the instrument.

Fixed-return option
Amex's name for a binary option.

Flex option
A listed option, with a duration of up to three years, that has negotiable terms as opposed to the standard option whose terms are set by the Options Clearing Corporation's listing regimen.

Floater
Industry jargon for a debt instrument whose interest rate is changed periodically in accordance with present interest rate conditions.

Floating for floating
An agreement between two or more counterparties to exchange floating-rate cash flows that are pegged to agreed-to indexes. One leg of the swap may be tied to the three-month Treasury bill rate, the other leg of the swap tied to the three-month LIBOR rate.

Floating-rate instrument
Debt instrument whose interest rate is adjusted periodically based on a referenced rate.

Floor broker
A member of an exchange who operates from the trading floor provided by a contract market and executes orders for others. The location on the trading floor may be a booth, post, or ring from which the broker operates.

Floor trader
A member who operates from a trading floor, making markets, adding liquidity, and executing orders against other members.

FNMA
See Federal National Mortgage Association.

Force majeure

An abnormal condition that prevents the carrying out of required assignments.

Foreign exchange

The exchanging of one currency for another.

Foreign exchange rates

The rates used in exchanging one currency for another.

Forward

An over-the-counter future product used mainly for postponing currency or interest rate transactions until a later time. The rate is negotiated today that will be used at a later time.

Freddie Mac

See Federal Home Loan Mortgage Corporation.

FRO

See Fixed-return option.

Fund manager

Manages a pool of money in an attempt to accomplish certain goals.

Future

An exchange-traded product that sets the price today at which a contract will be settled at, on a later date.

Futures commission merchant

An entity registered with the CFTC and NFA to transact business with the public, usually acting as a broker.

Futures exchange

A marketplace where futures contracts trade between members. Each exchange "lists" the products it chooses to offer (e.g., agriculture, metals, currency, interest rates, etc.).

FX

See Foreign exchange.

Gamma

Measures the degree of change of the option's delta to the price of its underlying security as it relates to a portfolio or strategy.

Gearing

The relationship of debt to equity. The higher the ratio, the more debt there is to equity.

Give up

Changing the name from the executing broker-dealer or original broker-dealer to the broker-dealer or other entity that will be the contra party responsible for settling the transaction.

Global economy

1. The global financial and economic status. 2. The effect of one nation's economy on the world.

Global Trade Repository (GTR)

DTCC repository for interest rate, credit, equity, and FX derivatives. The details of the participants' transactions are "booked" and retained at GTR, which acts as a third independent party to the transaction.

Globex

CME's virtual around-the-clock electronic trading platform.

GNMA

See Government National Mortgage Association.

Good till canceled (GTC) order

An order that remains in force until it is executed in the marketplace or canceled by the originator.

Good till "X"

An order to buy or sell an issue that is canceled after a specific time, "X."

Government National Mortgage Association (GNMA)

A federal agency, a division of the Department of Housing and Urban Development, issuer of pass-through securities. Also known as Ginnie Mae.

GSE

A government-sponsored entity created by an act of Congress. Federal National Mortgage Association (FNMA) is an example.

GTR

See Global Trade Repository.

Guaranteed bond

A bond that is guaranteed by a party other than the issuer. If the guarantor defaults, the investor may lose all of the investment. The exception is U.S. government debt, which is guaranteed by the U.S. government.

Hedge

A strategy that is structured to minimize or eliminate risk. Recent applications of the term, such as hedge funds, do not follow this definition.

Hedge risk

Possibility of a hedged position coming apart.

Hedgers

Those who use futures or other derivative products to offset or minimize risk.

Holder

Another name for the owner of an option.

Indenture

Details the terms under which the bond or other debt instrument was issued.

Index

The application of a mathematical computation involving the value of a set of products divided by a predetermined base amount to arrive at one representative figure. As the value of the products changes, the representative figure will increase or decrease.

Indexed portfolio

A portfolio of securities that is engineered to replicate the performance of an index, such as the Dow Jones Industrial Average.

Inflation swap

A swap composed so that the notional value can be adjusted at the end of the swap for the effects of inflation.

Initial margin

The amount required to be in a customer's account to satisfy a new position.

Institutional account

1. A customer's account that settles transactions through delivery vs. payment (DVP). 2. An account whose principal is created by law. Example: a corporation's pension fund.

Interest

The cost or charge assessed to the borrower for the use of the lender's money or other funds.

Interest only

Debt instruments are composed of two parts, principal and interest payments. This is the interest payment part of a stripped debt instrument.

Interest payments

Payments made according to a prearranged schedule for the use of borrowed funds.

Interest rate

Percentage of a loan's principal charged for the use of the funds.

Interest rate swap

Conversion of one rate to another (e.g., fixed rate for floating rate).

Internal audit

A review of the accounts in the books and records by employees of the entity.

International Security Identification Number (ISIN)
Twelve-digit global security identification number. A unique number that is assigned to each issue.

International Swaps and Derivatives Association (ISDA)
Group whose members aim to foster safe, efficient derivative markets and to develop documentation such as the Master Agreements.

In the money
In the case of call options: the amount by which the market value of the underlying asset exceeds the strike price. In the case of put options: the amount by which the strike price of the option exceeds the market value of the underlying asset.

Intrinsic value
A value that must be present in the pricing of a product. In option products, for example, it equates to the "in the money" sum that an option may have.

Introducing broker
A firm that is registered with the appropriate authority (e.g., FINRA, NFA) to conduct business with the public but uses the services of a clearing firm to settle the public's transactions.

Inverse floater structured product
One that is designed to move contrary to the market. For example: An interest payment on a bond is divided into two parts: the floater and the inverse floater. As market interest rates change, the rates paid by these two parts change accordingly.

I/O
See Interest only.

ISDA
See International Swaps and Derivatives Association.

iShares
ETFs that are sponsored and administered by Barclays Global Investors.

ISIN
See International Security Identification Number.

iTraxx
A credit default swap index primarily used in Europe.

Jelly roll
An option strategy whereby options with a set strike price and expiration month are rolled into a later expiration option with the same strike price.

Joint venture

A pooling of funds in an attempt to achieve a one-time goal.

Knock-in option

See Barrier option.

Knock-out option

See Barrier option.

Laspeyres index

One of two standard methods for calculating indexes. The formula uses a continuous base.

LEAPS

See Long-term Equity AnticiPation Securities.

Leveraged contract

Contract based on the use of loans and/or derivatives products to control the acquisition or sale of an asset of much larger size. Example: borrowing against the value of an owned asset to acquire another much larger asset.

Leverage exchange-traded fund

An ETF on which derivatives are used to augment the return.

Leverage swaps

Swap in which one of the legs is expressed as a multiple of the notional value.

Leverage transaction merchant (LTM)

A party who is actively engaged in the facilitation of leveraged contracts.

LIBOR

See London Interbank Offered Rate.

Limit order

An order entered into a market that sets the maximum price to be paid (buy) or the minimum price to be received (sell).

Liquidation

The closing of a derivative position.

Lombard rate

A rate set by the Deutsche Bundesbank for short-term lending rates collateralized by securities.

London Interbank Offered Rate (LIBOR)

An average of the interest rates London banks charge one another for borrowing funds.

Long

An owner's position in a security, derivative, commodity, or currency.

Long-term Equity AnticiPation Securities (LEAPS)

Listed equity options that have an expiration date as far out as three years. In the option's final year it reverts to the standard option format.

LTM

See Leverage transaction merchant.

Maintenance margin

The minimum amount of equity required to maintain positions in a margin account. In an account containing common stock, FINRA regulations state that the equity cannot be less than 25 percent of the market value. Broker-dealers set higher requirements.

Margin

Minimum amount of equity required in an account to acquire or sell short products.

Margin call

The calling for additional collateral in an account to cover a deficiency.

Market-linked investments

See Structured products.

Market makers

Traders that trade for their own account and risk, thereby adding to market liquidity. Many markets mandate that their market makers make two-sided quotes (bid and offer). In some cases, market makers are referred to as dealers.

Mark to market

Process by which the monetary values in an account are adjusted to their current market value.

Market risk

Risk of adverse market conditions, such as the changing of interest rates or the liquidity of the particular issue drying up.

Master Agreement

1. Developed by the ISDA, forms the core of an agreement between a derivative's participants. 2. One of five parts to the umbrella master agreement, sets the standard the participants will operate under.

Moody's

One of three major rating services. The other two are Standard & Poor's and Fitch. Moody's is most noted for its bond-rating capabilities.

National Futures Association (NFA)

Industry group promulgating rules to protect the integrity of the market and whose membership includes all parties operating on future exchanges.

National Securities Clearing Corporation (NSCC)

Division of DTCC. Clearing corporation for equities, exchange-traded funds, corporate and municipal debt, as well as closed-end investment funds and unit investment trusts.

Negotiated swap rate (NSR)

Swap rate that is set at the beginning of a swaption. It becomes the effective rate if the swaption is elected.

Net asset value (NAV)

Share price of open-end mutual funds and other related securities. It is computed by adding the value of the portfolio to money awaiting investments less operating expenses divided by the number of shares outstanding.

NFA

See National Futures Association.

Nominal value

See Notional value.

Nominee name

Owner in registered name only, but not the name of the actual principal or beneficial owner. It is a registration name used by custodians and other financial institutions which is accepted by industry participants and used to expedite trade settlement and other related actions.

Notional value

A value that exists in name only. A $1,000 bond trading in the market for $900 has a dollar value of $900 but a notional value of $1,000.

NSR

See Negotiated swap rate.

OID

See Original issue discount.

Open interest

The number of contracts of a derivative product that are outstanding (live) at a specific time.

Open repo

See Open repurchase agreement.

Open repurchase agreement

A repurchase agreement where the termination or closeout date is unknown at the time the repurchase agreement is set. Two transactions occur at the same time. One is selling an issue on inception date (trade date) for settlement (settlement date) on the inception date. The other transaction is buying the issue back using the inception date today (trade date) for settlement at a date that will be determined at the later time (settlement date). Either party to the repo can close out the contract with twenty-four hours' notice.

Option

A derivative product that grants its owner the privilege but not the obligation to take market action for a predefined period of time at a predetermined price.

Option combination

The purchase *or* sale of puts *and* calls on the same underlying issue with different option series designation.

Option spread

See Spread.

Option straddle

See Straddle.

Original issue discount (OID)

1. A bond issued at a discount that pays interest only at maturity. The difference between the price paid and par, paid at maturity, is the interest earned. 2. A bond issued below its face value (par). The portion or all of the discount will be taxed as interest income.

Over-the-counter

Trading in a nonregimented exchange market.

Over-the-counter option

An option not traded on an exchange where all parts are negotiated.

Paasche index

One of two standard methods used for calculating indexes. The base used for calculations is updated periodically.

Paper profit

A make-believe profit that would have been real *if* the position had been closed out.

Par

The face amount of a debt instrument. A $1,000 bond trading at $1,000 is trading at par.

Parity

When two or more securities are exchangeable for one another at equal value. For example: A $1,000 bond is convertible into 20 shares of common stock. The bonds and the common shares would be at parity if the bonds were trading at $800 and the shares were trading at $40 ($40 × 20 shares = $800).

Par value

1. A figure assigned to common and preferred stocks. 2. Concept used to convert shares to dollars on the company's balance sheet. 3. A value assigned to "percent" preferred stocks and used to compute preferred shares' dividends.

Pass-through security

An asset- or mortgage-backed security that passes through debt payments and interest to the security's owner. For example: each month the owner of a GNMA mortgage-backed pass-through security receives the mortgage interest payments and the amount of mortgage principal that has been paid down by the homeowners.

Physical settlement

The use of the referenced asset in transaction settlements, either by actual movement or by book entry. One party delivers the asset and the other party pays cash or its equivalent for it. In the case of a cash settlement one party pays the other the amount due according to the contract.

Preferred stock

Nonvoting ownership shares of a corporation that has prior claim to dividends and assets over the common stock. Preferred shares are supposed to pay a stipulated rate of dividend.

Premium

1. In a debt instrument, the amount paid over par. 2. In an option, another name for the price. 3. In insurance, the periodic cost for the policy. 4. In trading, the amount paid over fair value.

Price-weighted index

Index whose value is computed on the prices of a set amount of shares of the component securities.

Principal

The actual amount invested as apart from interest.

Principal only

A debt instrument that does not make interest payments, but is issued as a discounted instrument that pays out its full principal amount at maturity. Some government bonds are stripped into two parts and sold as interest only and principal only instruments.

Put

A product that gives its owner the privilege of selling the underlying product at a predetermined price during a specific time.

Put bond

1. A bond that contains a feature that allows the bondholder to sell the bond back to the issuer under preset terms. 2. A feature in some bonds that allows the issuer to mandate that the bondholder sell the bond back to it under fixed terms. (Resembles a call feature.)

Put or call swap

In either type of a fixed-for-floating rate swap that contains this feature, the floating leg of the swap can use the option to terminate the swap.

Recovery rate

The amount or percentage rate that is expected to remain after bankruptcy.

Redemption

The retirement of an instrument, usually for a payment of cash.

Referenced security or referenced asset

The underlying issue or entity that the swap or derivative is based on.

Refunding

The issuance of a new debt to pay off an old debt. The U.S. Treasury refunds its maturing Treasury bills by issuing new Treasury bills.

Registered employee

A person who has satisfied the requirements of a regulatory authority to carry out the responsibilities of his or her occupation.

Regulation T

U.S. Federal Reserve regulation governing the lending of money by broker-dealers to clients.

Regulation U

U.S. Federal Reserve regulation governing the extension of credit by banks to clients for security transactions.

Repo

See Repurchase agreement.

Repurchase agreement (Repo)

Two transactions are set up at the same time. One is selling an issue on the inception date (trade date) for settlement on the same day (settlement date). The other transaction is buying the issue back using the inception date as the trade date (trade date) for settlement on another known date (settlement date). Both legs of the repo values and applicable rates are known at inception.

Reverse conversion

An option strategy involving the selling short of a stock, the buying of a call, and the selling of a put on the same stock with both options having the same expiration date. No matter which way the stock's price moves, the exercise of the option will cover (close) the position.

Rho

Measures the change in time value of an option, or other derivative, as interest rate changes.

RIC

Reuters Instrument Code.

Risk arbitrage

Taking security or other financial positions based on an event that may or may not occur. Company A is rumored to be interested in acquiring the shares of Company B. If it happens, what effect will it have on the securities? Or if it doesn't, what will the effect be?

Risk-free arbitrage

Trading on an aberration in prices between the same products (e.g., the converted value of an American depositary receipt [ADR] and its foreign shares).

Roller-coaster swap

A swap in which the periodic payments increase or decrease according to an agreed-to schedule.

S&P

See Standard & Poor's.

Scalpers

Futures traders who trade on the spread between bids and offers.

Schedule

1. Part of the ISDA Master Agreement setting forth the responsibilities of the transaction. 2. Any listing of responsibilities executable by a particular party.

Securities Industry and Financial Markets Association

See SIFMA.

Securitization

The process by which financial assets are pooled together in a single new product and sold piecemeal, thereby spreading risk of default over many owners.

SEF

See Swap exchange facility.

Separate trading of registered interest and principal securities

See Stripped bond.

Series

1. In options, the strike price and expiration date. 2. In municipal bonds, subissues of the same bond.

Settlement date

The day there is supposed to be an exchanging of assets to satisfy the terms of a transaction.

SFR

See Swap fixed rate.

Shark note

A short-term note referenced to an index, with a knock-out option.

Short position

1. A short position requiring a covering action at a later time (e.g., selling stock short that must be bought back eventually); a nonderivative product. 2. A short derivative position requiring action only if and when acted upon by a long position (e.g., a seller of an option only has to act if the option is exercised by the option owner). 3. A position requiring the eventual delivery of a product (a future product short position). 4. A bookkeeping balance.

Short sale

Selling something that is not owned or intended to be delivered with the intention to buy it back at a lower price at a later date.

SIFMA

Securities Industry and Financial Markets Association. An organization made up of industry broker-dealers and other related interests.

Single-name swap

Swap between two parties and a single currency.

Sinker

A short name for a sinking fund—see Sinking fund.

Sinking fund

A fund that is set up by the issuer that permits the issuer to reacquire its own bonds from its earnings. The bonds are then retired.

Sovereign

That which belongs to a country.

Sovereign debt

Loans made directly by a country's government.

Sovereign risk

Concern that a foreign government: 1. may default; 2. may intervene during the life of a swap or other derivative; 3. may take market action that could negatively affect an ongoing contract.

SPAN margin

See Standard portfolio analysis.

SPC

Special purpose corporation—see Special Purpose Vehicle.

SPDR

Spiders or Spyders. ETFs on the S&P 500 index, managed by State Street Global Advisors.

SPE

Special purpose entity—see Special Purpose Vehicle.

Special Purpose Corporation

See Special Purpose Vehicle.

Special Purpose Entity

See Special Purpose Vehicle.

Special Purpose Vehicle

An entity that manufactures credit derivative securities.

Speculator

A trader who risks capital trying to outguess the market or effect of events and maintains positions for short periods of time.

Sponsor

The originator who presents an ETF product plan to the regulatory authorities.

Spread

1. The difference between two related prices. 2. In options, the buying *and* selling of equal numbers of puts *or* calls having the same underlying but different series. 3. Buying and selling equal numbers of different related future contracts to take advantage of an aberration in their prices. 4. The difference between the bid and offer of a quote.

SPV

See Special Purpose Vehicle.

SR

See Swap rate.

Standard & Poor's

One of three major rating services. The other two are Moody's and Fitch.

Standard & Poor's 500
A free-float capitalization-weighted stock index.

Standard margin
See Initial margin.

Standard portfolio analysis
System used by futures exchanges to analyze complex accounts to determine maximum risk.

STANS
See System for Theoretical Analysis and Numerical Simulations.

Straddle
The purchase *or* sale of puts *and* calls on the same underlying issue with the same option series designation—see Option combination.

Street side
That part of a transaction or entry affecting the operation processing accounts of the firm.

Strike price
A predetermined price at which an option, or other similar type of derivative, would transact an exchange of assets (trade).

Stripped bond
A bond where the interest and principal are divided into two different payment streams, interest only and principal only. *Strip* stands for Separate Trading of Registered Interest and Principal Securities.

Structured product
A product comprising a discounted bond and a derivative, such as an option.

Swap
A product in which assets, liabilities, or cash flows are exchanged.

Swap agreement
An ISDA contract that details the terms of the swap.

Swap broker
A firm that acts as a conduit between parties but does not take a position or risk.

Swap dealer
A firm that takes positions and trades against counterparties.

Swap exchange facility (SEF)
Third-party clearing facility mandated by the Dodd-Frank Act.

Swap fixed rate

The current rate applicable to swaps.

Swap interdealer broker

A broker whose clients are dealers that work between dealers dispensing information and generating liquidity.

Swap payer

Party to an interest rate swap that pays the fixed rate of interest.

Swap rate

The rate applicable to an ongoing swap or a swap rate negotiated in advance.

Swap receiver

Party to an interest swap that received the fixed rate of interest.

Swaption

An option to enter into a swap agreement at a later time.

Synthetic option

Using two of the three—puts, calls, and the underlying issue—to replicate the third. Example: long a call and short a put on the same underlying issue replicates the market price movement on the underlying.

System for Theoretical Analysis and Numerical Simulations (STANS)

System used by Options Clearing Corporation to analyze complex accounts to determine maximum risk.

Taker

Another name for the owner of an option. Term used in such countries as the United Kingdom.

Tau

Measures an option's premium change as the underlying security's volatility changes.

Term sheet

Contains full description of the derivative, issuer, underlying product, and features.

Theta

Reflects the daily decay of the time value of an option premium.

Tick

Minimum trading price movement assigned to a product.

Time value

That portion of an option's premium that is over and above its intrinsic value. The value dissipates as time passes.

TomNext
Settlement date for the trade is trade date plus two days.

Tomorrow next
See TomNext.

Total return index
Index whose received value feeds from three sources: the components of the index, revenue generated from collateral, and adjustments to the value of the index.

Total return swap or total rate of return swap
A derivative in which one party transfers both market and credit risk to another party in return for an income flow plus protection of original value.

Trade date
The actual day a trade occurs.

Trade date + 3
Trade settles three days after trade date.

Traders
Term is usually applied to market makers who trade for their own account and risk.

Trading lot
The regular trading size of a product (e.g., U.S. common stock = 100 shares).

Tranche
One section of several that compose an asset-backed security.

TROR
See Total rate of return swap.

TRS
See Total return swap.

Trustee
Individual or entity responsible for the safety and security of assets and the adherence to rules and regulations governing that responsibility.

UIT
See Unit investment trust.

Underlying issue
The asset that is behind the derivative.

Unit investment trust (UIT)

Established by assembling a nonmanaged fixed portfolio with a fixed maturity date and selling shares in it.

U.S. Treasury bills

Short-term instrument of the federal government.

U.S. Treasury bonds

Long-term instrument of the federal government.

U.S. Treasury notes

Intermediate-term (from one to ten years from issuance) instrument of the federal government.

U.S. Treasury rate

Benchmark interest rate used for other loans.

Valuation date

The day that the required money computations of a transaction are determined.

Value at risk

A guesstimate of potential loss that could occur over a set period of time, based on historical events.

Value-weighted average price

Method used to establish the basis for daily and final settlement prices for U.S. Treasury futures.

VAR

See Value at risk.

Variation margin

The mark to market on positions that are maintained in a futures account.

Venture capital

Investment in start-up companies or "one shot" opportunities.

VIX

CBOE's Volatility Index, which measures near-term market expectation as reflected by the S&P 500.

Volatility

The price movement range of a product or market over a predetermined period of time.

Volatility Index

See VIX.

Volcker Rule

Named after Paul Volcker, former Federal Reserve chairman; part of the Dodd-Frank Act that separates a bank's proprietary business from its customer business, thereby reducing the potential for conflicts of interest.

VWAP

See Value-weighted average price.

WAC

See Weighted average coupon.

WAM

See Weighted average maturity.

Weighted average coupon

Used in pricing a basket of different couponed debt securities.

Weighted average maturity

A weighting formula used to amortize the maturity of a pool of loans or a basket of debt instruments.

Writer

A party that sells the right, but not the obligation, to buy (a call) or sell (a put) an underlying product for a specific period of time.

Yield

The periodic return on an investment over and above the principal. See Current yield, Yield to maturity, Yield to call.

Yield curve swap

Swap based on the spread between two points on the yield curve.

Yield to call

Debt instruments that have a call feature usually have a call price. Yield to call uses the call price instead of par.

Yield to maturity

The return on an investment that includes the amortization or depletion of the difference between current market value and par or face value.

Zero-coupon bond

A discounted bond that pays its interest at maturity; an OID offering.

Zero-coupon swap

A fixed or floating rate against a zero-coupon bond.

INDEX

accreting swaps, 177
accumulation swaps, 177
actively managed certificate
    (AMC), 67
All Ordinaries index, 258
"all or none" transactions, 143–44
American Petroleum Institute No. 4
    index (API 4), 148
American Society for Testing and
    Materials, 147
anonymity, need for, 176
appreciating swaps, 177
Argentina Stock Exchange, 259
asset-backed securities, 208
asset swaps, 178–79
associated persons (APs), 139
"at the money," definition of, 77
Australian Stock Exchange, 258
authorized participants, 50, 52

banks, *see* investment banks;
    mortgage bankers
Barclays Global Investors, 49, 52
barrier options, 110–12
basis points, 24, 205
basis price, 19
basis spread, 24
basis swaps, 179, 180–81, 188–89
BBC Global 30 index, 260
bear spreads, 90–91
beta, 95–96
bilateral netting, 249, 250
binary options, 108–9
BlackRock, 49
bonds, 4, 11–12, 186

convexity of, 32
corporate vs. municipal, 20–21
covered, 216–17
fixed-income, 19
interest only/principal only, 33–35
pricing of, 29–33
put, 17–18
ratings of, 24–25
serial form of, 21
sinking fund provision for, 15–16,
    18–19
zero-coupon, 228
see also callable bonds
Bovespa (Bolsa de Valores do Estado
    de São Paulo) index, 259
Brent crude oil, 146–47
BRIC (Brazil, Russia, India, China)
    countries, 219
broker-dealers, 5–6, 13, 104, 213, 234,
    235, 241
bull spreads, 87–90
buyer, definition of, 70
buy/write strategies, 5, 83–85, 113–15,
    219–20

CAC 40 (Cotation Assistée en
    Continu) index, 258
callable bonds, 12–18
    as beneficial to issuer, 13
    partial, 13
    refunding of, 16–17
    rule-of-thumb method for,
        14–15
    sinking fund provision for, 15–16
callable/putable swaps, 180

capital requirements, 238
capped options, 105–6
capped swaps, 180–81
carbon dioxide emissions, 148–49
cash flow, 171, 179, 184–85
cash settlers, 80
CBOE Futures Exchange (CFE), 136
Central Appalachian Coal Future, 147
central clearing parties (CCPs), 27, 243
certificate of deposit (CD) rate, 179
Chicago Board of Trade (CBOT), 136, 249
Chicago Board Options Exchange (CBOE), 105, 136, 239, 240–42, 262
Chicago Climate Exchange (CCE), 136
Chicago Mercantile Exchange (CME), 127–28, 136
circus swaps, 181–82
class, definition of, 72–73
clearing corporations, 27, 51, 64, 73, 104–5, 107, 142, 143, 156, 161–62, 163, 164, 166, 209, 210, 222, 233, 239, 242, 245–49, 272
  benefits of using, 254–55
clients, 5, 247
CME Clearing, 144
CME ClearPort, 144, 147
CME Globex, 142, 143, 147
CME Group, 136, 142–44, 146, 164, 233
coal futures, 147–48
coffee futures, 145–46, 150–51, 166
collateral, 23
collateralized bond obligations (CBOs), 206–7, 214–15
collateralized debt obligations (CDOs), 4, 206–17
  risk and, 206
collateralized loan obligations (CLOs), 206–7, 215–16
collateralized mortgage obligations (CMOs), 8, 178, 206–14
  GNMA-backed, 207–11
  nongovernment-backed, 213
  REMICs and, 211–12

TBA pools of, 209–10
  tranches in, 212–14, 215
commercial paper, 11
commodities, 63, 177, 219, 230, 233, 262
  exchange-traded (ETC), 48, 63–64
  swaps, 182–84
  see also futures products
Commodity Exchange Act (1936), 127, 232, 233
Commodity Exchange Authority, 232
Commodity Futures Trading Commission (CFTC), 127, 137, 232, 237, 247
  divisions of, 233–34
  Dodd-Frank and, 239
commodity pool operators (CPOs), 137–38, 233
Commodity Price Index, 262
Commodity Research Board (CRB), 262
commodity trading advisors (CTAs), 138, 233
compound options, 112–13
confirmation (terms) sheet, 72
constant maturity swaps, 184
Consumer Confidence Index (CCI), 261
Consumer Price Index (CPI), 261–62
cost of carry, 152
cost of funds index (COFI) rate, 179
coupon rates, see interest rates
covered bonds, 216–17
covered call, definition of, 83
CRB BLS indexes, 262–63
CRB Futures Price Index, 262
credit, 5
  risk and, 22–25, 66
credit default swaps (CDSs), 144, 194–201
  assessing risk in, 195–97
  counterparties in, 194–95, 198
  ISDA master agreement for, 199–201
  marketability of, 196–97
  negotiation of, 197–98
credit events, 194
Creditex, 144
credit scores, 23
credit swaps, 178
creditworthiness, 22–23, 175
  fluctuation in, 25

CSX coal future, 147
Cubes, 50, 55
currency transactions, 246–47
  exchange-traded (ETC), 48
  options, 81–82, 116–17
  swaps, 177, 179, 181, 184, 187–88
current (spot) market indexes,
  262–63
current (spot) market price,
  123, 126
CUSIP number, 20–21
customized (one-off) transactions,
  26, 27, 44, 105, 166, 225,
  239–40

DAX (Deutscher Aktien IndeX),
  258, 260
day orders, 140
debt instruments:
  bellwether, 25–26
  investment-grade, 23
  pricing of, 29–33
  trading of, 19–20
debt markets:
  global economy and, 8–10
  interest rates and, 28–35
  liquidity of, 11, 26, 176, 242
  overview of, 8–21
  risk in, 22–27
  see also specific markets
default, definition of, 198
delivery versus payment (DVP)
  rule, 52
delta, 96–97, 98, 103
Depository Trust & Clearing
  Corporation (DTCC),
  51–52, 222
  Mortgage-Backed Securities
  Division of, 209, 210, 239
Depository Trust Company (DTC), 13,
  51–52
derivatives:
  of benefit to issuer of underlying
  product, 3–4
  capital requirements and, 238
  definition of, 3
  indexes and, 262–63
  investment banks and, 6–7
  of no benefit to issuer of underlying
  product, 4
  processing of, *see* transaction
  processing

types of, 3–4
  see also specific derivative products
Deutsche Bank, 67–68
diagonal spreads, 92
DIAMONDS, 50, 55
"discount," meaning of term, 19
dividends, 112
Dodd-Frank Wall Street Reform and
  Consumer Protection Act (2010),
  10, 11, 236, 238, 263–64
  Commodities Futures Trading
  Commission and, 239
  OTC derivatives and, 238–39
  processing and transparency
  issues addressed by, 238,
  242–44, 245
  SEC and, 239
Dow Jones Industrial Average, 50,
  256, 257
down-and-out call option, 110
down-and-out put option, 110
DownREIT, 45
duration, Macaulay vs. modified,
  32–33

EDGAR (Electronic Data Gathering,
  Analysis, and Retrieval), 231
electronic commerce networks
  (ECNs), 49, 54
electronic trading platforms, 141–42,
  143, 239, 243
EMIR (European Market
  Infrastructure Regulation), 10,
  238, 264
emissions contract futures,
  148–49
Equifax, 23
equity-linked notes, 227–28
Euribor (Euro Interbank Offered
  Rate), 34, 35
Euronext, 258
European Central Bank, 10
European Market Infrastructure
  Regulation (EMIR), 10,
  238, 264
"Ex by EX," 108
excess return trackers, 67
exchange rates, 168
exchange-traded commodities (ETC),
  48, 63–64
exchange-traded currencies (ETC),
  48, 65

exchange-traded funds (ETFs), 39,
45–46, 48–62, 95
creation of, 50–53
definition and types of, 49–50
global, 56–58
grantor trusts, 58–59
indexes and, 262
inverse, 59
leveraged, 55–56, 59
margining of, 60–62
mutual funds vs., 53
open-end, 55
redemption of, 51
strategies for, 53–55
trading of, 51–53
UIT vs. mutual fund form of,
54–55
exchange-traded notes (ETN), 48,
65–67
risk in, 66–67
exchange-traded products, 39, 48–68,
239, 249
exercise capabilities, for options,
77–79
exercise price, 78–79
Experian, 23
expiration dates, of options, 73–74

Fannie Mae (Federal National
Mortgage Association),
211–12, 213
federal funds rate, 34, 35
Federal Home Loan Mortgage
Corporation (Freddie Mac), 20,
211–12, 213
Federal National Mortgage
Association (Fannie Mae),
211–12, 213
Federal Reserve Board (FRB), 231,
234–35
fiduciary responsibility, 13
financial crisis (2008), 10–11, 228
Financial Industry Regulatory
Authority (FINRA), 45, 62, 66,
231, 234–35, 236
Financial Times London Stock
Exchange (FTSE 100; "Footsie")
index, 258
Fitch, 23
fixed-for-fixed swaps, 181, 186–88
fixed-for-floating swaps, 179, 180–82,
185–86

Fixed Income Clearing Corporation
(FICC), 105
fixed return options (FROs), 108
fixed- vs. floating-rate debt
instruments, 11–12
flex options, 107
floating-for-floating (basis) swaps, 179,
180–81, 188–89
floor trading, 141–45, 243
foreign exchange, 116–17
forward contracts, 165–68
forward currency market, 166–68
forward rate agreements (FRAs), 165,
168–70
Frankfurt Stock Exchange, 258
Freddie Mac (Federal Home Loan
Mortgage Corporation), 20,
211–12, 213
FTSE 100 (Financial Times London
Stock Exchange; "Footsie")
index, 258
fuel futures, 146–47
Fund Analyzer, 235
funds, availability of, 9, 10–11
futures commission merchants
(FCMs), 138, 142, 144, 152–53,
161–62, 233, 247
futures margins, 152–64
initial, 152–53
leverage in, 159–61
SPAN, 161–63
variation, 153–54, 161
futures market, 137–51
associated persons (APs) in, 139
bids in, 139
commodity pool operators (CPOs)
in, 137–38
commodity trading advisors (CTAs)
in, 138
electronic trading platforms in,
141–42
futures commission merchants
(FCMs) in, see futures
commission merchants (FCMs)
hedgers in, 123–24, 125, 126, 137,
139, 149, 164
leverage transaction merchants
(LTMs) in, 138–39
limit orders in, 140
list of U.S. exchanges, 136
"market if touched" orders in, 141
offers in, 139

order and report requirements for, 149–51
orders in, 140–41
producer-user relationship in, 123–24
speculators in, 124–25, 139, 149
stop orders and stop limit orders in, 141
time constraint orders in, 140
traders in, 137
trading floors in, 141–45
futures products, 72, 82, 121–36
contracts for, 129–32
definition of, 121–22
delivery months for, 128
exchange for physical (EFP) in, 163–64
exchange for related positions (EFRPs) in, 164
liquidity and, 124–25
list of, 132–35
market risk and, 123–28
market value volatility and, 125–27
options on, 161
pricing of, 123–25, 152
quality requirements for, 150–51
and volatility of underlying issues, 92–93, 99, 125, 153

gamma, 98, 103
Ginnie Mae, *see* Government National Mortgage Association (GNMA; Ginnie Mae)
global economy, debt markets and, 8–10
global warming, 126
GNMA, *see* Government National Mortgage Association (GNMA; Ginnie Mae)
Goldman Sachs, 263
good till canceled (GTC) orders, 51, 140
Government National Mortgage Association (GNMA; Ginnie Mae), 20
CMOs issued by, 207–11, 239
future product of, 128
grantor, definition of, 70, 71
grantor trusts, exchange-traded, 58–59

Hang Seng index, 258
hedgers, hedging, 22
futures and, 123–24, 125, 126, 137, 139, 149, 164
swaps and, 175, 194
Hedge Street, 136
holder, definition of, 70, 71, 241
Hong Kong Stock Exchange, 258
horizontal spreads, 92
Housing and Urban Development Department, U.S., 207
housing market, 10

IBEX 35 index, 258
income writing strategy, 109
see also buy/write strategies
indexes, 256–63
capitalization-weighted, 256–57
derivative products and, 262–63
economic, 261–62
floating adjusted weighting, 257
formulas for, 260
general market, by country, 257–60
portfolios and, 262, 263
price-weighted, 256
index-linked notes, 227–28
index options, 80–81
inflation swaps, 184
initial margin, 152–53
initial public offering (IPO), 6, 7
Intercontinental Exchange (ICE), 136, 144–45, 146, 147–48
interdealer brokers (IDBs), 144, 176
interest:
as expense, 9
taxes on, 20
interest rates:
debt markets and, 28–35
factors affecting, 8–9, 28
fixed vs. floating, 11–12, 185
forward contracts on, 167
forward rate agreements and, 168–70
long-term vs. short-term, 185
rho and, 98–99
risk-free (Treasury bill), 112
interest rate swaps, 184–89
fixed-for-fixed, 186–87
fixed-for-floating, 185–86
scheduling payment in, 189

International Securities Exchange, 117, 249

International Swaps and Derivatives Association (ISDA), 198, 235–36
master agreement of, 199–201, 236

"in the money," definition of, 76

intrinsic value, 76–77, 80, 85, 91, 97, 98–99, 100, 101, 112, 117, 204, 284

inverse floater structured products, 226–27

Invesco PowerShares, 50

Investment Advisors Act (1940), 231, 232

investment banks:
capital requirements of, 238
role of, 5–7

Investment Company Act (1940), 40, 55, 231, 232

investment-grade securities, 23

IPC index (Índice de Precios y Cotizaciones), 257

IPSA (Índice de Precios Selectivo de Acciones), 259

ISE (Istanbul Stock Exchange) 100 index, 259

iShares, 49

joint ventures, 41

Kansas City Board of Trade (KCBT), 136

knock-in, knock-out options, 109–12

KOSPI Composite Index, 259

Laspeyres Index, 260

Lehman Brothers, 66

leverage transaction merchants (LTMs), 138–39

LIBOR (London Interbank Offered Rate), 24, 34, 35, 179, 188, 203

LIFFE CONNECT, 142

liquidity, 11, 26, 66, 107, 108, 124–25, 176, 242

London Stock Exchange, 63–64, 258

longevity of loans, interest rates and, 9, 28

Long-term Equity AnticiPation Securities (LEAPS), 75, 106

"long the option," definition of, 70

Macaulay duration, 32–33

Madrid Stock Exchange, 258

margin, margining, 38, 117
Dodd-Frank and, 243–44
ETFs and, 58, 59, 60–62, 64
spreads and, 86, 88–89, 118–20
straddle position and, 120

market-linked products, see structured products

market makers, 50, 52, 176, 242

market risk, 25–26, 66
futures and, 123–28
swaps and, 175

markets:
spot (current), 123, 126
see also debt markets

Markets in Financial Instruments Directive (MiFID), 238

mark to markets, 153–54, 246

matching facilities, 249

mergers and acquisitions, 6

Merrill Lynch HOLDRS, 59

MerVal (Mercado de Valores) index, 259

Minneapolis Grain Exchange (MGEX), 136

modified duration, 32–33

monetary policy, 9

Moody's, 23

mortgage-backed securities, 10, 43–44, 178
see also collateralized mortgage obligations (CMOs)

Mortgage-Backed Security Division (MBSD), 209, 210, 239

mortgage bankers, 208

mortgages, 178, 206
REITs and, 43
subprime, 10, 23

mother and daughter options, 112–13

municipal bonds, 19, 20
corporate bonds vs., 20–21

mutual funds, 36–42
closed-end, 39–41
exchange-traded products vs., 39, 43
REITs and, 45
unit investment trusts, 41–42

mutual funds, open-end, 36–39
break-point sales charges for, 37–38

closed-end funds vs., 40–41
  net asset value of, 38–39, 40
  no-load, 37

Nadex, 136
NASDAQ 100 index, 50, 262
NASDAQ Composite index,
    257, 258
NASDAQ OMX Futures Exchange
    (NFX), 136
National Exchange of India, 259
National Futures Association (NFA),
    137, 233, 237
National Securities Clearing
    Corporation (NSCC), 51, 105
net asset value (NAV), 38–39, 40, 53
netting:
  bilateral, 249, 250
  nonnetting vs., 249
  unilateral, 243, 246, 250, 251–52
Newcastle coal futures, 148
New York Board of Trade
    (NYBOT), 136
New York Mercantile Exchange
    (NYMEX; COMEX), 136
New York Stock Exchange
    (NYSE), 105
  see also NYSE Amex; NYSE
    Liffe US
Nifty index ("Nifty Fifty"), 259
Nikkei 225 index, 259
no-load funds, 37
nonnetting, 249
North American Securities
    Administrators Association
    (NASAA), 45
notes, 11
  exchange-traded (ETN), 48
  structured, see structured notes
notional value, 177–78, 185
  principal amount vs., 193
NYSE Amex, 108
NYSE Liffe US, 136

OEX (S&P 100 index), 257
OEX options, 262
Office of the Comptroller of the
    Currency (OCC), 230–31
oil contracts, 125
OneChicago, LLC, 136
one-off (customized) transactions,
    26, 27, 44, 105, 166, 225, 239–40

open outcry, 141–42, 143
operational risk, 27
Options Clearing Corporation (OCC),
    73, 104, 107–8, 222, 239,
    242, 243
options dealers, 104
Options Price Reporting Authority
    (OPRA), 242
options products, 69–82
  American form of, 78, 223
  barrier, 110–12
  binary, 108–9
  call, defined, 69–70
  capped, 105–6
  class of, defined, 72–73
  compound, 112–13
  currency, 81–82, 116–17
  European form of, 78, 117,
    222, 228
  exchange-traded, 4, 73
  exercise capabilities for,
    77–79
  expiration date of, 73–74
  fixed return (FROs), 108–9
  flex, 107
  on futures, see futures
    products
  index, 80–81, 262
  intrinsic value of, 76–77
  knock-in, knock-out, 109–12
  LEAPS, 75, 106
  liquidity of, 73–74, 272
  orderly issue of, 242
  over-the-counter (OTC), 73, 104–5,
    107, 108, 241
  position terminology in, 70–71
  premium of, 76–77, 96–97,
    99–100, 112
  privately placed, 4
  put, defined, 69–70
  rainbow, 115–16
  series of, defined, 73–74
  standardization of, 242
  strike (exercise) price of, 73–74,
    78–79, 104
  structure of, 72–74
  symbology of, 75–76
  synthetic, 113–15
  type of, defined, 72–73
  uncovered, 89
  underlying issues of, 71–72,
    96–97

options products, strategies for, 79–80, 83–94
   beta and, 95–96
   buy/writes and, 5, 83–85, 113–15, 219–20
   delta and, 96–97, 98, 103
   gamma and, 98, 103
   multiple options and, 88–89
   option premium and, 96–97, 99–100
   rho and, 98–99
   spreads and, *see* spreads
   straddle and, 92–94, 99, 113, 120
   tau and, 99
   theta and, 99
"out of the money," definition of, 77
over-the-counter (OTC) markets, 40, 44, 45–46, 144, 176
   Dodd-Frank and, 238–39
   forward contracts in, 165–68
   options in, 73, 104–5, 107, 108, 241

packaged products, *see* structured products
pass-through securities, 128, 207–8, 239
Paulson, Henry, 216
Philadelphia Board of Trade (PBOT), 136
PHLX, 117
Platts CAPP Rail (CSX) OTC assessment, 147–48
portfolios, indexing of, 262, 263
precious metals, forward contracts on, 167
premium, definition of, 19, 71, 76
premium reducers, 85–86
present value, formula for, 29–30
pricing:
   current (spot), 123
   of debt instruments, 29–33
   of futures, 123–25
   transparency of, 107, 242–43
principal amount, notional value vs., 193
proprietary trading, 11, 107–8
put bonds, 17–18

rainbow options, 115–16
rating agencies, 23

real estate investment trusts (REITs), 43–47
   equity, 43
   as global product, 46
   investing in, 44–45
   mortgage, 43–44
   mutual funds and, 45
   popularity of, 43
   qualifications for, 46–47
   registered vs. privately placed, 44–45
   taxes on, 46
   termination of, 47
Regulation T, 231, 234–35
REMICs (real estate mortgage investment conduits), 211–12
reporting authorities, 242, 248
repositories, 253–54
reserves, 10–11
Retirement Calculator, 235
retirement plans, 37
reverse convertible products, 228–29
rho, 98–99
Richards Bay coal futures, 148
rights, 4
risk, 10, 238
   in binary options, 108
   of buy/write strategies, 84–85
   credit, 22–25, 66
   in credit default swaps, 195–97
   ETNs and, 66–67
   futures margins and, 161–63
   hedging of, 22
   interest rates and, 9, 28
   liquidity, 66, 107, 108
   market, *see* market risk
   operational, 27
   spreads and, 85, 86–87
   systemic, 236
roller-coaster swaps, 189–90
rule-of-thumb (ROT) method, 14–15, 29

Sallie Mae (SLM Corporation), 215
S&P 500 index, 49, 52, 95, 127, 257, 262
S&P Global 1200 index, 260
S&P GSCI index, 263
S&P 100 index (OEX), 257, 262
S&P TSX Composite index, 257
Sarbanes-Oxley Act (2002), 231
scalpers, 125

Securities Act (Truth in Securities Act, 1933), 218, 231
Securities and Exchange Commission (SEC), 6, 40, 44, 50, 218, 230–31, 234–35, 236, 242
  divisions of, 231–32
  Dodd-Frank and, 239, 243
Securities Exchange Act (1934), 59, 231
Securities Industry and Financial Markets Association (SIFMA), 236
seller, definition of, 70
senior debt, 65
series, definition of, 73–74
settlement, 255
Shanghai Stock Exchange, 258
short-term paper, 11
"short the option," definition of, 70–71
Singapore Stock Exchange, 259
sinking fund provisions, 15–16, 18–19
SLM Corporation (Sallie Mae), 215
Société d'Investissement à Capita (SICAV), 68
South Korean Stock Exchange, 259
soybean futures, 125–26
  sample contract for, 130–32
special interest vehicle (SIV), 215
special purpose vehicle (SPV), special purpose entity (SPE), 215, 217
speculators, futures and, 124–25, 139, 149
Spiders (Spyders; SPDRs), 49, 55
spot (current) market indexes, 262–63
spot (current) market price, 123, 126
spreads, 85–92, 113
  bear, 90–91
  bull, 87–90
  diagonal, 92
  horizontal, 92
  margin and, 86, 88–89, 118–20
  as premium reducers, 85–86
  as risk reducers, 85, 86–87
  vertical, 92
SSE (Shanghai Stock Exchange Composite Index), 258
Standard & Poor's, 23
  see also OEX (S&P 100 index); S&P 500 index; S&P Global 1200 index; S&P GSCI index; S&P TSX Composite index

standardized portfolio analysis of risk (SPAN) margin, 181–83
State Street Global Advisors (SSGA), 49, 50
step-up swaps, 177
straddle positions, 92–94, 99, 113, 120
Straits Times index, 259
strike price, definition of, 73
structured notes, 223–26
  equity-linked, 227–28
  index-linked, 227–28
  inverse floater, 226–27
structured products, 218–29
  definition of, 4–5, 218
  investment banks and, 6–7
  objective of, 219
  reverse convertible, 228–29
subindexes, 260
SunGuard, 142
swap brokers, 173–74, 175, 182, 244
swap dealers, 174–75, 244
swap execution facility (SEF), 238
swaps, 171–93
  accreting, 177
  amortizing, 177
  asset, 178–79
  callable/putable, 180
  capped, 180–81
  circus, 181–82
  commodity, 182–84
  constant maturity, 184
  credit, 178
  credit default, see credit default swaps (CDSs)
  currency, 177, 179, 181, 184, 187–88
  fixed-for-fixed, 181, 186–88
  fixed-for-floating, 179, 180–82, 185–86
  floating-for-floating (basis), 179, 180–81, 188–89
  hedging of, 175, 178
  inflation, 184
  interest rate, see interest rate swaps
  notional value in, 177–78, 185, 193
  options on, see swaptions
  overview of, 171–73
  participants in, 173–76
  roller-coaster, 189–90

swaps *(cont.)*
  total rate of return (TROR), 190–92
  yield curve, 192–93
  zero-coupon, 193
swaptions, 202–5
  call vs. put, 204
  receiver vs. payer in, 203–4
  types of, 203
synthetic options, 113–15
systemic risk, 236

taker, definition of, 70, 71
tau, 99
taxes:
  on interest, 20
  on REITs, 46
TBA (to be announced) pools, 209–10
theta, 99
Thomson Reuters, 142
time value, 76, 79–80, 93–94, 96, 97,
    98–99, 100, 102, 103, 112
Tokyo Stock Exchange, 259
Topix index, 259
total rate of return (TROR) swaps,
    190–92
total return trackers, 67
trackers, 67–68
trade date plus three (T + 3) rule, 52
trading floor, 141–45, 243
tranches, 212–14, 215
transaction guarantee, 255
transaction processing, 238–55
  customized vs. noncustomized
      products in, 239–40
  Dodd-Frank and, 238, 243–44
  evolution of, 240–44
  nonsystemized, 244–45
transparency, 107, 242
  Dodd-Frank and, 238,
      242–43, 245
TransUnion, 23
Treasury bill interest rate, 112
Treasury bills, 17, 19
Treasury bond future, 128
Treasury bonds, 20–21, 105, 128
  as interest only/principal only
      instruments, 34–35
Treasury debt instruments, 8
Treasury Department, U.S., 17

Trust Indenture Act (1939), 231
Truth in Securities Act (Securities
    Act, 1933), 218, 231
type, definition of, 72–73

Undertakings for Collective
    Investment in Transferable
    Securities (UCITS), 67–68
underwriting, 6, 7
unilateral netting, 243, 246, 250,
    251–52
unit investment trusts (UITs),
    41–42, 49
units, 4
unsecured debt, 65–66
up-and-out call option, 110
up-and-out put option, 110
UPREIT, 45
U.S. Treasury rate, 34, 35, 179, 188

value at risk (VAR), 153
Vanguard, 50, 262
variation margin, 153–54, 161
venture capitalists, 41
vertical spreads, 92
VIPERs, 50
volatility:
  of currencies, 65
  futures products and, 125–27
  of indexes, 95–96
  of underlying issues, 92–93, 99,
      125, 153
Volcker Rule, 11

warrants, 4
Washington Post, 198
weighted average coupon (WAC), 211
weighted average maturity
    (WAM), 211
West Texas Intermediate (WTI) oil,
    146–47
writer, definition of, 70, 71, 241

yield, credit risk and, 23–24
yield curve swaps, 192–93

zero-coupon bonds, 228
zero-coupon swaps, 193
Z tranches, 214